MASTERING

Digital 2D and 3D Art

Les Pardew
Don Seegmiller

THOMSON

COURSE TECHNOLOGY

Professional ■ Trade ■ Reference

A DIVISION OF COURSE TECHNOLOGY

Mastering Digital 2D and 3D Art

ISBN: 1-59200-561-6

Library of Congress Catalog Card Number: 2004108527

Printed in the United States of America

04 05 06 07 08 BU 10 9 8 7 6 5 4 3 2 1

SVP, Thomson Course Technology PTR:
Andy Shafran

Publisher:
Stacy L. Hiquet

Senior Marketing Manager:
Sarah O'Donnell

Marketing Manager:
Heather Hurley

Manager of Editorial Services:
Heather Talbot

Associate Acquisitions Editor:
Megan Belanger

Senior Editor:
Mark Garvey

Associate Marketing Manager:
Kristin Eisenzopf

Marketing Coordinator:
Jordan Casey

Project Editor:
Jenny Davidson

Technical Reviewer:
Kelly Murdock

PTR Editorial Services Coordinator: Elizabeth Furbish

Copy Editor:
Kim Cofer

Interior Layout Tech:
Shawn Morningstar

Cover Designer:
Mike Tanamachi

Indexer:
Kelly Talbot

THOMSON

™

COURSE TECHNOLOGY

Professional ■ Trade ■ Reference

Thomson Course Technology PTR, a division of Thomson Course Technology ■ 25 Thomson Place ■ Boston, MA 02210 ■ http://www.courseptr.com

Acknowledgments

Don Seegmiller

I acknowledge my family and their support in helping me with this book. To my wife, without her support and love this project would not have been possible. She is my constant inspiration. To my three children, Jennifer, Nicole, and Andrew, who help keep my vision clear and my perspective correct. They all are what matters most.

Les Pardew

No book is an easy task. In creating this book I had extensive help and support from a number of amazing people. First of all, I thank my Father in Heaven for giving me the talents I have and helping me to develop them. I thank my family for helping and supporting me through the many hours of work involved in putting this book together. In particular I want to thank my wife for her love and trust.

We both want to acknowledge the effort of the many great people at Thomson Course Technology, who have helped in countless ways. We thank the editors, designers, and others for their insights and help. Without them this book would not have been completed.

About the Authors

Les Pardew was born and grew up in Idaho. His hometown was a small farming community where he learned the benefits of hard work. His graduating high school class only numbered 33 individuals. From this small beginning, Les has grown to become a recognized leader in interactive entertainment.

Les is a video game and entertainment industry veteran with over 20 years of industry experience. His artwork includes film and video production, magazine and book illustration, and more than 100 video game titles. He is the author or co-author of five books: *Game Art for Teens*, *Beginning Illustration and Storyboarding*, *Game Design for Teens*, *Mastering Digital Art*, and *The Animator's Reference Book*.

Les started his career in video games doing animation for *Magic Johnson Fast Break Basketball* for the Commodore 64. He went on to help create several major games, including *Robin Hood Prince of Thieves*, *Star Wars*, *Wrestle Mania*, *NCAA Basketball*, *Stanley Cup Hockey*, *Jack Nicklaus Golf*, *Where in the World/USA Is Carmen Sandiego?*, *Starcraft Broodwars*, *Rainbow Six*, and *Cyber Tiger Woods Golf*, to name a few.

Pardew is an accomplished teacher having taught numerous art and business courses, including teaching as an adjunct faculty member at Brigham Young University's Marriott School of Management.

He is a business leader, founding two separate game development studios. He is also a favorite speaker at video game conferences and events.

Les is the father of five wonderful children and the grandfather of one beautiful granddaughter. He loves being with his wife and children both at and away from home. Deeply religious, he devotes 20 to 30 hours a week to leading and counseling a congregation of university students at Brigham Young University. "With all of the blessing the Lord has given me, I feel a solemn responsibility to help others."

Don Seegmiller was born in Provo, Utah, and grew up in both California and Colorado.

He has been an artist as long as he can remember. "Creating images for either myself or others has become such a part of my life that I cannot imagine not being able to pursue this activity."

He attended Brigham Young University from Fall 1973 until graduating Spring 1979 with a Bachelor of Fine Arts in Graphic Design with an emphasis in Illustration. Before graduation, he was hired by the David O McKay Institute of Education as their full-time graphic designer/illustrator. While employed at Brigham Young University, he began to paint egg tempera paintings on the side. In the Fall of 1980, with three paintings under his arm, he traveled to Santa Fe, New Mexico, seeking representation in one of its many art galleries. He found representation in Wadle Galleries Ltd. Within a year, his work was selling well enough that he was able to pursue painting full time. At this same time his medium switched and he took up oil painting. Known as a "Classical Realist," he is one of the finest figure artists working today.

While his work has been represented by many major art galleries, the majority of his work continues to be handled by Wadle Galleries Ltd. of Santa Fe. Over the course of the last 20 years, his work has been shown from England to Hawaii. He has painted over 400 paintings and is included in many private and public collections. He does commission portrait work occasionally. His work hangs in the permanent collection of the Springville Museum of Art and his paintings have been featured in all the major western art magazines. He occasionally is asked to teach oil painting workshops and has been listed in Who's Who.

Don teaches senior-level Illustration, traditional head painting, figure drawing, and digital painting for the Department of Visual Design at Brigham Young University. He has become one of the foremost digital painters in the country. He has been teaching since 1995 and finds that his students are a constant source of energy and inspiration. He is currently developing an online course for the Academy of Art University of San Francisco about Digital Illustration.

From 1995 until the summer of 2002 he was the Art Director of Saffire Corporation, a video game developer. During his tenure at Saffire he worked on video games for clients ranging from Sony to Nintendo.

He is a regular speaker at the Game Developers Conference, where he has done full-day tutorials on character design and digital painting in 2002, 2003, and 2004. In 2005 he will again be doing a full-day tutorial.

His work is featured in the Painter 6 and 7 Wow Books, *Step by Step Electronic Design*, and both Spectrum 7 and 8, the premier showcase of fantasy and science-fiction illustrators.

Recently he has been working with Corel Corporation producing art for their releases of Painter 7, 8, and IX. He continues to work with Corel on additional projects.

Don has also recently worked with the publisher Charles River Media to write and illustrate the books *Digital Character Design and Painting* and *Digital Character Design and Painting: the Photoshop Edition*.

He loves working on different subjects for different clients while continuing to oil paint for his gallery in Santa Fe. His clients have ranged from video game companies including Blizzard, Sony, Nintendo, Ensemble Studios, and others, to doing work for comic book publishers promoting new licenses, to doing magazine and book covers for clients such as Random House, Scholastic, Parachute Publishing, and others.

Don travels extensively doing workshops and seminars for different groups including the Ringling School of Art, Ensemble Studios, University of California at Irvine, Disney, The Association of American Medical Illustrators, and others.

He currently resides in Orem, Utah, at the base of a 12,000 foot mountain, which gives an ever-changing vista and inspiration. "My life centers on my family."

Don is an avid fly fisherman who enjoys the solitude of a quiet evening on a trout stream with one or two good friends.

Contents

3   Digital Painting   49

4   Digital Portrait Painting   61

9   Texturing 3D Models   231

10   Lighting and Rendering   287

Index   315

Introduction

Welcome to digital art. A fascinating new world of creative possibilities awaits you in this book. In its pages you will find techniques and methods of painting that would be impossible to achieve in traditional art. You will also be able to explore the amazing possibilities of 3D digital art creation.

Over the last several years many artists have found the unique possibilities of creating digital art. The computer has freed artists from the worry of ruined surfaces, toxic chemicals, and expensive materials.

The computer has replaced most traditional media in commercial art. Now instead of painting on canvas, many commercial artists paint on the computer. The computer has found its way into the studios of artists, architects, designers, and fine artists. This is due in part to the fact that printing, video, games, and even film are all edited or laid out digitally. But it might have even more to do with the powerful tools available for digital artists.

Tools for creating digital art are pushing the envelope of creative possibility. Not only are they accurately simulating traditional media like watercolor, oil paint, air brush, or others, they are also providing new and better ways of accomplishing difficult tasks. What used to take artists hours to accomplish can now be completed in a few short steps. For example, repetitive objects can be duplicated easily in a digital art program rather than painting them individually. Smooth gradations and large areas of color can be applied to a painting instantly. Mistakes can be removed with little or no effort.

Digital art has also enabled artists to do what was impossible using traditional methods. Artists are no longer limited to painting on a single surface. The simulated surface texture can change as the artist wishes during the course of the painting. Even oil and water can mix in digital art. If the artist wants to have part of a picture look like an oil painting and part look like watercolor, there is no problem digitally.

The addition of 3-dimensional art to the digital artist's arsenal of tools opens possibilities of creation that transcend anything available in traditional media. 3D digital art has opened the door for creating art that almost appears to have a life of its own. It combines the possibilities of sculpture and architecture to the creation process without the need to buy a single block of granite. It also gives the artist complete control over lighting and environments. What's more, everything can be changed and adjusted to exactly what the artist wants and viewed from any angle the artist desires.

With all of these exciting possibilities in digital art, it is about time that a book dealt with the subject in a way that helps the traditional artist make the move to digital media. This book is designed to give the traditional artist a glimpse into the fascinating world of digital art. It has a number of step-by-step projects that show how to create both 2D and 3D art. It also contains a number of helpful hints and suggestions for the type of digital art programs that are appropriate for different objectives.

Reading this book and following the many projects in it should help to build a better understanding of digital art creation. It should also lay the foundation for further study in the field.

1

The Computer as an Art Tool

The very first artist probably used a stick to create the first drawing. Although sticks are great tools for many purposes, they are somewhat limited in their versatility as an art tool. From that early time until today, artists have searched to find better tools and media to create their art. This search has taken artists through cave paintings, to frescos, to oil paintings, to airbrushes, and finally, to digital art.

The tool for the digital artist is the computer. For many artists the computer is the ultimate art tool. This is probably due to the versatility and flexibility of the computer. No other art tool has the breadth and depth of possibilities.

This book takes a look at the creation of digital art. It is designed to help the artist achieve mastery over the media, and it covers both 2D and 3D art creation. The first half of the book shows you how to create great 2D artwork and paintings. The second half of the book explores digital art creation with the use of 3D art tools.

What Is Digital Art?

So what is digital art anyway? And where did it come from? Well, it all starts with a pixel.

A *pixel* is a small, square dot of color. An image on a computer screen is made up of many tiny pixels, and each pixel can change in both value and color. By changing individual pixels, the artist can change the picture.

Pixels have RGB or CMY values. RGB stands for Red, Green, and Blue. RGB colors are the standard for digital art that will not be printed, such as computer games and motion pictures. Art that is printed commonly uses CMY values, which stand for Cyan, Magenta, and Yellow, the same colors used in color separations. Both scales are numerical systems that assign a color and value based on numbers. The term *digital art* comes from the fact that the art is based on numbers, or in other words, digits.

Figure 1.1 shows a close-up view of a digital image of a human eye.

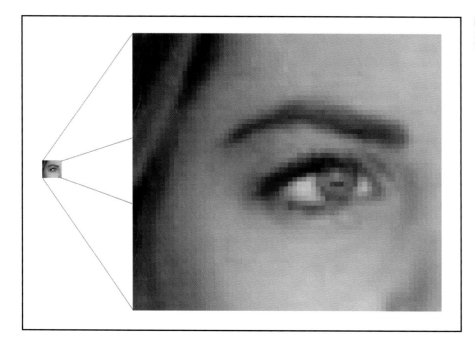

Figure 1.1 When a digital image is blown up, the individual pixels become apparent.

As the picture in Figure 1.1 demonstrates, each pixel has a value and a color. In a way it is like a very detailed mosaic tile picture.

Origin of Digital Art

The first digital art goes back to even before the pixel was developed. Back when computers were in their infancy, the pioneers in the industry used printouts rather than computer monitors. The first digital art was created as dots on paper. Some of the earliest computer games were Teletype games where the players would send updates to each other as printouts.

As display technology increased, digital graphics creation moved from the printer to the computer monitor. These early monitors were monochromatic and designed for text, not for graphics. Regardless, artists found ways to create art even if it was only one color.

Most people mark 1963 as the origin of digital art when Ivan Sutherland invented Sketchpad. Sketchpad allowed the artist to use a light-pen device to work on vector images on a vector graphics display monitor. Vector graphics are lines and curves derived from mathematical formulas.

Note

Vector graphics and raster images will be covered later in the chapter.

Later in that same decade the raster image was invented and pixels came into being. A *raster* is the pattern of dots that form an image. Raster images are made up of horizontal lines of pixels, and the number of horizontal lines and the number of pixels in each line determine the resolution of the computer monitor.

The first raster images were very blocky because those early computers were not powerful enough to project very many pixels. The progress of raster images can be seen clearly in the evolution of characters in games. Figure 1.2 shows a very early game character. The image is in one color and the pixels are very large. This character is only five pixels wide and five pixels high.

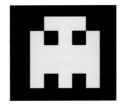

Figure 1.2 Early game characters were one color and very blocky.

The Move to Color

It didn't take long before scientists learned how to change the colors on computer monitors. The computers were still considered business or research tools and not art tools, but the artist was not to be denied. Programmers with interest in creating graphics on the computer started writing programs to create digital art.

During this time another important event was taking place: The personal computer was introduced to the market. These early machines were not very powerful compared to the big mainframe systems, but they did do something that changed the face of computing forever. They put computers in the hands of millions of people, some of whom were interested in creating art. Many of these people were the ones who started writing graphics programs for the personal computer, which were the forerunners of the programs we use today.

Figure 1.3 shows an early game character. Notice that he has more pixels and different colors than the earlier character. He is 16 pixels high and 7 pixels wide.

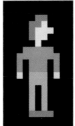

Figure 1.3 Early color game characters were limited in their number of colors.

This character has four colors. In those days many systems were limited in how many colors they supported. Some had set colors like the old IBM PCs. Others allowed some variations in color.

Progress was being made every day in computer graphics. With each succeeding year, systems were introduced that boasted higher resolutions and more colors. Figure 1.4 shows a game character with a 16-color variable palette. More colors meant artists could start shading their characters. Notice that the game character is starting to take on a sense of volume.

In the late '80s, games were becoming more realistic, but they still looked blocky. The same thing was true for all digital art. Variable colors gave digital artists a chance to start creating more realistic digital pictures. It was during this time that desktop publishing was developed, the laser printer was invented, and people started to look at the computer as an art tool rather than just a business machine.

Figure 1.4 When variable colors became available, game characters started taking on a sense of volume.

With a greater emphasis on graphics, personal computer systems entered a whole new path of evolution, bringing about better display systems and higher resolutions. The game characters went from being about 30 to 60 pixels high to around 200 and displays went from 320×200 to 640×480 resolutions. Figure 1.5 shows a game character at about 180 pixels high.

Figure 1.5 Greater resolution meant more detail for computer game characters.

More Power Brings Better Tools

Once computers became popular for desktop publishing, the race for creating better graphics tools started in earnest. Now developers had a real market for their programs because artists in large numbers were buying computers and software. This paved the way for companies like Adobe and Corel to create software for personal PCs and sell the software directly to the general public rather than only to art production companies.

Computer manufacturers and chip makers were intrigued by this new set of computer users. Artists wanted the fastest systems with the best graphics capabilities. They were driving the high end of computer usage and represented a substantial market for the most expensive machines.

Within a few short years the entire landscape of personal computers changed. System memory and processor speeds increased dramatically. Digital input devices like tablets were developed. Computer monitors became larger. Graphics cards were developed, which gave computer systems added graphic punch. The rapid advances moved the personal computer from a tool for hobbyists to a tool for graphics professionals.

3D Makes Its Move

3D digital art started in applications like military simulators. The simulators were custom-built computers tied to hydraulic systems to simulate aircraft or vehicle motion. The first simulators were not photo-realistic but they did give the trainee a feeling of being in a real environment. The advantage of these simulators was that the trainee could make mistakes without danger of getting hurt or destroying valuable military vehicles or airplanes.

It soon became apparent as graphic power increased that digital art could be used in motion picture productions. At first digital 3D art was used to augment physical models or to enhance special film effects. As time went on, however, digital 3D art started to be used more and more until entire movies like *Toy Story* and *Dinosaur* were done with digital art and no live actors.

Most of the initial 3D graphics for motion pictures were all created on high-powered systems called workstations. These graphic workhorses were specially designed computer systems with the most powerful graphics hardware available. They were significantly more expensive than personal computers, and they ran specialized software that was also very costly. The workstation's life, however, was destined to be short-lived.

As more and more people purchased personal computers, the prices for computers started to fall. This was driven in large part by competition from computer and chip manufacturers to get computers into as many homes as possible and the fact that mass production made individual systems less expensive to build. So while personal computers were advancing daily in power and sophistication they were also becoming more affordable. The more expensive process of building workstations had no chance of competing with the onrush of the PC.

As PCs became more powerful, high-end 3D software migrated from the workstation to the standard off-the-shelf PC. This move opened the door for digital artists everywhere to be able to create beautiful 3D digital art.

Figure 1.6 3D characters replaced 2D characters in video games.

Digital 3D art was also entering the computer and video game world. Home PC and video game consoles were rapidly gaining in power. In the mid 1990s, the video and computer game industry moved from primarily using 2D art to using 3D art for most games. Though very blocky at first, video games with 3D characters were readily accepted by the public. Game players liked the idea of games with 3D characters and environments.

PCs were not the only systems to advance rapidly in computing power. Video game systems were also becoming more powerful. By the late 1990s and early 2000s, game systems were capable of almost lifelike graphics. Figure 1.6 shows a character from one of these systems.

Figure 1.7 shows a timeline with the evolution of the game character to show how digital art has advanced over the years.

Moving forward, there are limitless possibilities for creating digital art. Many off-the-shelf PCs are powerful enough to handle complex digital composition. Software like Photoshop, Painter, Corel DRAW, Maya, 3DS Max, and many others have come down in price along with hardware to create an environment that favors the artist. Artists are free to create incredible art with advanced tools, and the future looks to only get better for the digital artist.

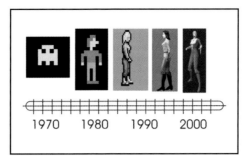

Figure 1.7 The timeline shows the advance of digital graphics in video games.

The Tools of the Trade

Understanding how to create digital art starts with understanding the tools. Any artist who works in traditional media like oil paint or watercolor has to have a good knowledge of the paint, the painting surface, and the brushes used to create his or her art. Digital artists may work on a computer but they still need to understand how to use the digital tools—that is, software programs—for creating art.

The selection of graphics programs for the digital artist is large and sometimes confusing. Although many programs are similar, they all have differences that can cause the digital artist problems when trying to complete a work of art. This book does not cover every program available to the digital artist. Instead, the book focuses on specific tools with enough depth that you will be able to gain proficiency with the program.

Two basic types of digital art programs are covered in this book: 2D and 3D. 2D digital art programs are basically image editing and creation programs. They include drawing, painting, and photo retouching software. 3D digital art programs are art development tools for creating 3D models, which then can be animated and rendered. Both types of programs are very complex software, but at the same time they are not difficult to use from an artist's standpoint.

2D Art Programs

Before we get into a discussion about the programs available to you, the digital artist, to create your 2D imagery, we need to discuss for a moment the different 2D image types.

2D computer art falls into two very distinct categories: vector-based images and raster-based images. It would be very hard to understand 2D computer art and how to create it without first defining and discussing the differences of these two major types of images. Both types of art have advantages and disadvantages and your knowledge of the two will help you decide which will be most appropriate for your particular task.

Although vector and raster images are very different, it is important to remember that all digital art when viewed on a computer monitor is displayed as pixels on the screen.

We begin our discussion by talking about raster computer images.

Raster Images

Raster images, also called bitmaps, are very common. Most of the images that you see on a computer screen are probably raster images. This type of image is created by such programs as Corel Painter and Adobe Photoshop. All photographic images that you see on the computer are raster images. Raster images are made up of pixels displayed on the computer screen.

A pixel is defined as "the smallest discrete component of an image or picture on a CRT screen (usually a colored dot); the greater the number of pixels per inch the greater the resolution." This definition is from www.freedictionary.com. What this rather wordy definition says is that all images that are viewed on a computer screen are made up of very small, individual squares of color called pixels. Each pixel can have only one color displayed at a time but they are so small on the screen that as you view them, your eye visually mixes adjacent colors and you see smooth transitions between different colored areas. The typical color monitor can display between 72 and 96 pixels per inch depending on your specific monitor and the screen resolution you are displaying.

The pixels of an image are not just randomly placed. They are arranged in an orderly grid and are square in shape. Figure 1.8 shows a small raster-based image that has been enlarged to show the individual pixels.

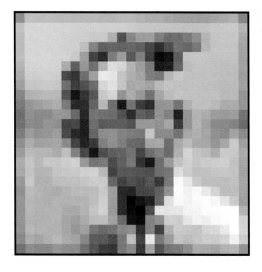

Figure 1.8 A small image enlarged to show the individual pixels.

Even the large areas of solid color are made up of individual pixels, but because they are of the same color, you cannot see a separation between them. Notice that the smaller image appears at a size that is similar to what you would see displayed on your monitor and how the colors seem to merge smoothly with one another. This brings up the next important thing you need to know about raster-based images, and that is the issue of the image's resolution.

Often when you are discussing or listening to discussions about pixel-based images, you will hear them discussed in terms of resolution. What exactly does the resolution of an image mean? The resolution of an image is simply the way of describing the number of pixels displayed within a specific unit of measure. On the computer screen this is described as the number of "pixels per inch," or ppi. As stated earlier, the typical screen resolution of an image is between 72 and 96 pixels per inch. In print, the resolution of an image is described as the number of "dots per inch," or dpi. The average printer connected to a computer will need an image that is somewhere between 200 and 300 dots per inch to get a good print. For all practical purposes, ppi and dpi can be thought of as the same thing.

Understanding this difference between screen resolution and print resolution is critical to your success as a digital artist. When thinking about printing your digital art, you can think of pixels and dots as being the same size. Knowing this, you will be able to estimate just how big an image displayed on your screen will print. Assume the image you have displayed on your screen is about 300 pixels wide or about 4.16 screen inches at 72 pixels per inch screen resolution. How big will it print? The simple formula is to divide the size of your screen image by 300 or the resolution of your printer. In this case, an image that displays 300 pixels wide on your screen will only print 1 inch wide. Unless you are looking for a very small print, this will not do. If you want a printed image that is 3 inches wide you would need an image that is 900 pixels wide on the screen. This size image would display on your screen at about 12.5 inches wide at a 72 dpi screen resolution. This shows you that you should not be fooled by the image displayed on your screen, thinking that it will print at the same size you are viewing. Not understanding the difference between screen and print resolution is one of the most common mistakes of beginning digital artists.

There is one more thing you need to be aware of when working with raster images. Raster images are resolution dependent. This means that you will not simply be able to increase the size of the image on your screen to get it to print out without the quality of the image suffering significantly. That is, your 300-pixel-wide image in the previous example could not be increased to 900 pixels wide without a great deal of damage to the way the image looks. It would indeed print 3 inches wide on your printer, but the results would not be acceptable. This is also why an image that is 300 dpi, when opened in your image editing program, appears so large.

When you change the resolution and size of an image in your image editing program, you are doing so through that program's ability to resample the image. A number of different and complex ways of resampling an image are currently used. It is enough for us as artists to realize that whenever you resample an image using any method, you are changing the image in a fundamental way. If you increase the size of the image, the program has to invent pixels to be placed beside the original pixels to make the image larger. The program usually accomplishes this by looking at the pixels surrounding the newly created ones and averaging the color and value of the created pixel. When you make an image smaller, you are asking the program to essentially throw away pixels of the original image and hope it makes good choices. Both generally do not give good results. If you need to resample an image up in size, try to not make the image more than twice as large. You can resize a 300-pixel-wide image up to about 600 pixels wide without suffering a significant loss of quality to the image.

Always take into consideration the final use of your art and create the image to a size that is appropriate. If you are creating an image that will only be used on-screen, the image will be smaller than one that you want to create for print purposes.

Many different formats exist in which you can save your raster images, and the good news is that it is relatively easy to change the image into a different format if needed for a different purpose. Also, for the most part, raster images in almost any format are easily viewable by others using a number of image viewing programs, many of which are available on the Internet for free.

The most important things to remember about raster or bitmap images are the following:

- Bitmap images are made of pixels.
- Bitmap images cannot be made either larger or smaller without some loss in the image quality.
- There are very many different formats that bitmap images can be saved as and they are generally easy to convert between images.

Vector Images

Although there are many reasons why you might want to use a program to create vector-based art, that is not the focus of this book and vector art will only be introduced here.

Vector art is a very different type of image when compared to raster-based art. Vector images are made up from many individual objects arranged to create an image. These objects can be as simple as a straight line, a curved line, a simple shape, or a complex shape. The individual elements, their complexity, and their arrangement is limited only by the skill of the artist. All of these objects are defined by mathematical formulas and are very easily moved and manipulated within an image. Because these independent objects are defined by mathematical formulas and not pixels, vector images can be enlarged or reduced without affecting the quality of the image. After all, a circle is a circle no matter how big or small it is.

Vector images are the image types created by programs such as Adobe Illustrator and Corel DRAW. Vector images are very good for representing linear objects. Producing linear art much as you would with pen and ink and flat-colored styles of art are the strength of vector programs. Vector-based programs are getting better at creating more complex images but they are not at all suited for producing images with a photographic or painted feel.

Vector images display on your screen as pixels and are converted to a pixel-based image within the program you are using to print. You should always make it a point to save your images in their vector format even though you will ultimately need to convert the image to a raster format. There are not as many vector formats available as there are raster-based formats, and converting between formats is sometimes not very easy.

A few things to remember about vector images are:

- Vector images are made of individual objects combined to create an image.
- Vector objects can be transformed and manipulated with no loss of quality to the image.
- Vector images must generally be converted to raster (bitmap) images before they are printed.
- Fewer vector image formats are available to the digital artist than raster formats, and there is sometimes difficulty when converting one vector format to another.

Most of the art you will be creating as a digital artist will be raster based (bitmaps), so this will be the focus of the rest of the book when dealing with 2D art. Many good 2D art programs are available out there. Some are geared toward manipulating photographs and correcting the look of images, some are made for the sole purpose of digital painting, some are for drawing and producing more graphic looking images, and some are made to be very accurate for scientific and industrial applications. Many are made so they have the ability in the hands of a skilled user to cross boundaries and be used for a number of different projects.

The programs range in price from very expensive, such as Adobe Photoshop, to some that are actually free. As with many things in life, you often get what you pay for and the features in a program such as Photoshop are almost too numerous to name and definitely geared toward the professional digital artist. Some of the less expensive and free programs have a very limited range of features and yet are no less useful to the beginning or professional digital artist.

Figure 1.9 A digital painting created in Painter.

The program used in this book is Corel Painter. Corel Painter, now in its ninth version, is the premiere digital art creation tool. There is not another program available at any price that, when matched with a skilled artist, can produce as beautiful results. Figure 1.9 shows a digital painting created in Painter.

This mid-priced digital painting program is unmatched in its ability to create digital art that mimics traditional media. Not only are you able to imitate the look of traditional mediums, but you can combine digital media that you could never mix in the traditional world. For example, it is very easy to combine an oil paint and watercolor look within Painter.

Painter is being used more and more across many different artistic disciplines to create art. Users include medical illustrators, game developers, digital photographers, concept artists, illustrators, and plain old fine artists. More and more artists who are interested in digital art as a hobby are discovering the almost unlimited potential of Painter. You can find additional information about Painter at www.corel.com.

Our focus in the 2D section of this book is the creation of digital art that looks like a painting, and all the tutorials in this book have been created using Painter.

The people at Corel have kindly allowed us to include a 30-day evaluation copy of Painter on the companion website www.courseptr.com/downloads. In addition, you will also find many custom brushes, patterns, and paper textures created expressly for you to use as you paint.

3D Art Programs

Many great 3D software programs are available from which an artist can choose to create art. 3D programs are typically more expensive than 2D programs because of their greater complexity. Some of the most popular 3D programs are:

- Maya—www.alias.com
- 3D Studio Max—www.discreet.com
- Softimage—www.softimage.com
- Formz—www.formz.com
- Cinema 4D—www.maxon-computer.com
- LightWave—www.newtek.com

All of these 3D programs have features that make them unique, but they are all similar in many ways as well—the choice of which one to use will depend on your individual preferences.

For this book we will focus on Maya, which is created by Alias, because it has one of the largest user bases. It is also one of the most flexible programs, allowing for the greatest artistic expression. Maya is widely used in both the motion picture and video game industries. It is also one of the best 3D programs for creating digital art. Figure 1.10 shows a scene from a video game. The characters and environment were all created in Maya.

Note

Maya is the product of the folks at Alias. They have generously created a learning edition of their software. The Maya, Personal Learning Edition is a full-featured product made for educational purposes and is not intended for commercial use. If you don't have any experience working in Maya and want to try it out, try the learning edition to see if you like it. It can be downloaded from www.alias.com.

Figure 1.10 Maya is widely used in video game productions.

3D Digital Art

3D digital art is the building of 3D virtual environments, objects, and characters for use in the creation of digital pictures. The pictures may be individual works of art or they may be connected in a series like in video productions or games.

The 3D digital artist, rather than creating a 2D painting of a subject, creates everything in virtual 3D and then renders the image on the computer. Rendering is the process of creating a 2D image of a 3D scene. After the rendering the 3D digital artist may enhance the image with 2D painting techniques.

Some digital artists use 3D simply to set up scenes or characters, whereas others use 3D for the entire picture. A lot depends on the effect the artist is working toward and the knowledge the artist has of both 2D and 3D image creation techniques.

In addition to creating single images, 3D art is used extensively for animation where multiple images are rendered in sequence to show movement. This is how 3D art is used in motion pictures.

Advantages of 3D Digital Art

3D art offers many advantages to the digital artist. These advantages are flexibility in camera angles, duplicating objects, and reusing scene elements.

Flexibility

The biggest advantage of 3D digital art is that the artist can create many pieces of art from the same assets. For example, the artist might be working on a scene with several figures in a hotel lobby. With 3D art techniques the artist first creates the lobby and then populates it with the furniture, fixtures, and figures. This takes some time but once everything is in place, the artist is able to view the scene from any angle and move figures and furniture for multiple pictures from the same basic assets. In 2D, changing views would require the artist to create an entirely new painting.

Duplicating Objects

3D art also has the advantage of duplicating objects. Figure 1.11 is a screen shot from Maya. It shows a room with several columns. Creating this room in a 2D paint program would require the artist to paint in each column. In a 3D program the column is created once and duplicated. Then the duplicate columns are placed in their appropriate locations within the scene.

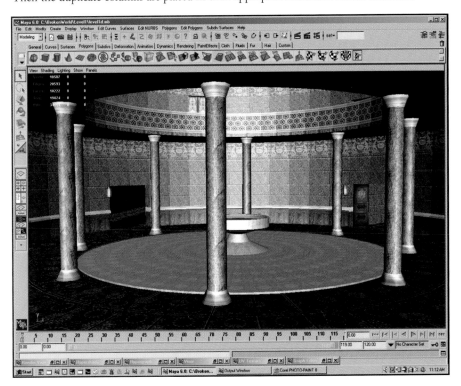

Figure 1.11 3D objects like these columns can be duplicated.

Reusing Scene Elements

3D objects are reusable. If, for example, you create a chair in a 3D program, that chair can be reused for other pictures without having to re-create it. This allows for many advantages to the 3D artist. The more scene elements the artist creates in the process of his work, the larger his library of scene elements becomes. He can then choose elements for upcoming pictures from those he has already created, saving time and money in the process. This can be a big help to artists who deal with the same subject matter extensively.

An artist who specializes in architectural renderings does not have to paint in individual trees if the work is done in 3D. Several types of trees can be created in 3D and then saved to the artist's library. All the artist then has to do is load one or more of the trees into the 3D scene of the building and place them in the scene.

Modifying Objects

3D objects can be easily changed or modified, creating new scene elements without having to completely rebuild them. The changes can be as simple as changing the surface of the object to give it a different look. For example, a building can go from a brick surface to stucco by simply changing the texture used in the model. A tree can be scaled to give the artist a variety of sizes without rebuilding the tree.

Some changes may be complex such as changing a human character from a businessman to a construction worker, but starting out with a human model still saves extensive modeling. 3D artists often create extensive 3D libraries of their work and instead of building new models, they often will take models that are similar and modify them to meet the needs of a new project.

3D Digital Art Creation Methods

3D digital art can be created in a number of ways. These methods include polygons, NURBS, and subdivision surfaces, among others. The method used for creating 3D digital art depends on the final purpose of the art. Polygons are best for situations in which there are heavy limitations on the display of the art, like in video games. NURBS are better for smooth, rounded surfaces where the final image is a rendering. Subdivisional surfaces are a blend of polygon and NURBS modeling techniques that have advantages for both limited and rendered applications.

Polygons

A polygon is a flat plane defined in 3D space by three or four vertices. The word *vertices* is the plural for vertex, which is a single point in 3D space. If a polygon is defined by three vertices, it will be a triangle. Triangle polygons are often referred to as *tris*. Figure 1.12 shows a single polygon with three vertices. The vertices are the yellow dots at the corners of the polygon.

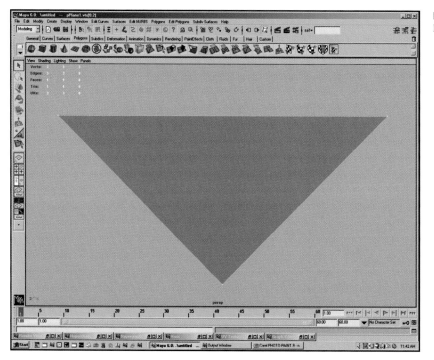

Figure 1.12 A three-sided polygon has three vertices.

If a polygon is defined by four vertices, it will have four sides. Four-sided polygons are often referred to as *quads*. Figure 1.13 shows a four-sided polygon.

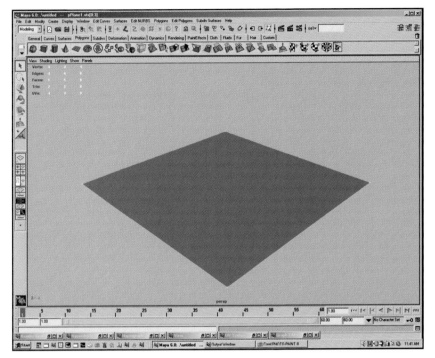

Figure 1.13 A four-sided polygon has four vertices.

Four-sided polygons are the most common type of polygon used in creating models. Three-sided polygons are the basic rendering polygon. Many rendering programs for games and other real-time applications will only work with three-sided polygons. Because of this, many 3D programs allow the artist to create the models using four-sided polygons and then convert them to three-sided polygons when the artist is finished. This process is called *triangulation*, but it doesn't refer to locating something on a map.

NURBS

NURBS is an acronym that stands for Non-Uniform Rational B-Splines. I am sure this has some meaning to a mathematician, but for the artist it means that NURBS are models created with curves. Figure 1.14 shows a NURBS sphere next to a polygon sphere. The NURBS sphere is rounded, whereas the polygon sphere is made up of many flat planes.

The advantage of using NURBS for rounded surfaces should be obvious. NURBS models are great for creating smooth rounded surfaces like balls or a human hand. A NURBS model can be easily modified to change the shape of a curve. Figure 1.15 shows the NURBS model modified to a new shape. Notice that the curves are still smooth.

The problem with NURBS models is that working with curves can sometimes be difficult, especially when fine detail is needed or when models need both rounded and flat surfaces or creases. NURBS models are also a problem when it comes to specific rendering engines. Most real-time rendering engines do not support NURBS surfaces, so the models have to be converted to polygons before they can be rendered.

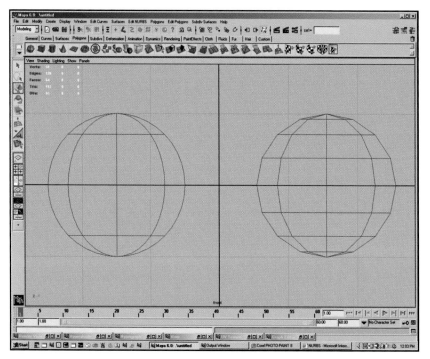

Figure 1.14 NURBS models are made up of curves, whereas polygon models are made up of flat planes.

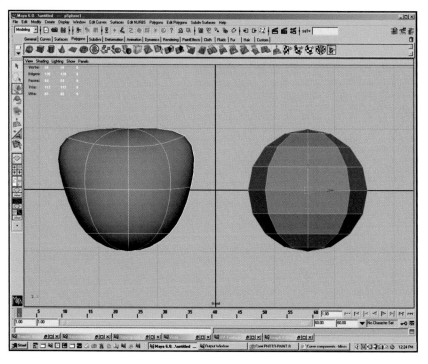

Figure 1.15 The NURBS model remains smooth when the shape is changed.

Subdivision Surfaces

A *subdivision surface* is a hybrid between polygons and NURBS in that it combines the best features of both methods. Subdivision surfaces allow the use of a single surface to model complex shapes. The single surface can have different levels of detail in different areas. For example, when modeling a hand greater detail can be in the areas of the fingernails and less detail in the areas of the palm. This ability to subdivide areas of a model is where subdivision surfaces get their name. Figure 1.16 shows three spheres. The one on the left is a NURBS sphere, the one in the middle is a polygon sphere, and the one on the right is a subdivision surface sphere. Examples of building models with these three methods are shown later in the book.

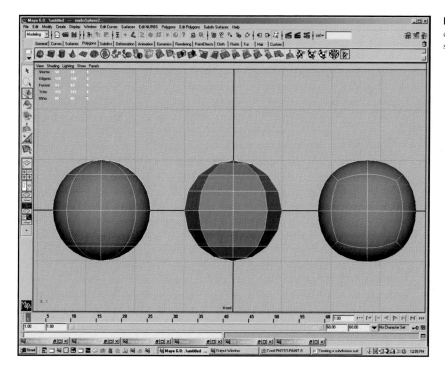

Figure 1.16 These spheres were created using NURBS, polygons, and subdivision surfaces.

Summary

This chapter covered the following topics:

- A brief introduction to digital art.
- A history of digital art tracing its origin and development to the present.
- A basic overview of the two main and very different types of 2D images. These include raster (bitmap) images and vector images.
- A very brief introduction to Painter, the program that was used to create the 2D tutorials within this book.
- A short list of 3D art programs.
- An explanation of 3D digital art with some of its advantages for the digital artist.
- A description of 3D modeling methods with examples.

The following chapters give several hands-on examples that demonstrate how to create digital art. Each chapter gives step-by-step demonstrations to help you learn by doing. Talking about art is okay if you are not interested in becoming an artist, but to really understand how to create digital art, the artist needs to actively create. We hope you will enjoy the demonstrations and try a few.

2

Digital 2D Art and Photo Manipulation

You no longer have to pay a premium price for the basic system to get you started on your way to creating 2D computer art or exploring digital photo manipulation. The cost of becoming a digital artist gets less expensive each year. The first part of this chapter introduces you to what you need to begin your trip of digital artistic discovery, and the second part explores some exercises with photo manipulation.

What You Will Need

First and foremost you need a computer. Will just any computer do? Well, for the most part, just about anything that you buy at your local computer store or even your discount outlet will be adequate for our future tasks. The system requirements for a computer used to create 2D digital art are, as a general rule, not nearly as substantial as computers used to create 3D art.

The first choice you will need to make is what type of computer you will purchase. Will it be an Apple computer or a Windows-based computer, often just referred to as a PC, that you choose? Which platform is best for the digital artist?

Users of both will sing the praises of their particular operating system. The truth is that they are both great. In the past, most graphic artists used Apple Macintosh systems for their work and it became known as the machine of choice for artists. In fact, many printers and service bureaus would not accept files unless they were in a Macintosh format. The times have changed, and nowadays you will find professional artists using both Windows and Apple systems. And printers no longer require files to be in Macintosh formats. Which should you choose?

There are a couple of things that distinguish the two types of computers from each other.

- **Price**. You will as a general rule pay more for an Apple computer than you will for a Windows-based machine. This is due largely to more competition between manufacturers in the Windows-based computer market.

- **Ease of use**. Many users will tell you that there is no easier computer to use than an Apple. Others will tell you that both are just as easy to use anymore. You should probably choose what you are most comfortable with.

- **Available software**. If you are going to use the computer for things other than creating digital art, you should probably consider purchasing a Windows-based machine. There is more software available for the PC, especially if you plan to play games.

Aside from those few reasons, there is not really a right or wrong answer. Many artists find themselves using both in their work. Oftentimes, they will have one type at the office and the other at home.

Whichever you choose, you will need to consider a few things when purchasing a computer to use for digital art.

This section lists some things that you should look for and be aware of when you purchase that computer.

Memory

The most important consideration when purchasing a computer for 2D art purposes is the amount of memory installed. Most systems that you can purchase nowadays will have at least 256 megabytes of memory already installed. This should be your minimum target amount. Many systems will have 512 megabytes of memory, which is more ideal. As your skill increases, you will probably want to increase this amount to 1 gigabyte or even more.

If you are upgrading your current machine, adding more memory will be the most cost-effective and inexpensive upgrade you can make to give your computer better performance.

The CPU

The CPU is the heart of the computer. It goes without saying that the faster the processor, the less time you will have to wait for things to happen on your computer. Any processor that is faster than about 700 MHz will be just fine for most 2D art tasks.

The Hard Drive

Bigger is better. You will be saving the images that you create, and you may save many versions of the same image as you are creating it. You will want as large a hard drive as you can afford. Most computers these days come with at least a 40-gigabyte hard drive, and this will be adequate. If you can afford a larger one, by all means get one. You can never have too much hard drive space.

In addition to hard drives, most computers also come equipped with a CD burner and sometimes even a DVD burner. Burnable CDs cost less than five cents each, so there is no good reason not to back up your work at the end of each painting. If you are lucky enough to have a DVD burner, backing up your work will be even more convenient because you can get many more images on each disc.

The Monitor

Your computer's monitor may be the part of the computer that has the longest lifespan. It is not uncommon to use a monitor long after the computer it was originally purchased with becomes obsolete. You may consider using the monitor that came with an older computer since it still works fine, but if you are using a monitor that is more than three or four years old, consider purchasing a new one. The clarity and brightness of a new monitor will be worth the price.

Most computers today come with at least a 17-inch CTR monitor. If you can afford a larger monitor, by all means, get it. You will not regret your decision. Most professional computer artists use at least a 21-inch monitor and many are using dual-monitor setups. If you can afford one of the new LCD monitors, you may want to consider this as an option because, as a rule, they are very bright and have good color. Before you purchase your monitor, make sure that you do the research to find out which one is the right model for you; you may be using this monitor for many years. If possible you should see the monitor in action at a local computer store before buying. Prices can vary widely, so shop around.

If you can afford it, consider purchasing two monitors to use at the same time. This is a great setup because you can put your reference materials on one screen and your painting program on the other. You won't have to switch between programs, or windows within programs, to see your painting and your reference. Some programs even allow you to span the two monitors, so you will have lots of space for your actual painting. If you decide to use two monitors, make sure that the video card you have will support both. If it doesn't, you will have to add an additional video card or get a new one that has dual-monitor support.

The Video Card

Without a good video card, the best monitor in the world will not display good images. The best consumer-grade video cards are made for game enthusiasts and are also fantastic cards for the digital artist. You want a card with at least 32 megabytes of video memory. It is good advice to stick with one of the major video card manufacturers' products as their technical support and the availability of drivers will be better than an off brand. It is just as important to do your research about these different manufacturers' cards and then shop around to find the best card in your price range for the task at hand. Most of this information is easily accessible on the Internet and in computer-related magazines.

There you have it. These are the basic components of the computer that will serve you well as a digital artist.

The following sections discuss some additional things you might want to consider buying to make your experience more pleasant.

A Stylus and Tablet

A tablet and stylus really is a necessity when painting digital art. Although you can create very beautiful digital 2D art using a mouse, you will have a much easier time if you have a stylus and a tablet. Painting with a mouse can be likened to painting with a bar of soap—you have about the same amount of control.

The best tablets are made by Wacom. Wacom has just come out with its new Intous 3 tablets, and they come in sizes ranging from 4"×5" to 12"×18" in size. You can still purchase the Intous 2 models, which are less expensive than the new model, and if you look harder, you might still be able to find used Intous 1 and even Art Pad models. They will all pretty much work the same, except the new Intous 3 has some buttons and touch pads built into the tablet that may make your work easier. Your decision should be based on the amount of desk space that you have and your budget. With limited desk space, or if you are going to be traveling and using your tablet with a notebook computer, you will probably want to opt for the 4"×5" model. Most people find the 6"×8" size to be the perfect compromise between cost and size. It is small enough to fit on most desks and big enough that you will not feel cramped when you are drawing and painting. Wacom also has a model called the Graphire, which is a good alternative if you are on a budget. Of course, you may want to investigate other companies that manufacture tablets as well so that you can shop around to find the best buy.

A Scanner

You will need some way to get sketches that you draw into the computer, and the easiest way is with a scanner. Scanners are available in almost every store that sells computer accessories. The prices of scanners start right around $50.00 and go up from there. You can find a good and very serviceable scanner for less than $150.00.

Do not be seduced by the scanning resolution advertised on the box. Many scanners nowadays will scan at resolutions greater than 4800 lpi interpolated and 2800 lpi hardware resolution. Lpi stands for lines per inch, and the only reason you may ever need a resolution over 2800 lpi is if you are scanning film or slides, and only then if your scanner has that function. Different manufacturers advertise different resolutions, so read the box before you buy. You will hardly ever need to scan something at a resolution that is greater than 600 lpi, and more often than not, you will not need to scan at a resolution greater than 300 lpi for superb quality printing. If you are only going to be working at the screen resolution, you will be scanning at less than 100 lpi. The point of all this is that you should not spend more money to get higher resolution scans unless there is a very good reason to do so.

A Digital Camera

Another piece of equipment that you should consider purchasing for your digital toolbox is a digital camera. For most of your paintings, you will want reference materials to refer to while painting. Although it is not a problem, and is often encouraged, to copy someone else's paintings while you are learning, there will come a time when you will need materials of your own to aid you in creating your digital paintings. A digital camera with a 4-megapixel image will be quite adequate, and the prices are continuing to fall.

A Printer

You may indeed want to get a printer, but there are two ways to think about what type of printer you get. A good printer will cost you $200.00 or more and is a good investment, but it will only print on 8½"×11" paper. If you are planning to print larger than that, the cost of the printer will go up dramatically. You can buy serviceable printers for less than $100.00 with quite good color. So how do you make a decision on what printer to buy? If you are going to do a lot of larger-format printing, you probably want to go with a more expensive printer. But if you are going to print only your best images at a larger format, go for a less expensive printer to proof your work and then take the file to be printed at any one of the many print shops available in almost every city. These print shops have better printers than most of us can afford and they usually keep up with the new technology. A big plus is that you will not be paying for bad prints. On the downside, the price of the prints will be slightly higher.

If you acquire all the items discussed so far, you will have a good setup and you'll be ready to embark on your journey to being a 2D digital artist. The only thing missing is software. Which software should you choose? The next section looks at a number of different applications that are easily available to the beginning 2D digital artist.

Digital Painting Software

When you begin looking around the Web, catalogs, or retail stores for 2D painting software, the first thing you will notice is that very few applications are called "painting" software. Most the software you will find is called "image-editing" software. An example of image-editing software would be Adobe Photoshop. This particular program is made specifically for manipulating photographs or already-produced images. This does not mean that image-editing programs cannot be used for painting. In fact, most of these applications have numerous painting tools included with their image-editing capabilities. An example of software created specifically for digital painting would be Corel Painter. This type of software is specifically for image creation from scratch though you can also use it to edit images.

The discussion starts with a list of free software and ends with a list of some of the more expensive applications. This is by no means a comprehensive list, but it will give you a place to start looking. Also, be aware that new programs are appearing every day so you should always be on the lookout for interesting and new programs that could make your artistic expression easier and more interesting. Because this list is not a review of the mentioned programs, if you are interested in what others think or want a review before downloading or purchasing these programs, I suggest you look on the Web. A good site that generally has reviews and recommendations for graphics software is http://graphicssoft.about.com/. If you are downloading the program, you will probably find that the Web site you download the program from will have reviews from different users.

Free Software

The following programs are fantastic in at least one respect—they are all free for you to use. Also be aware that number of features is not always that important for basic painting processes although as a general rule, it is good to experiment with what is available. Some of these programs have many features, whereas others only have a few, so use whatever will get the job done for you. Let's start with some software for the PC:

- **GIMP for Windows.** Originally developed for Linux users, this program has an interface and some features that are similar to Photoshop. http://www.gimp.org/

- **Art Rage.** Probably my favorite of the bunch. It has tools that really leave you feeling like you are using real paint on the computer. http://www.ambientdesign.com/artrage.html

- **Pixia.** An English version of a free image-editing and painting program originally from Japan. http://park18.wakwak.com/~pixia/

Here are a few for the Mac platform:

- **Future Paint.** This program is compatible with Mac operating systems up through OS X and offers quite a few features. http://www.stazsoftware.com/futurepaint/

- **Rainbox.** A free program, although not necessarily a true painting program. You can make some rather wild designs using it. It is a simple enough program that children will have no trouble using it. http://www.axlrosen.net/rainbox.html

- **Pixen.** This is a small painting program that excels at doing very small images and "pixel" art. This program is best suited for very small paintings built pixel by pixel. If you have lots of patience and a meticulous way of working, you might enjoy building images this way. http://www.opensword.org/Pixen/

You can find other free programs out there if you look around a little bit. If you are new to digital painting, try some of these applications just to get a feel for painting on the computer. A good source of free and shareware software is www.simtel.net in their graphics section.

Shareware Graphics Software

Shareware is not free software, but software that the author lets you try out to see if you like it before you buy it. Sometimes the program is a full version with all features available, and sometimes it is a limited version with features disabled. The next few programs are shareware or relatively inexpensive. Most have a demo version that you can download.

These programs are for the PC:

- **Photobrush.** This is a rather nice program with some very good features. It has brushes that give a natural feeling along with tools that are useful for photo editing. http://www.mediachance.com/pbrush/

- **Project Dogwaffle.** How is that for a name for a painting program? This is a very good program as far as its brushes go and it has a few features that you won't find in any other program regardless of cost. In particular, it has brushes that operate on a particle-based system, making the painting of things such as fields of grass, trees, and other repetitive objects easy and interesting. http://www.squirreldome.com/cyberop.htm

- **Ultimate Paint.** This is a full-featured painting and image-editing program. It is a fast and easy program to use with many quality effects that you can apply to your images. However, effects and plug-in filters are not really ways of painting on the computer; they are quick means of changing the way an image looks. http://www.ultimatepaint.com/

These programs are for the Mac:

- **Rainbow Painter.** This is an interesting program with a rather unique interface. It has many features, including more than 60 different effects that you can apply to your painting. http://www.rainbowpainter.com/

- **Future Paint.** This is a program that is bristling with features, including many different effects. In addition to painting and creating images, Future Paint has file management features, such as the ability to convert files in a folder from one format into another format, and creating thumbnails. http://www.stazsoftware.com/futurepaint/

- **Painting.** This is a very simple yet powerful painting program. It doesn't have many bells and whistles, but this is a good program if you want to just paint a picture. http://www.sarwat.net/painting/

Once again, numerous other programs are available. This is simply a small sampling of a few programs that are either free or inexpensive. Depending on the depth of your pockets, any of these would be a great starting place to learn some of the basics about 2D digital art.

Here now are some of the ultimate 2D digital painting programs. These programs are all available for both the Mac and PC except for Paint Shop Pro, which is PC-only, and Studio Artist, which is Mac-only.

- **Adobe Photoshop.** This is the granddaddy of all 2D image-editing programs. It is used by most professionals in all industries that create digital imagery. It is also the most expensive of the programs mentioned here, costing upwards of $600. If you are a student or associated with a school, college, or university you will be able to find a copy for around $250. You will need to do your shopping to find the best deal. Coupled with the price is a steep learning curve—it takes lots of work to understand all the features that this program has to offer and how to use them to best advantage. Although the brushes in Photoshop are getting better and better in every new version, it was never meant to be a painting program first and foremost. It is a very flexible and powerful image-editing, painting, almost-anything-you-want program. Photoshop is not for everyone, but if you are willing to devote the necessary time and effort to learn it, you will have the ultimate image-editing tool that will also work extremely well when you want to paint. A huge number of third-party books have been written for Photoshop that are dedicated to almost anything you would ever want to use the application for, from making Web graphics to retouching photographs to painting 2D textures for video games. http://www.adobe.com

- **Corel Painter.** Just as the name implies, this program is for painting. Far and away the finest painting program available at any price; nothing compares when it comes to being able to mimic traditional artistic media with digital tools. This program also has a rather steep learning curve, but it is about half the price of Photoshop. Painter ships with hundreds of brushes, which is way more than you will ever need, but part of the strength of this program is the ability to customize and create your own brushes. It is often difficult to tell if a painting was done with traditional media or Painter when looking at a print. Along with Painter's superb image-creating features, it also gives you the ability to paint animations in much the same way a traditional animator would. Painter will be the program that is used in the tutorials throughout this book. http://www.corel.com.

- **Jasc Paint Shop Pro.** This PC-only program has always been looked upon as kind of an inexpensive Photoshop wannabe. In the past this has been to some degree true, but no longer. With the last few versions, the program has come into its own and now has a very capable set of painting and image-manipulation tools. It also has a large and loyal user base. Paint Shop Pro has recently been acquired by Corel, so look for it under its new owner's name. http://www.corel.com

- **Corel Photo Paint.** This is part of the Corel Graphics Suite. It is a very capable image editor with some of the best selection tools available. It has some brushes that you won't find in any other image editor. To get the best bang for your buck, Photo Paint is one of the best buys around. http://www.corel.com

- **Synthetik Studio Artist.** This is a Mac-only application that can "automatically paint and draw." Although you can paint with Studio Artist, it is really for the most part a super cloning program that works just as well on animations. It ships with more than 3000 painting presets that are completely editable. Studio Artist is a complicated program to master, but worth the effort. http://www.synthetik.com

I would like to mention one more program that is a rather strange yet powerful application, but that is in a class of its own. Z-Brush is like nothing else out there. It is a relatively expensive program with an unusual interface that can be confusing when learning it. It is not only a painting program, but also a true 3D modeling program that excels at creating creatures and organic shapes. When not creating in 3D, you can paint with this program but the difference is that your pixels not only have an x and y orientation, but also will paint with true depth. Z-Brush calls its pixels "pixols" to indicate that they have z-axis information. Pixologic, the maker of Z-Brush, calls this "painting in 2.5D." When painting with depth, you are able to change the lighting on the scene and it will update in the painted image. If you are looking for something unusual, new, and full of creative potential, you can do a lot worse than Z-Brush.

Now that you have had a very brief overview of some of the 2D software available, including an interesting 2.5D painting program, you have a choice to make. Which tool are you going to use to become a 2D digital artist? That decision will be up to you, but the rest of the 2D sections in this book use Corel Painter IX because of the strength of its painting features and, in particular, the brushes and their ability to interact with paper textures. A 30-day demo version can be downloaded for either the Mac or PC at www.corel.com.

Let's Get Started

Often as artists when we are trying something new we will become frustrated not only by our unfamiliarity with the new tool we are using but also by our perceived skills or lack thereof in creating images. We are most often our own worst critics. Because of this tendency, our first foray into the world of 2D digital art will try to ease some of this frustration by introducing digital art created using photographs. This will remove the self-imposed pressure on our drawing and painting skills and let us concentrate on becoming more familiar with the new tools we will be using. Let's leave the drawing and painting skills to further development in later chapters and just have a bit of fun in this one.

Without further delay let's start making digital art based on a photograph.

The current generation of digital painting software makes the creation of art from photographs very easy. You can create an image that looks like a traditional oil painting, a watercolor, a pencil sketch, a pastel painting, and even creations that look like something entirely new and different. The results that are possible are limited only by your imagination.

In this part of the chapter, you'll take a photograph and run it through a number of different methods to make it look like something entirely different. You can manipulate an image in a number of different ways to make it look like a painting. Some methods are better than others, and this chapter looks at several techniques.

You may be wondering why you would want to do this, and there are several good reasons. If you are a professional or amateur photographer you may be looking for that little extra something that will set your work apart from other photographers. Transforming all or a part of your original photograph into an image that looks like it was created by artistic means different than photography could be that different touch. If you are an illustrator who works in the digital realm, you may want to experiment with a different look for a particular job. Being able to change the look of your image from, say, watercolor to pastel could be just what a particular job needs to be successful. Not only will the ability to change the look of the image be valuable, but you will always have the original to fall back on. You do not have to worry about ruining any of your work while experimenting. Your range as an artist has just increased immensely.

In this chapter of the book, you will take a photograph of your choice and do several different things to change its look. First, you will simply use a plugin filter that is available for any program that supports Photoshop-compatible plugin filters and play with the different settings to see what can be done virtually automatically to any image you have. After this first section using the Virtual Painter plugin filter, you will take your photograph, and in a more artistic way change its appearance to resemble an oil painting, an impressionistic painting, a watercolor, and a pastel painting. Once you have seen what can be done in these few examples, a whole new world of creative photo manipulation will be opened to you, whether you are a photographer or an artist.

Used in the first few examples manipulating an image is a Photoshop-compatible plugin filter called Jasc Virtual Painter, and it is available for trial download at http://www.jasc.com/products/vpainter/vptrialreg.asp?. This plugin filter should be installed in the Painter Plugins directory.

Although most image-editing software has the ability to alter an image using effects and plugin filters, this tutorial uses Painter because of the ease and control that you as the artist have over the process.

Manipulating a Photograph to Create a Digital Painting

This first tutorial uses Corel Painter IX to take a photograph and make it a painting. Not only will you make it a painting, but you will make it into multiple paintings that look like different media. The techniques used are really quite easy to learn, but depend on you to master for the best results. It is assumed, though, that you know how to do the following:

- Open an image in Painter.

- Clone an image.

- Perform basic layer functions.

- Navigate in Painter and find the brushes, paper textures, effects menus, and so on.

- Generally correct the color balance, contrast, and lightness or darkness of the photograph.

This chapter briefly touches on these subjects, but if you want an in-depth understanding, you should consult the Painter manual. The techniques demonstrated will work with any version of Painter from 7 on.

You are, of course, welcome to do any of the initial photo adjustments in a different program, such as Photoshop or any other program you are comfortable with. This chapter does not cover general photo-correction techniques. If you are interested in photo-correction techniques, there are many good books available at your local bookstore in the computer graphics section. There is also a very good and active website that is devoted exclusively to photo retouch, restoration, and manipulation. Its web address is http://www.retouchpro.com.

What Type of Photograph Should I Use?

Because this tutorial will work with any photograph you have on hand, it is not necessary that you use the one in the example. The photograph that I am using was taken from the Corel Stock Photo Collection 4. Also, it is not necessary that you use a portrait photograph because these methods will work well with any subject matter. Find a photograph that you are fond of and let's have some fun making it into something different.

The techniques that are demonstrated will work best with a photograph that is not too large or too small. The size of the image is important only because the settings shown for the tutorial are for an image that is about 1500 pixels in the largest dimension. If you use a photograph that is larger or smaller, you will need to adjust the settings to get similar results.

The photograph that you choose should have the following attributes:

- A good and wide range of values.

- Forms that are well defined and easily recognizable. A camouflaged hunter in the forest would not be a good choice, for example.

- A wide range of colors for interest. You could just as easily use a black-and-white photograph, but the effect will be easier to see in color.

The photo used in this tutorial has good lights and darks, good color contrasts from bright reds to deep blues, and would be recognizable if blurred or distorted heavily. Figure 2.1 shows the original photograph.

Photoshop Compatible Plugin Filters

Figure 2.1 The original photograph.

Plugins are small programs that you can install and use within such programs as Photoshop, Painter, Paint Shop Pro, Corel Photo Paint, and others. Some plugins are meant to accomplish very specific tasks, such as creating seamless textures, making buttons for Web pages, swapping color channels, and so on. The plugin used in this section is Jasc Virtual Painter. A demonstration version can be downloaded at http://www.jasc.com/products/vpainter/vptrialreg.asp? The specific use of this particular filter is to alter the look of a photograph to make it look more like a painting.

A number of other plugins are available that specifically are used to make an image look more like a painting. If you would like to find out more about different plugin filters available, there is a website called The Plugin Site—http://thepluginsite.com/. Another good site is Free Photoshop, http://www.freephotoshop.com/. Between these two sites you can find out just about anything you would want to know about plugin filters.

Photographers are using plugins more and more to add a little something different to the look of an image. Although some of these plugin filters work better than others, most are not very creative because they simply require you, as the artist, to make small changes in a predefined set of features. There is nothing wrong with using these plugin filters, but you will be much happier and more creative with the techniques that are described a bit later.

Images Created Using Jasc Virtual Painter

Figure 2.2 An Oil Painting filter applied to the photograph.

The next few images show the results of applying the Jasc Virtual Painter plugin filter to the original image. These few examples are but a fraction of the available options using this particular plugin filter. If you have downloaded and installed the free demo version, by all means try different settings and experiment. The filter can be found under the Effects menu in Painter.

This section does not go into using the filter because it is very self-explanatory. Figure 2.2 shows the original photograph with an Oil Painting effect applied using the default settings in the Jasc Virtual Painter. Try different settings to see various results.

This particular filter produces an interesting, subtle result. Figures 2.3, 2.4, and 2.5 show the same photograph with a Silk Screen, Drawing, and Pastel effect applied, respectively. All of these effects were applied using the default settings in Jasc Virtual Painter.

As you can see from these examples, the filters change the photograph in subtle to extreme ways. Whether you like the effect is strictly a personal decision, but using plugin filters is really nothing more than letting the program do the work for you.

You should understand that when you use these plugins, they change your original image in a fundamental way. Because of this, it is good to make sure that you are working with a copy of the image and not the original. If you work with the original and accidentally do a "Save" and not a "Save As" command, you will have overwritten the original file and it will no longer be available.

Setting Up Your Image in Painter

In this section you will be using Painter without any additional plugins to create images that look more like they were painted with various different mediums. All of the techniques are compatible with Painter 7 on. First, here's the general procedure for setting up your image so it is ready to work with:

1. Open your image in Painter.

2. Go to the Effects menu and choose Tonal control. Use the options to make any adjustments you want as far as contrast, how light or dark the image is, and color. Do whatever you want to make the image a satisfying starting point. You can make all of these adjustments from within the Effects/Tonal Control menus. Figure 2.6 shows the location of the Tonal Controls menu.

3. In the File menu, select Clone. An exact duplicate of your original photograph is created, as shown in Figure 2.7. Painter automatically names this image "Clone of (*whatever your original image was named*)." The image is not saved at this point, so save your image and remember to save often. If the computer happens to crash, anything that you may have done will be lost. This cloning feature is a great way to make sure that you never destroy your original—simply make sure you are working on the clone image. There is no limit to the number of clones that you can create. If you clone the clone, Painter will just add another "Clone" to the image name. Be sure to check the image name often because it can sometimes be confusing with two initially identical images displayed on the screen at the same time as to which you are working on. Figure 2.7 shows the photograph cloned and displayed in front of the original image.

Figure 2.3 The photograph with the Silk Screen effect applied.

Figure 2.4 The photograph with the Drawing effect applied.

Figure 2.5 The photograph with the Pastel effect applied.

You can minimize the original image to make sure that you do not paint on the original, but do not close the image. If you mistakenly close the image, you will not have a source image to build your new painting from. Painter will default to one of its patterns as the clone source. If you have closed the image, simply open it again and in the File menu select Clone Source and choose your original image's name.

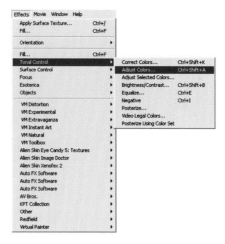

Figure 2.6 The Tonal Control menu.

4. Select the entire image using the Select menu or the keyboard shortcut (Ctrl+A on the PC or Command+A on the Mac). Press the Backspace key to clear the image. Your canvas is now blank. At the top-right corner of the image is a small button that looks like two overlapping squares. This is the Tracing Paper button. Toggle this button and your original photograph is displayed as if it were reduced in intensity by 50 percent. Figure 2.8 shows the cloned image compared to the original with an arrow pointing to the Tracing Paper button.

Notice how much lighter it appears. The display you see is not actually on the cloned image, and you can turn it off by clicking the button again. It is simply a ghost of the original image that you can use for reference.

Toggle off the Tracing Paper button. It does not need to be displayed for the next steps. Select the Cloners from the Brush Selector. The Brush Selector is located in the upper-right corner of the Painter screen and the Cloners icon looks like a rubber stamp tool.

Figure 2.7 The cloned image of the photograph. Notice the name of the image.

Figure 2.8 Toggle the Tracing Paper button so you can see the "ghost" image.

5. Select the Soft Cloner brush variant from the many different cloning brush variants available and draw in your image. The Soft Cloner will draw an airbrushed replica of the original image. Figure 2.9 shows the location of the brushes as indicated by the red arrow and some strokes made in the cloned image.

Figure 2.9 The Cloners location and some strokes made in the image with the Soft Cloner variant.

This brush variant does not make a very dynamic representation, but illustrates the point of how these Cloners work. The Soft Clone variant will be used to good advantage in later steps.

Automating the Process

There are many Cloners to explore, but first, let's automate the process a bit. Sometimes when you are working on a large image you may find it advantageous to let the computer do much of the initial work with Painter's Cloners.

1. Select the entire image and clear it. Do not close the original image. Minimize it to the bottom of the screen and get it out of the way. Choose a different Cloner for this demonstration.

2. Select the first Cloner, Bristle Brush Cloner, and set its size to about 10 pixels. To the right of where you just picked this brush is a small black triangle. Click this triangle and select Record Stroke. Draw a single stroke on your canvas. Figure 2.10 shows the location of the Record Stroke menu item.

Figure 2.10 The Record Stroke menu item.

3. When you have a stroke recorded, go back to the same menu and select Playback Stroke. Tap with your stylus or click your left mouse button anywhere in the image, and the stroke that you recorded will be painted automatically. Every time you touch the canvas with your stylus or click the mouse button, another stroke will be painted. Figure 2.11 shows the image with some recorded strokes being used to paint the cloned image.

4. Select the entire image and clear it by using the Backspace key to get a blank canvas.

5. Go back to the same menu accessed by the small triangle on the right side of the brushes and select Auto Playback. Without having to do a thing, the canvas is being filled in with your recorded stroke in a random fashion. You can let the auto stroke completely fill the canvas, or anytime you want to stop filling with the stroke, click with your cursor anywhere in the image. Figure 2.12 shows the cloned image about half filled using the Auto Playback feature.

Figure 2.11 A recorded stroke being used to paint the cloned image.

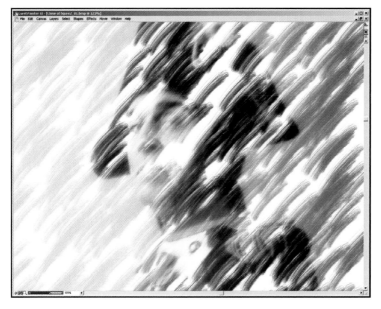

Figure 2.12 The canvas is being filled with the recorded stroke using the Auto Playback feature.

Using some of these techniques, go ahead and paint the cloned image entirely.

6. Record a new stroke using a larger brush size of about 40 pixels. Auto Playback the stroke until the canvas is covered. Because you are letting the computer paint with a bigger brush, the image is slightly fuzzy and blurry, but it is best to always start with a larger stroke. Figure 2.13 shows the canvas covered using the large brush stroke.

Just as in traditional painting, you do not want the same amount of detail over the entire image. Start out with a large brush over the entire canvas and gradually use a smaller brush where you want the clearest and most detail.

Figure 2.13 The cloned image completely painted using a large recorded stroke with Auto Playback.

Now make the brush size smaller, about 10 pixels in size. Record another stroke in a different direction and instead of using Auto Playback, check Playback Stroke. Tapping the stylus or clicking the left mouse button, work in the areas where you want greater detail. In the example image, this is in the face and medals. When you have enough refinement in these areas, stop. Figure 2.14 shows the image after using a smaller stroke to define the details.

Figure 2.14 Add some details using a recorded stroke of a smaller brush.

You should now have a pretty good-looking image. A lot of how the image ends up will depend on the brush that you are using. In some cases you may even want to add some of the original image back into the clone to accentuate the details a bit more. If you do this in a very subtle way, you will not impact the painted look. The best Cloner to use for this final finishing work is the Soft Cloner. Select the Soft Cloner brush variant and using about a 10-pixel size, add in some additional detail in the areas where you want greatest emphasis. In the case of the example this is in the eyes, nose, mouth, and some of the medals on the uniform. See Figure 2.15.

Figure 2.15 Use the Soft Cloner brush variant to add the finishing touches to the painting.

In the preceding section you saw a basic a way of using Painter's cloning feature as well as the cloning brushes to transform a photograph into an image that looks more painted than photographic. This section explores a few more of the cloning brushes and techniques to use them with a more hands-on approach rather than using Painter's automated features.

Creating an Oil Painting Look

So let's try something different and create a new image that has the look of a traditional oil painting.

1. Select the whole image and backspace to a new blank canvas.

2. Pick the Flat Impasto Cloner brush. This is an interesting brush in that it paints not only to color, but also paints to an imitation depth. In Painter this ability is called Impasto. A whole set of Impasto brushes come standard with Painter, but the brushes used to demonstrate this Impasto effect are included with the Cloners.

3. Set the size of the brush to about 36 pixels. If you use Impasto brushes that are too small, the results will not look as much like a painting. This is because when using smaller-sized Impasto brushes, you will get artifacting as the program tries to give depth to the stroke. Often this will look like small white specks or white lines through the color.

4. Turn on the Tracing Paper and quickly paint in the contours of your main object. You're just going to use this as a rough guide, so it doesn't need to be exact. Paint in the image using the brush. In the background, experiment with the direction of the stroke. Some directions will produce more pleasing results. Try making rounded strokes with the brush. You will notice that the paint is built up with a three-dimensional feel. Figure 2.16 shows the painting in progress. Notice that the three-dimensional feel is particularly visible in the lighter areas of the background. Impasto brushes tend to work best in areas without tiny details.

Figure 2.16 Paint with the Flat Impasto Cloner brush to get a three-dimensional look.

You can turn off the three-dimensional effect if you want to see how the colors are being painted. To do this, click the impasto icon, which is the little blue star-shaped icon three spots below the tracing paper icon. Figure 2.17 shows the location of this feature indicated by the red arrow and with the effect turned off so you can see how the painting looks with only two-dimensional brush strokes.

If you click this icon to activate it but are not using an Impasto brush, you will not see any change in the image.

5. Using the Soft Cloner brush, add some detail back into any area you think may need some more. Figure 2.18 shows very subtle use of the Soft Cloner brush to add a touch of detail back into the face, and in particular, the eyes.

Be careful when using some of these three-dimensional cloning brushes—even with an image that is very strong visually. Choosing the wrong brush can change an image so much that it becomes almost unrecognizable or at the least unattractive. Figure 2.19 shows the image painted using the Texture Spray Cloner. As you can see, the texture is so strong that, although it's an interesting effect, it is too much for the painting.

Figure 2.17 Click the impasto icon to turn off the three-dimensional effect.

Even if you over-texture your painting, you can fix it. To do so, select the Flat Impasto Cloner brush.

1. Select the Record Stroke menu item.

2. Record a circular stroke.

3. Auto Playback the stroke and let it fill in most of the canvas.

4. Before the Auto Playback completely finishes covering the canvas, stop it. Bits of the original texture will still show through the current strokes, giving a nice randomness to the image. It now looks more than ever like a wet oil painting. Figure 2.20 shows the resulting image.

Figure 2.18 A little detail added into the eyes and face using the Soft Cloner brush.

Creating an Impressionist Look

Let's try something new in this next example. Before clearing your canvas of the oil painted photo, take the eyedropper tool which is located in the Painter toolbox and sample a darker color from your image. In the example photo, the selected color is the deep blue/purple color from the right side of the painting. Make the secondary color active and select one of the lighter colors in your image (in the example image it is the light purplish color).

Figure 2.19 An over-textured painting created using the Texture Spray Cloner.

1. Clear the image using the technique used in earlier examples.

2. Open the Gradient palette by going to the Window/Library Palettes menu and Show Gradients. The default shortcut key combination is Ctrl+8.

3. Fill the image with a linear gradient ramping from the dark color on the left of the painting to the light color on the right using the Paint Bucket tool. If when you fill the canvas your gradient travels in the wrong direction, launch the Gradient palette and use the small red dot to set the direction that you want the gradient to fill. Figure 2.21 shows the Gradient palette with the correct direction for the fill shown on top of the filled image.

Figure 2.20 An oil painting created from a photograph using an Impasto brush and the Auto Playback feature.

4. Select the Impressionist Cloner brush and set the brush size to 50 pixels. Begin painting in the background areas, eventually covering the whole image. Try not to cover the background completely. If you need to see the original image as reference, simply turn on the tracing paper. Figure 2.22 shows the results so far, and frankly, it does not look like much at this point.

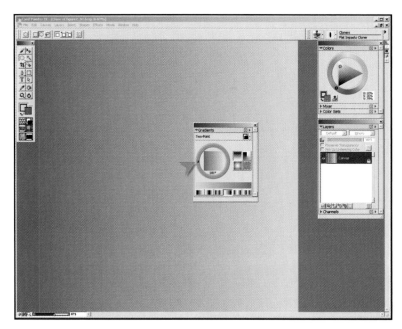

Figure 2.21 The Gradient palette and the filled image.

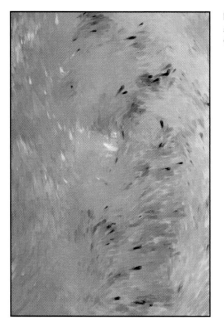

Figure 2.22 The painting after using a large version of the Impressionist Cloner brush.

5. Reduce the size of the brush to about 25 pixels and continue to paint the image. Concentrate more and more on the center of interest. If you want to see the underlying photo, turn on the Tracing Paper. Figure 2.23 shows the painting with a smaller brush used in the areas that needed to be developed more fully and the Tracing Paper turned on to help keep your strokes in the areas you want them.

Figure 2.23 The image after using a smaller brush with the Tracing Paper turned on.

Figure 2.24 shows just how abstract the image is at this point in the painting process and yet it is very much like an impressionistic painting.

Use a smaller brush of about 10 pixels in size to paint in areas of greater interest in your image. This will begin to let details emerge from all of your strokes. Figure 2.25 shows the example image with the smaller brush used mainly on the face, showing some details emerging.

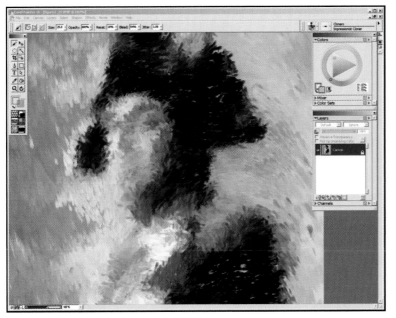

Figure 2.24 The same image with the Tracing Paper turned off showing a very abstract image.

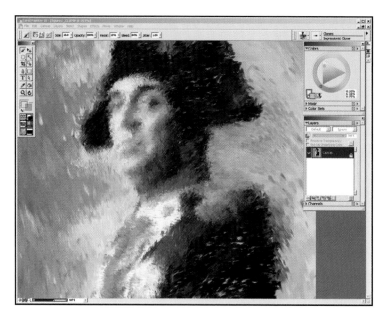

Figure 2.25 Use a smaller brush in the areas of greater interest.

Figure 2.26 shows the final image using a still smaller brush. No matter how small you use this particular variant, you will never get a great degree of detail, so once again switch to the Soft Cloner. In the example image you will see the results of using the Soft Cloner in the eye areas. You still can see the strokes created using the Impressionist Cloner but with a slightly clearer view of the eyes.

Creating a Watercolor Look

Up to this point you have been using techniques that in some ways represent oil painting. Now, let's switch gears a bit and paint a watercolor painting.

The brushes available on the Digital Watercolor brushes menu are not cloning brushes, but there is an easy way to make them cloning brushes. By doing so you can use the techniques described earlier to achieve

Figure 2.26 The final image with a touch of Soft Cloner.

many different effects. To change any brush to a cloning brush, simply click the rubber stamp button on the Colors menu. Clicking this button causes Painter to pick up color from the clone source. Figure 2.27 shows the location of this button.

1. Clear the image as before.

2. Select the Digital Watercolor brushes and choose the Simple Water variant. Make sure you are selecting the Digital Watercolor brushes and not the Watercolor brushes. They are different types of brushes.

3. Click the rubber stamp button on the Colors palette to change the Simple Variant brush into a cloning brush. Once again, set the brush to a larger size of about 30 pixels. Be careful if you are not using a very fast computer because some of these brushes are very processor-intensive. If your computer is a bit slower, use a smaller brush.

4. Go ahead and paint over the entire image with the larger water-color brush. Your results should be similar to Figure 2.28.

Figure 2.27 The rubber stamp button on the Colors menu.

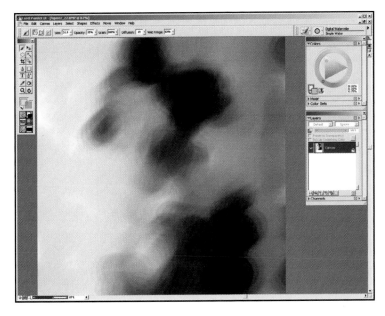

Figure 2.28 A basic block-in using the Simple Water variant of the Digital Watercolors.

5. Make the size of the brush smaller and continue to paint across the painting. Figure 2.29 shows the entire painting.

The painting is getting close to complete.

6. Make the brush even smaller and do some final work in the areas where you want the greatest amount of detail. Figure 2.30 shows the results of using a small watercolor brush on the example image.

7. You can use the Soft Cloner technique described earlier to bring in just a touch more detail if you'd like, but first you need to dry the watercolor layer. The reason that you dry the Digital Watercolor layer is to essentially lock the way the Digital Watercolor strokes look. If you do not dry the layer and change the Digital Watercolor brush, the whole painted image will change. While it is not necessary to dry the layer to use a Cloner, it is a good habit to get into when using any Digital Watercolor brush. To do this, select Dry Digital Watercolor in the Layers Menu. Figure 2.31 shows just a touch more detail added using the Soft Cloner.

Figure 2.29 Use a smaller watercolor brush across the entire painting.

You now have an image that looks like a watercolor painting. Pretty easy wasn't it?

Creating a Pastel Look

The final technique in this chapter shows the procedure for creating a pastel painting.

1. Select the entire image and clear the canvas as described earlier.

2. When the canvas is cleared, fill it with a cool, mid-value gray color. The canvas is filled with color because pastel papers are generally a color other than white. In fact, pastel paper can be almost any color imaginable. It is important to remember that when you are trying to duplicate a traditional media feel with digital tools, you should use colors and textures that would be found in those media.

3. In the Brush Selector Menu, pick the Chalk brushes and then select the Variable Chalk brush variant.

4. Set the grain to about 15 percent and the opacity to 50 percent in the top Property Bar.

5. Click the rubber stamp button in the Colors palette.

6. Beginning with a big brush that is about 20 pixels in size, start painting but don't try to completely cover the underlying paper. Figure 2.32 shows the initial rough-in.

7. In gradual steps, reduce the size of the brushes as you did in the earlier images to refine the details as you go. Figure 2.33 shows the image almost finished. You have to admit, the painting looks very much like a pastel painting.

8. And now the final touch. There is one additional step you can take that will increase the illusion of a pastel painting. From the Effects Menu, select Surface Control and choose Apply Surface Texture. The options box shown in Figure 2.34 appears.

Figure 2.30 Use an even smaller brush to add some finishing touches in the areas of greatest interest.

Figure 2.31 Dry the Watercolor layer and use the Soft Cloner brush to add just a touch of detail.

Figure 2.32 Beginning the pastel painting.

9. Move the Shine slider all the way down to "0" since pastel paper has no shine. Move the amount to about 20 percent and leave everything else at the default setting. Click OK. A nice texture is applied to the image that will enhance the illusion of a pastel painting. The complete painting is shown in Figure 2.35.

Figure 2.33 The almost finished pastel painting.

Figure 2.34 The Apply Surface Texture options box.

There you have it. Several easy and vastly different ways of converting photographs into works of art that mimic traditional mediums. The advantages of these methods are vast when compared to simply running a plugin filter. Using these methods, you as the artist are in total control of the results.

Figure 2.35 The finished painting.

Summary

In this chapter, you learned a few very important things to do when working in Painter to create works of art from your photographs, including the following:

■ What to look for in a basic computer that will be used for creating digital art.

■ A very brief look at the differences between choosing a Macintosh or PC-based computer.

■ Useful accessories you may want to purchase.

■ A brief look at some of the different software options available to the 2D digital artist.

■ How to use Photoshop compatible plugin filters.

■ How to record a stroke and how to draw with it or paint an image with it automatically.

■ How to take normal brushes and make them behave as Cloning brushes.

Hopefully you had fun and learned many different ways to change your photographs. Based on what you have learned, you can see just how many different options are open to you when using many of the other features available in Painter.

The next chapter illustrates how you can paint an original work of art within Painter starting with only a rough sketch.

3

Digital Painting

In this chapter we now go from using a photograph to creating a digital painting from scratch. Don't worry about making an exact copy of the image that I will paint. The subject matter is easy to draw and will look better with some of your own personality showing through. Use this and the following 2D tutorials as general guides to learning the techniques presented and not as images you must copy. Now, let's get started.

Creating a Digital Painting
Using Corel Painter IX

In the demonstration in the following section you will be painting an image using digital watercolor and pastel. You will use just a few of Painter's other brushes in the very early and final stages of the painting. You have lots of brushes to choose from, but part of the point of this tutorial is to show that you need only a few brushes to paint a very acceptable painting.

In this first 2D painting tutorial, you will be painting a fantasy landscape using watercolor and pastel. Because this is about creating an image and not necessarily about how to use the program, please consult the Painter manual or online help for answers to any questions you have about Painter-specific operations. Having said that, this first image is an easy image to paint, so you will not be using some of the more advanced features available in Painter. It is assumed, though, that you know how to do the following:

- Create a new image in Painter.

- Set your individual Painter preferences in the program, especially the brush-tracking feature that tells the program how to react with your individual hand pressure.

- Basic layer functions such as creating, rearranging, and changing the composite method of individual layers.

- Navigate around Painter and find things like individual brushes, different paper textures, and choose colors.
- Load custom paper libraries.

Although this tutorial briefly touches on these things, you should consult the manual for most questions. The techniques demonstrated will work with any version of Painter from 7 on up. To keep this tutorial as simple as possible, you will use only default brushes that are provided with Painter. The paper library used is Don's Paper and is available for download at the publisher's website at http://www.courseptr.com/downloads.

Starting the Painting

Start Painter, load the Don's Paper paper library, and create a new image that is 900×900 pixels at 300 dpi. This will give an image that will print 3×3 inches. You will gradually enlarge the size of the image as you develop the painting. It is sometimes good to start painting on an image that is slightly smaller in both the horizontal and vertical dimensions than you will need for the final output so that you can block in color and develop the composition of the painting quickly. As you paint you will gradually enlarge the image's dimensions so you will be able to put in more and more details without ruining the initial color composition.

Select the Fine Tip brush from the Felt Pens category of brushes, and roughly sketch in a house shape using a mid-value gray color. Feel free to be as creative as you care to be and do not feel it is necessary to just copy what I have drawn. Do not draw the details yet, and because we all have a tendency to revert to what I call "coloring-book mode," do not draw a detailed and defined contour. There is a tendency to want to just fill in the lines if you have a too-carefully drawn outline. Figure 3.1 shows a very rough house shape sitting on a small hill with some short cliffs surrounding it. The general idea is derived from thatched cottage houses of the English countryside.

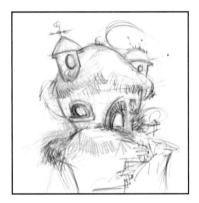

Figure 3.1 The very rough house shape sketched on the hill.

As mentioned, the image printed at this size will be 3×3 inches. Although the house would be fine to paint as it is, it might be a lot more interesting to look at if additional height were added to the cliffs. To do this you will need to resize the image you are working with. Find the Canvas menu item in the top menu bar and select Canvas Size. A dialog box displays asking you how many pixels you want to add to each of the sides. For now, add another 900 pixels to the bottom. This does not change the size of the actual drawing as resizing the canvas would. It simply adds additional pixels around the image. Figure 3.2 shows the options box that is displayed when you select the Canvas Size menu item.

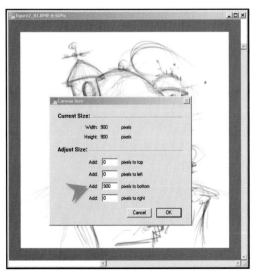

Figure 3.2 The Canvas Size options box with 900 pixels entered in the bottom box.

Tip

It is worth noting that you can also add negative values in these boxes, and area will be subtracted from the image.

Often you will find as you are painting that you will want to add or take away portions of the canvas to achieve a stronger composition. This is very easy to do in the digital painting world, whereas it might be impossible to enlarge a canvas in the traditional painting world.

Paint in some higher cliffs in the newly added bottom portion of the canvas. Keep things loose and subject to change should you change your mind. Save your image. Make it a practice to save your image before every major change you make just in case you change your mind and need to revert to an earlier version. Figure 3.3 shows the image with the newly drawn cliffs.

Pick the Simple Water brush from the Digital Watercolor brushes. Pick a rough paper texture. Set the opacity of your brush to a lower setting somewhere between 10 and 20 percent and, starting with lighter colors just as you would in traditional watercolor, begin to paint in the sky and cliffs. Change colors in the color picker. Try to give the sky a rather stormy look. Do not worry about blending the colors. You will notice that the edges of the strokes will blur slightly. Figure 3.4 shows the initial digital watercolor strokes over the sketch. Notice that there is not a lot of effort made to stay in the lines.

Continue adding color, getting darker and darker with your strokes. Notice how dark the cliff color is becoming where you are adding shadows. Add some greens to vaguely represent vegetation around the bottom of the rocks. Switch between different paper textures as you work. Using lots of textures will help keep the image lively and interesting to look at. Also vary the scale, brightness, and contrast of the paper textures to get a variety of different looks. Use the cobblestone paper texture to add some round, rocky shapes to the cliffs. Figure 3.5 shows the buildup of the textures and colors all over the image.

Add more and darker colors and begin to paint some color into the house. You have probably noticed by this time that there is no effort to cover the initial sketch. In fact, these watercolor brushes are transparent and are not able to cover the sketch. This is not a concern. Notice all the different textures that are being used as we paint with the digital watercolor. Figure 3.6 shows the many different textures being used as we paint.

At this point, you have established the color scheme and have also decided where the light and dark areas are painted.

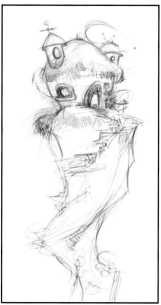

Figure 3.3 The house sitting on very high cliffs.

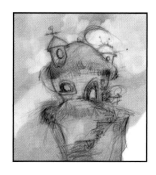

Figure 3.4 The first watercolor strokes into the sky.

Figure 3.5 Use darker watercolor strokes to build up the image.

It should be noted too that the image is still in a very flexible stage and it is very easy to experiment and make changes if you want to. Figure 3.7 shows what your image should look like at the end of the watercolor stage.

Figure 3.6 Use many different textures in the watercolor stage of the painting.

Now switch to the Variable Chalk brush from the Chalk brush category. This is a very good brush that will help cover the underlying image and still interact with paper textures, so you will not lose the nice textures you have developed to this point. Set the brush's opacity to around 40 percent, the brush grain to about 20 percent, and the size somewhere around 20 pixels. Begin painting in the sky using the same paper textures that you used when watercolor painting. This particular brush will fill in the paper texture if you press hard on your stylus. The lighter you press, the more texture that will be apparent. Look at the left side of the painting in Figure 3.8 where the sky meets the vegetation and you will see an example of this brush's ability to use the texture.

Figure 3.7 The end of the watercolor stage showing the color scheme and the different value relationships throughout the image.

Select different paper textures that resemble rocky surfaces, and paint into the cliffs and house. Using carefully selected paper textures will make it look like you did a great deal of work on the painting to give the rocky surfaces their character, when in reality, getting this effect is simply a matter of the right paper texture and brush combination. Your audience will be impressed with all your hard work and you never need tell them just how easy the effect was to achieve.

We are going to assume the light source is coming in high and slightly to the right side of the image. This will make it possible for our objects to grow darker as they recede toward the back side, giving a very strong silhouette for the cliff and the house. Paint some dark greens, going lighter as you get to the top surfaces of the grass. Notice that the original drawing is beginning to be covered by the pastel strokes. Figure 3.9 shows the rocky textures and grassy areas in development.

Figure 3.8 The very rough texture where the sky meets the vegetation is created by light stylus pressure and a small grain setting using the Variable Chalk brush.

Now is a good time to decide if the image should be larger to get the level of detail you anticipate wanting in the end. This image is slightly small to give a good print, so you need to now make it larger. Unlike the earlier step of adding additional pixels around the periphery, you will simply enlarge the image. Doing this too often or to a significantly larger size will decrease the quality of the painting, but enlarging an image to no more than 200 percent will generally not do noticeable damage to the image. Go to the Canvas menu in the top menu bar and select Resize. Increase the size of the painting from 900 pixels in the horizontal dimension to 1500 pixels. This is not quite 200 percent, so you will notice very little damage to the quality of the image. The vertical dimension will increase proportionally to reflect the change in the horizontal dimension. Figure 3.10 shows the Resize options box.

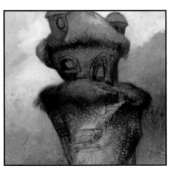

Figure 3.9 The rocky textures and grassy surface.

Continue to use the same brush and begin to develop the look of a thatched roof to your house. Invert the paper texture by clicking on the Invert Paper button on the Paper palette. This will enable you to select a lighter color and paint in the tops of the rocks on the side of the house instead of the gaps between the rocks. Inverting the paper texture is a great trick to use to once again look like you have done a great deal more work than you actually have. Draw and paint in more detail into the door and window areas using colors sampled from within the image. Your image should look similar to Figure 3.11.

Not much has been done in the background or cliffs since the initial lay-in of color, so now is a good time to move to these areas. It is never a good idea to complete one area of a painting before the others because there is a chance that the finished area will look completely out of context and wrong when viewed against the rest of the painting. Still using the Variable Chalk brush, fill in some of the brown areas of the cliff. Switch paper textures to something with a vertical direction, and paint in some of the green areas to give a vague feel of vegetation growing upward. Figure 3.12 shows the image at this point.

Switch to the top part of the painting and use the Variable Chalk brush to clean up and paint the sky to a more finished state. All of the colors that you are painting with at this point in the process should be sampled from within the painting and you should rarely have to go to the color wheel to select a color.

Once again save your work. It cannot be stressed enough that you save often. There is nothing more frustrating than working for two or three hours and having a computer crash and losing all your work.

Figure 3.13 shows the whole painting at this point in the process.

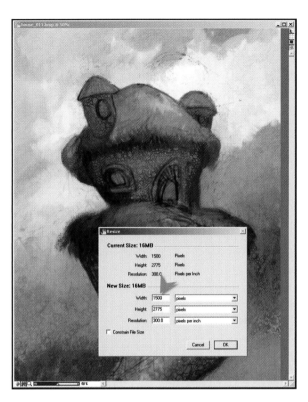

Figure 3.10 The Resize options box.

Figure 3.11 The thatched roof, window, door, and rocky wall are painted into the image.

Figure 3.12 Add brown color into the cliff and paint some abstract green vegetation in the bottom of the image.

Figure 3.13 The whole image to this point in the painting.

The painting is just a little boring at this point, so add a point of interest by painting some light coming out of one of the windows using some bright orange and yellow colors. This will do two things: It will add a bright spot of color that will help lead the eye to the center of interest, and it will also add just a touch of mystery to the painting.

Continue working on the windows of the house, including the dark one in the tower. Paint some light from the window onto the grass to give contrast and the feeling of depth in the image. Figure 3.14 shows what the finished windows should look like.

Figure 3.14 Paint light spilling out of the window onto the grass.

It is time to get working on the cliffs. They are boring and without form and need a lot of help to make them look interesting. Using a smaller-sized brush of about 15 pixels, draw some cracks and crevices into the main forms, letting some of the textures already there suggest shapes to you. If you are getting too much texture showing through your stroke and want a more solid line, increase the grain slider to about 25 percent.

Figure 3.15 shows these cracks drawn somewhat following the form to help lead the eye to the house on the top.

Using colors that are both lighter and darker than the base color, develop some form in the rocks, as shown in Figure 3.16. Remember to take into account that the light is coming from the upper right. Once again, use your imagination to make these rocks look interesting. Creativity is one of the most important keys to interesting paintings.

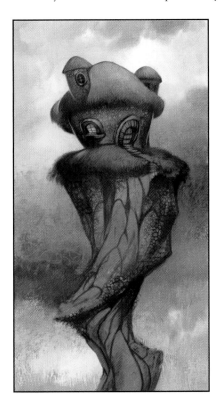

Figure 3.16 Add some form to the rocks using colors that are both lighter and darker than the base color.

Figure 3.15 Use a smaller size Variable Chalk brush to draw the main cracks and creases into the cliffs.

Figure 3.17 shows the complete image and illustrates how developing the form in the rocks helps define the path the eye takes, and generally makes the image more interesting.

Once again, select some of the paper textures that look like rocks or cobblestones, increase the contrast of the paper, and using a large brush with a light touch, paint some of the rounder rocks back into the large forms you painted in the previous step. Paint them on the lower edges of the large rocky forms to give added visual weight to these areas. If you just randomly painted the textures all over the rocks, it would fragment the larger forms visually. Figure 3.18 shows the textures painted.

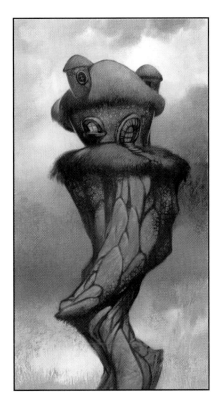

Figure 3.17 The entire painting.

You are now getting close to the end of this painting and will be adding a few finishing touches. Add a little additional interest to the tops of the cliffs by painting in some hanging vines. Paint these using the same brush that you have been using but switch to a paper texture that is full of round, leaf-like shapes. Create a new layer to paint on in case you make a major mistake or decide you do not like the look of what you are painting. If you do, you can simply clear or delete the layer.

Starting with the darkest darks for the leaves, paint in some hanging vines of random lengths. When you are satisfied, pick a slightly lighter color and paint in some more leaves. It is important to vary slightly the size of the paper texture so that the lighter leaves do not line up exactly on top of the darker ones. You want to go for the look of very detailed painted leaves without the pain of painting each one individually. This is easily accomplished by careful choice and use of different paper textures. Figure 3.19 shows the painting with hanging vines added.

Using the same technique described in the previous step, add some lighter leaves as shown in Figure 3.20.

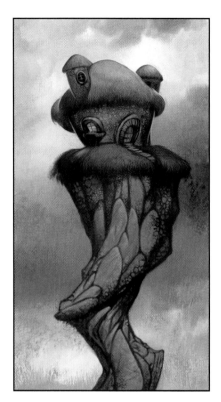

Figure 3.18 Add smaller rocky textures back into the larger forms.

Figure 3.20 Add some lighter leaves.

Figure 3.19 Paint some dark and mid-value hanging vines on a new layer.

Add a few flowers to give a bit of bright color to this relatively subdued color scheme. Still using the Variable Chalk brush but in a smaller size, paint in some yellow flowers in the grass. For a bit of additional color, add some purple flowers to the hanging vines. Do not overdo it—just a few here and there will suffice. Figure 3.21 shows the results.

The top contour of the house is a little boring, so add something to help break the contour. How about a chimney? Create a new layer to paint on just in case you do not like the result. Let's base our chimney roughly on the chimneys found on English cottages. Begin by painting in a cylindrical shape. Do not worry if your cylinder is not symmetrical since nothing about our house is. Add the two smoke stacks on top of this cylindrical shape. Paint the main body of the chimney in a similar fashion that the walls of the house were painted in, using the same texture to give continuity between the two. For the small smoke stacks, simply paint them in a solid color to give a terra-cotta feel.

Figure 3.21 Add flowers to the vegetation.

The chimney would not be complete without a little smoke. This not only adds visual interest, but once again adds to the underlying story that viewers will envision in their minds. Paint the smoke on a new layer using a variety of default Airbrushes. You might also want to add some small brightly glowing embers to the smoke. Experiment until you get the look you want. Figure 3.22 shows smoke rising in a breeze from the house's chimney.

Figure 3.22 Paint a little smoke on a new layer.

In these days of high technology, what abode would be without a television and a few antennas on the roof? Sometimes it is a very good idea to add something that is completely out of context to an image. Here, the addition of modern antennas adds a bit of humor to the image. Paint these on a new layer using the Variable Chalk brush. Your painting should look similar to Figure 3.23. Save your image again.

Figure 3.23 Paint a few antennas on the top of the house.

Now add the final touch. Using the Glow brush with your color set to a rich red color, add a subtle but bright glow around the window, as shown in Figure 3.24.

The complete painting is shown in Figure 3.25.

Figure 3.24 Add some glow to the window.

There you have it. An interesting and relatively easy painting to complete.

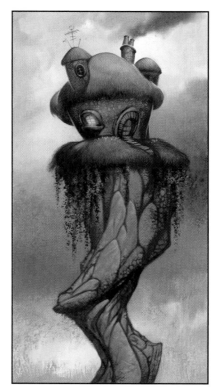

Figure 3.25 The finished painting.

Summary

Painting and drawing on the computer is so very easy, and this section was a good initial foray into the world of digital painting. The subject matter was relatively simple yet useful to demonstrate different painting techniques. The techniques are simple but achieve results that look much more labor intensive. You have learned how to use brushes and paper textures to your advantage as well as enlarging and changing the format of your painting to suit your creative ends.

You have also learned a few very important things when working on this image that you will use as you continue to paint in the 2D digital world:

- Save your work a lot. Hard drive space is not as valuable as your time.

- You need not use every brush or feature of a piece of software to get stunning results.

- When you are experimenting with something new, make sure that you do it on a new layer so corrections or discarding the layer is easy.

Hopefully, you had fun and learned something while doing this tutorial. The next two chapters tackle two of the most difficult subjects for an artist to master in either digital or traditional media: the human face and the human figure.

4

Digital Portrait Painting

Painting the human face is often as difficult as painting the entire human figure. Whether you are using traditional media or digital, there are things you can do to help make the painting process easier, and that is the goal of this tutorial. If you can paint the human face, there is good reason to believe that you will be able to paint most any face of any character or creature with greater ease.

About This Tutorial

This tutorial once again uses Corel Painter. In this particular case, you will paint a face from a frontal, straight-on viewpoint because it is easier to explain specific principles about painting a face from this angle than from any other.

This painting will be of a generic face. The principles and procedures used are applicable to any portrait you may want to paint, but learning the basics of painting a face are easier if you are not as concerned with capturing a likeness. Although capturing a likeness is not particularly difficult, it does take greater concentration and better drawing skills than painting a generic face. Having said that, feel free to use any reference materials you might care to use for this tutorial. If you follow the tutorial you will be drawing the head from scratch; if you prefer, you can download "Chapter 4 Sketch" from the publisher's website, http://www.courseptr.com/downloads and begin using that sketch.

This tutorial is not meant to represent the best or only way to approach painting the face, but if you follow the tutorial relatively closely, you can build on what you learn to paint future portraits on your own.

The brushes that are used in this tutorial are available in this chapter's folder on the www.courseptr.com/downloads website. You can use them or create your own.

Before You Begin

These tutorials are not meant to be "how to use the software" manuals, but there are a couple things that you should know about Painter that will make following the tutorial easier, including:

- Where the different palettes and menu items are located.
- How to create and use layers, including changing the composite method of the layer.
- How to load the brushes that you have downloaded from the publisher's website, http://www.courseptr.com/downloads, into your copy of Painter.
- How to import custom palettes also available for download on Course PTR's website.

If you need information on any of these things, please consult the Painter manual or online help.

Although there are differences between the various versions of Painter, the techniques in this tutorial are applicable to all versions from version 7 on.

The Sketch Phase

Open Painter and import the custom palette called "Face Painting." This group of brushes contains both the custom and default brushes that are used in this project and can be downloaded from the publisher's website. If you are not able to import the palette or some of the brushes are missing, make sure that you have loaded all of the custom brushes you have previously downloaded into your copy of Painter. If you need instructions on how to load brushes, consult the Painter manual or sneak a peek at the next chapter on painting the figure, where the instructions are also given.

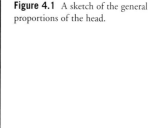

Figure 4.1 A sketch of the general proportions of the head.

1. Create a document that is 1200 pixels wide and 1500 pixels high, and sketch in a very basic head shape using "Don's Brush." Divide the head once vertically and three times horizontally, as shown in Figure 4.1. This gives you the basic head shape divided into the general facial proportions.

2. The drawing should be very sketchy. Using the same brush, draw the facial features onto your basic head shape. Sketch in the hairline and the ears. Remember that you are just indicating position at this time, so there is no need for great detail. Figure 4.2 shows the sketch at this point in the process.

Figure 4.2 The head sketch with features indicated.

3. Continue to refine the figure, adding the neck and shoulders as shown in Figure 4.3.

4. When you are drawing the beginning sketch it is also important to start to determine and indicate where your light and dark areas will be located. One of the darker areas in most faces will be in the hair. Using the same brush, paint in the darker

shape of the hair. It is important to remember at this point when painting without reference that you should keep things loose and subject to change. The hair is a good example of this because it is very likely to be changed as the painting develops. Figure 4.4 shows the sketch with the hair darkened.

Figure 4.3 Add the neck and shoulders to the sketch.

5. Copy the entire image using either the Select All menu command or the keyboard shortcut, Ctrl+A. Copy the entire selected image using either the menu command or the keyboard shortcut Ctrl+C. Paste the image back into itself using the keyboard shortcut Shift+Crtl+V. This keyboard shortcut will paste the copied selection back into the image in the exact coordinates that it was cut/copied from.

6. You now have a new layer that is an exact duplicate of your head sketch. Double-click this layer and name it Sketch. Change the composite method of this layer to Gel or Multiply so that all of the white becomes transparent, leaving only the sketch visible on this layer. This particular layer will only be used if you need to check your drawing's proportions at a future point in the painting process. Click the small eye icon next to the layer and hide this layer.

Figure 4.4 The sketch with the hair darkened.

7. Make sure that the canvas layer is active. Go to the Effects Menu and choose Surface Control > Apply Lighting as shown in Figure 4.5. Color the background with colors of your choice.

8. Figure 4.6 shows the Apply Lighting option palette, which gives you numerous options of how you can apply the effect to your image. Play with various settings and colors of light until you get a combination that you find attractive. You can add additional lights simply by clicking in the small preview

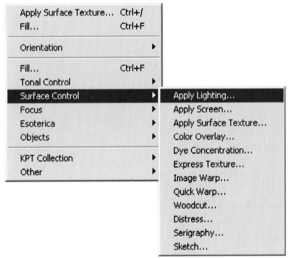

Figure 4.5 The Apply Lighting menu location.

of the effect. If you want to delete a light, click on its icon and press the Backspace key. If you need explanation or instructions on the different settings, refer to the Painter help file or the manual.

It is usually a good choice when painting the face to choose colors for the background that will contrast nicely with the skin tones. In this case the image was colored using an orange/blue combination. There is very good reason to add a color to your image before painting. If you paint on a white background, every color you use from the lightest lights down the value scale will look dark. By adding color to the background, you create a painting environment where you will be able to more accurately judge your values. In this particular case we added a lighting effect that gave a nice transition from a cooler color to a warm color and covered the canvas layer, yet allowed the sketch to show. As an alternate, you could just as easily have used a gradient or solid color fill using the paint bucket tool. If you choose to use the paint bucket tool, make sure that

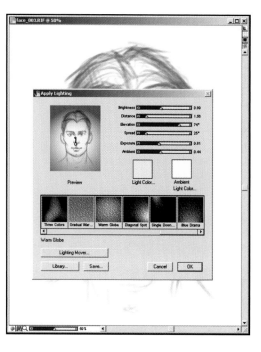

Figure 4.6 The Apply Lighting options palette.

you create and fill a new layer. With this new layer filled, you will need to change its composite method or opacity so you can see the underlying sketch. Drop the layer. If you simply fill the canvas layer the results will be unpredictable and not satisfactory. The whole point is to cover the white of the image so you are not painting on a very bright and light surface.

9. Save your work. The face with a lighting effect applied is shown in Figure 4.7.

Starting the Painting

Figure 4.7 The face sketch with a lighting effect applied.

Now that all of your preliminary work is finished, it is time to begin some real painting on the face.

1. Create a new layer. Double-click on this new layer and name it "painting layer." This new layer will be the layer that you do the actual painting on. Creating new layers to work on is a good habit to get into when you are making major changes or starting a new phase of your painting because it makes changing your mind or correcting mistakes very easy.

2. It is most important when painting anything from the imagination, and especially a face, to decide early on where the light in the image is coming from. In this case we will assume the light is coming from the upper right. Knowing the light source makes it possible to visualize where the light and shadow areas of the face will be. Using Don's Brush in a size of about 20 pixels, begin painting in large areas of value. Start by painting in all the shadow areas of the face as one shape. Also paint in some of the lighter colors in the forehead area. Try early to establish both the light and dark value areas in your painting so that you know the range of values you have to work with. Do not just fill in the areas as you would a coloring book.

In the initial stages of the painting, you will need to select your colors from the color picker. As you progress in the painting you will select more and more of your color from within the image itself. Figure 4.8 shows the newly created layer with both shadow and light colors applied.

3. Add some bright red colors into the cheeks, nose, and ears of the painting. When painting a human face, the face can be divided into three basic areas of color. From the hairline to the top of the eyebrows, the flesh is warm and slightly yellow in color. This area of the face is also generally lighter in value than the other areas of the face because it usually is facing the light source of a scene more directly. From the eyebrows to the bottom of the nose is a distinctly more red area. This includes the nose, cheeks, and ears. When painting a male figure, these colors can be exaggerated slightly to make the face look rugged, but you do not want to exaggerate much with a female face since a rugged looking female is not usually desirable. From the bottom of the nose to the chin is a distinctly cooler and slightly darker area. This is caused as the face begins to turn away from the light source. In the male face much of this color is also because of the beard. It is also noteworthy that as you paint the receding planes of the face, they can be slightly cooler in color in all areas of the face. Figure 4.9 shows a graphical representation of where these areas of color are located on the face.

4. While painting in the initial colors, do not worry about trying to get a nicely blended and smooth surface. At this point the goal is simply to establish the basic colors in the face. You will do the blending and smoothing of the colors later in the process. Figure 4.10 shows the painting with the bright red areas in the middle of the face, cooler colors in the chin, and warmer creamy colors in the forehead.

Checking for Accuracy

When you paint a face, it is a good idea to constantly check your drawing for accuracy and to check that the features are lined up correctly. This is very easy in a frontal view of the face using digital media and is one of the reasons we are painting a face from this view.

To check that the features are lined up correctly, make sure that the rulers are visible around the edges of the image. If they are not, go to the top menu bar and select Canvas > Rulers > Show Rulers. Once you have the rulers displayed you can arrange a series of guidelines to check the arrangement of the features. Of course this only works from this angle, but it will help get you in the habit of visualizing these alignment lines from any other angle from which

Figure 4.8 Paint a new layer with both shadow and light color to block in the main areas of the face.

Figure 4.9 The three areas of color within the human face.

Figure 4.10 The bright colors are painted in the face.

you may be painting the face. Figure 4.11 shows these alignment lines superimposed on the painting. As you can see, the features are generally correct in their placement although there are some drawing problems, such as one eye being larger than the other. This is not much of a concern this early in the painting if you are aware of the problem because it will be easy to correct. It is when you are further along and have the painting closer to finished that you will be more reluctant to correct mistakes. It should also be noted here that absolute symmetry between the sides of the face is not desirable. There is the temptation when checking the accuracy of your painting to correct any imperfections in the drawing by simply copying one side of the face, flipping it horizontally, and placing it on the opposite side. This will give your painting a distinctly strange appearance. In the real world no face is symmetrical, and all have slight flaws that give a person character. While you want an accurate drawing, you do not want symmetrical perfection.

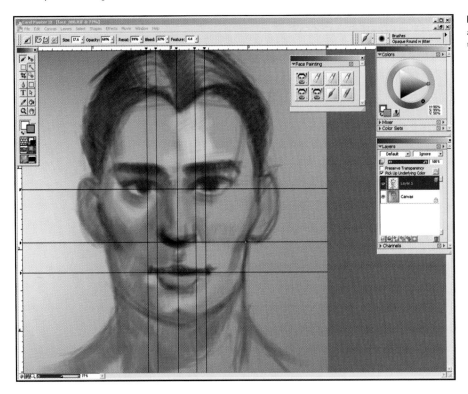

Figure 4.11 Alignment lines are placed over the face to check the placement of the features.

If you are comfortable with how the painting is proceeding, save your work.

Continuing the Painting

1. Continue to paint the colors of the face. Always be aware of the direction of the light falling on the face when you are working. In this painting, it is assumed that the light source is coming from the top right. Figure 4.12 shows the image with additional painting in all areas of the face. There is no need to worry about blending at this point.

2. All of the work on the painting so far has been done with one brush, Don's Brush. If you want to experiment with different brushes, please feel free to do so. The only point to painting the image with one brush is to show that you can be productive using just the basic features of any program. You need not be daunted by any program you may be trying to learn. Continue to paint on the face.

Figure 4.12 The painting showing additional work as you continue adding color.

3. At this point in the tutorial, the shadows are looking a bit light; darken them so there is a good difference in the values between the light and dark sides of the face. There are several ways to darken the shadows. You can select the shadow areas using the lasso tool and then adjust the Brightness and Contrast to get darker color or you can simply darken the shadows by painting darker color roughly over what you already have. Either will work just as well. In this particular case I do the latter. Generally when painting, you want to make sure that the darkest areas in the lights are not darker than the lightest areas in the darks. Figure 4.13 shows how the shadow side of the face has been reestablished. Notice that the strokes are still pretty rough and there has been no effort to refine the details. The goal is still to develop the color theme of the painting.

Figure 4.13 The shadow side of the face painted with darker color.

4. Figure 4.14 shows a close-up of the painting at this point. Notice that some of the background blues have been allowed to show through into the skin tones on the face, specifically around the eyes and lower cheek areas. This is a result of not trying to completely fill in between the lines. Allowing some background color to show through is a very good idea because a color harmony will be built throughout the painting.

5. Continue to paint into the face until you have the correct amount of colors and your values are established. There is no right way to determine when this is complete—for the most part you will need to rely on your feelings as an artist as to when enough is enough. Most of the colors that are being painted in the face are being sampled from different areas within the painting using the eyedropper tool and not from the color wheel. The eyedropper tool can be quickly accessed while painting using the Alt key. Press the Alt key, click with your stylus on the color that you want to pick in your painting, release the Alt key, and continue to paint with your newly selected color.

Figure 4.14 The painting showing where some of the background color has been allowed to show through the foreground colors.

Blending Your Colors

1. Select "Don's Blender" from the Brushes palette and smooth all the colors that you have painted. There are also a number of default blending brushes located in the Blenders brush category. Feel free to experiment with any of these additional blending brushes. Your painted face may look a little soft, but this is a good base for painting in the details in the following steps. Figure 4.15 shows the blended face looking slightly out of focus and soft.

Figure 4.15 The face with all the colors blended together using Don's Blender.

Rotating the Canvas

Do you find that drawing or painting strokes in one direction feels less natural than drawing/painting in another? Do you ever find yourself rotating a piece of paper as you draw to get a more comfortable angle for the stroke you are drawing? Painter has a feature that allows you to change the angle of the canvas and that can make your life a lot easier when doing this type of blending work. In fact, it can make your digital painting much easier in all phases of the process. You can rotate the canvas and paint on it in different positions simply by using a combination of keys on the keyboard.

1. Hold down the spacebar. Notice that your cursor changes to a hand shape and you are able to move the image all around the screen. This feature makes it very easy to move the image so that, for example, you can concentrate on the lower-right corner without having to paint in the lower-right corner of the screen.

2. If you hold down the spacebar and at the same time hold down the Alt key, you will see your cursor change to a small pointing hand. While holding these keys, click, hold down the stylus tip, and drag in your image. You can now rotate the canvas to any angle to facilitate the easy application of your strokes. When you are done, simply rotate the canvas to a new angle. When you want to return the canvas to the vertical position, hold down the spacebar and Alt key combination and tap with your cursor in the image. The painting will immediately return to vertical. Figure 4.16 shows the canvas rotated to a different angle.

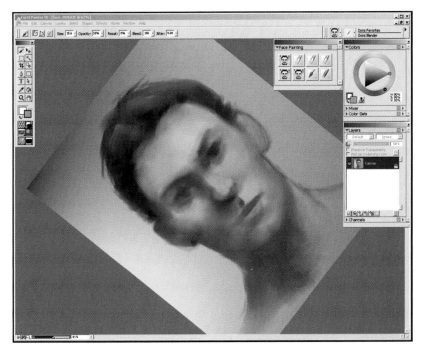

Additional Painting

1. Once the overall painting is blended, you can go in and begin to refine the individual features. You can refine the right eye using Don's Brush but in a smaller size. Also refine the nose and mouth on the right side of the face. This side of the face is beginning to take on a more solid appearance. Your painting should now look similar to Figure 4.17.

2. Using the same small brush, reestablish more of the drawing. Your painting should now look similar to Figure 14.18.

Painting is for the most part a simple matter of keeping the right colors in the correct size and shape next to their neighbors. In a way it is much like the old paint-by-numbers kits that we did as children. You moved across the picture, painting each shape with a specific color, and at the end of the process, you had a painting that looked something like the picture on the box.

In reality, painting is more complicated because you have to find these shapes yourself and determine what colors to use.

Figure 4.17 The painting showing more work refining the features on the right side of the face.

Figure 4.18 Refining the features of the face.

3. There are some very distinctive "landmarks" you can look for to help you paint the edges between the shapes you have found and help you keep your colored shapes in the correct places. As you paint any face, these landmarks tend to be the lightest and darkest spots of the face. Get these in the correct position and you are almost guaranteed to have correctly placed features. First look where the lightest spots are located—they are generally found where there is a quick change in the planes of the face. The amount of oil found on the skin can also be a determining factor. The general areas to look for the highlights in any face are circled in red in Figure 4.19.

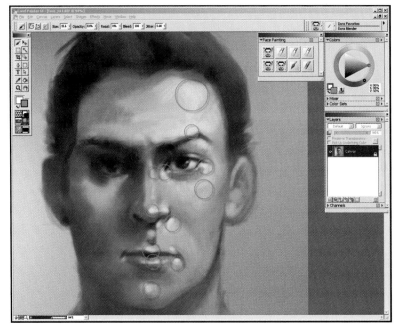

Figure 4.19 The highlights located on the face.

4. The dark areas also can act as similar landmarks. These are often located very close to the highlights. Make sure when you are painting to look for both these light and dark areas. Some of the dark areas to look for would be the corners of the eyes, the corners of the mouth, nostrils, edges created by the eyebrows, dimples in the cheeks and chin if present, and possibly the opening of the ear.

5. Using Don's Brush, continue to refine the features in both the light and dark areas of the face. Do some additional work in the hair. As you paint, sample the nearby colors. Although you are not blending with a blending brush, this will result in a soft transition between colors. At this point, your painting should look similar to Figure 4.20.

6. Feel free to use the blending brush if you want to, but make sure that you do not over blend and lose all the detail that you have been working so hard to establish. Figure 4.21 shows the whole painting to this point with some carefully controlled blending.

Figure 4.20 The face with more details painted in both the shadow and light areas.

7. One of the biggest complaints about digital paintings is that they often look so smooth that they lack character. The brush that has been used up to this point in the painting is a quick and useful brush, but does not have a great deal of character. To add a bit of character to your painting, switch brushes to one that will give you some more interesting texture in your strokes. Pick the Acrylics/Captured Bristle brush variant from the Face Painting palette and paint the face again. This brush is a default Painter brush and can also be found in the Acrylic brush category found in the Brush Selector. Figure 4.22 shows a close-up so the texture of the strokes is apparent.

Figure 4.21 The painting with selective blending.

8. Now the hair needs some work. So far we have not paid any attention to areas other than in the face, so let's get a little wild and do something interesting with the hair. Since you are going to be doing a little experimenting, you want to make sure that if you do not like your results, it will be easy to correct your mistakes. Create a new layer and name it Hair. Select the Dry Ink brush from the Face Painting palette. This is also a default brush and can be found in the Brush Selector in the Brushes or Calligraphy categories. This is a perfect brush for painting hair because you can go from a very narrow, single strand to a very wide multiple stroke depending on how much pressure you put on the stylus. Figure 4.23 shows an example of a stroke that can be made with this particular brush.

Figure 4.22 The Acrylic/Captured Bristle brush leaves a very textured stroke.

9. Paint some interesting looking hair on the new layer named Hair. Try going really ratty and freeform. Fortunately, if you do not like the look, you can clear the layer and try again. It will be easiest to use this brush to draw the hair if you rotate the canvas as described earlier in the tutorial to make drawing your strokes more natural. I kind of like this ratty look and decided to stay with it. Figure 4.24 shows the beginnings of the hair on its own layer.

Figure 4.23 A stroke made with the Dry Ink brush.

Figure 4.24 The hair painted on a new layer.

Finishing Touches

Figure 4.25 An almost finished eye.

It is now about the right time in the painting process to begin some finishing work.

1. Switch back to the face layer and use various brushes from the Face Painting palette to paint in an almost finished eye. Figure 4.25 shows a close-up of the work on the eye.

2. Using Don's Brush and the Captured Bristle acrylic brush, start the finishing process of the features in your painting. Refine the structure of the eye paying particular attention to the eyelids, placement of the corner of the eye and the eyebrow. Paint the detail in the nostril and wings of the nose. Give the lips some fullness and place the highlight at the corner. When you are satisfied with your work, save the image. Your painting should look something like Figure 4.26.

Figure 4.26 Add more detail to the features.

3. The contour of the face is rather ragged and sloppy looking. Go ahead and drop the face layer onto the canvas. Using the background colors and a large brush, clean up the contour of the face. Work back and forth between the face and background. If you only work with the foreground when refining the contour, there will be a very gradual expansion of the edges of the face and pretty soon the bounding edge of the face will be too large and the features will appear too small. By working with both the background cutting into the foreground and foreground working into the background, you will be able to control the contours more easily. When you are satisfied with the look of the contours of your painting, make sure to save your work. Figure 4.27 shows how the face will look with its contours cleaned up.

Figure 4.27 The face with cleaner contours.

4. Now would also be a good time to check the final alignment of the features. Make sure the rulers are visible and use guides to see how the features are lining up. Notice that in a general way, the features are still lined up as they should be, but also remember that the features do not need to be exact mirror images of each other. Remember, although symmetry is one of the things that we recognize as beautiful in a face, it is also very artificial looking if it's exact. In this particular painting the inside corners of the eyes line up pretty well but the outside corners are at different heights. The corners of the mouth line up pretty well as do the bottom edges of the nose. Figure 4.28 shows the painting with the guides displayed showing the alignment of the features.

5. When you are painting any subject matter, often the question will arise about where you should put the most intense and vibrant colors. A good rule of thumb is that the more intense colors in a subject will be found on the transition edge between the shadow and light

areas. The reason for this is quite simple. Light tends to wash out color, and you simply cannot see color well in the dark. Therefore, put your brightest colors on the edges between the two. Continue working on the forehead of the face, reinforcing that lighter and creamier skin tone. Notice that the color that is on the edge between the light and dark is much more vibrant. The ear is another area where bright color can and should be used. If you look at the painting, you can see almost pure red painted into the right ear. This is because as the light shines on the head, it is transmitted through the flesh of the ear. The effect is much like if you take a flashlight and hold it up closely to a cupped hand. The fingers of the hand become very red. Figure 4.29 shows the addition of the more vibrant colors in the forehead and ear.

6. Continue to softly blend the face a bit more. Figure 4.30 shows the result of careful blending. The goal of this blending is not to completely eliminate the strokes, but to soften them slightly.

7. Continue working on the shadow-side cheek, blending the colors to try to get the structure correct. There always seems to be one area that gives an artist trouble in any given painting, and the shadow-side cheek is that area in this image. When you are finished, your painting should look similar to Figure 4.31.

Artists have a tendency when painting on the computer, and indeed when painting in traditional media, to not use the full value range available to them. This tendency creates results that are generally slightly lighter and have less contrast than is desirable. Fortunately, this is very easy to correct in the digital world. Essentially what you do is add a slightly dark glaze over the entire image. This usually works best if you use the image itself as the glaze.

8. Select the entire canvas image where the face is painted. Copy and paste the selected image back into exactly the same spot on the original image. Now change the composite method from Default to Gel or Multiply. The image will now be very dark, so lessen the opacity of this new layer to somewhere around 40 percent, or whatever percentage you find attractive. The image should now be slightly darker, but also much richer looking with a wider range of values. Figure 4.32 shows the Gel layer with opacity of about 40 percent superimposed over the original face painting. Save your image, then drop the Gel layer down onto the canvas. Save the image again. This constant saving gives you the ability to back up a step or two should you decide that the direction you are heading with your painting does not look like you want.

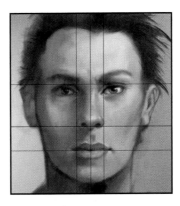

Figure 4.28 The guides showing if the features align well.

Figure 4.29 Vibrant colors added to the face.

Figure 4.30 A slight blending of the brush strokes.

Figure 4.31 More work in the shadow-side cheek.

9. Go back and do more finishing work on the face. Strengthen the drawing and reintroduce any highlights that were lost in the previous step. Your painting should now look similar to Figure 4.33.

Figure 4.32 The head painting with a Gel layer overlaid and dropped onto the canvas.

Figure 4.33 More finishing work is done on the face.

10. Let's get back and do a bit more work on the hair. Make sure that the hair layer is the active layer. Select the Dry Ink brush and while rotating the canvas as needed, paint in the rest of this guy's wild hair. Figure 4.34 shows the hair painted.

11. Using the same brush, add some small detail into the eyebrows using both light and dark colors. If you have a good base under these very fine strokes, it will not look like you have tried to paint every hair but will look a bit more realistic. Figure 4.35 shows the work on the eyebrows.

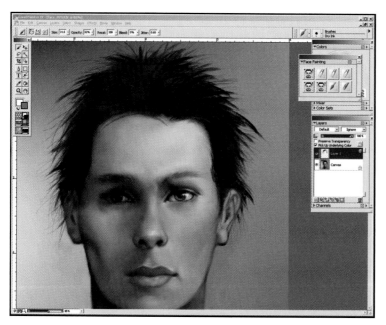

Figure 4.34 Finally, a full head of hair painted with the Dry Ink brush.

We are now heading into the finishing stages of painting a face. Add a new layer and using the Dry Ink brush add a few curls hanging over the forehead of the figure.

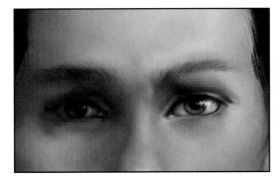

Figure 4.35 A bit of work on the eyebrows.

12. Next, add a "five o-clock shadow" on the chin. This is a feature that is very easy to overwork and difficult to paint with traditional methods, but is so easy to do in the digital world. To do this, create a new layer to work on and name it Whiskers. Select the Coarse Spray airbrush from the Airbrushes Category in the Brush Selector and a dark brownish grey color. With a light touch, paint in the whiskers on the face. Chances are that you will have whiskers that are much too dark and cover not only the areas that they should, but also the nose and lips, and some that are probably too high into the cheeks. Here is where the digital magic comes in. Reduce the opacity of the layer to a point where the whiskers blend in naturally. Using an eraser, lightly erase the stray whiskers. Your image should look a lot like Figure 4.36.

Figure 4.36 Whiskers and stray strands of hair painted onto the face.

You may have noticed that there are no whiskers above the upper lip. This was not an oversight, but left undone because in the final step you are going to add a small beard.

13. Create a new layer, name it Beard, and select the Dry Ink brush. Carefully paint in a beard. You are perfectly welcome to make the beard as long and shaggy as you want. Figure 4.37 shows a close-up of the painted beard.

For all intents and purposes, the painting of the face is finished at this point. The techniques used can be applied to virtually any face or portrait that you may want to tackle. While additional work would normally be done on some kind of costume and on the neck area, this tutorial just focuses on the face itself. Figure 4.38 shows our finished painting.

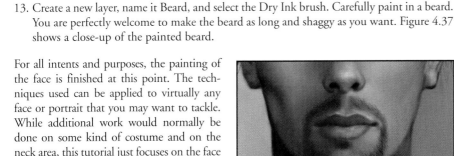

Figure 4.37 A beard painted using the Dry Ink brush.

Summary

If you follow the techniques described in this tutorial, you will have success. After a few successes, you will be able to build on these techniques with methods of your own and create completely original works of art with your own stamp of creativity. Most of these techniques could be adapted somewhat to any digital image-creating program.

Hopefully, you have learned a little more with each tutorial. In the next tutorial, you will paint a complete figure, and the human figure is considered by many artists to be the most difficult subject matter to master.

Figure 4.38 The finished painting.

5

Digital Figure Painting

Painting the human figure, be it digitally or in a traditional medium, is often quite daunting and intimidating for the artist. Sometimes the challenge can be almost overwhelming. Nevertheless, if you have the desire, you will succeed by following the steps in this tutorial.

About This Tutorial

Although this tutorial is not meant to represent the best or only way to approach the painting of a human figure, it is a good method to use. You will be using many of the same techniques and procedures you would use if you were doing a figure painting using oil paint. It is suggested that you follow the tutorial fairly closely and then build on the lessons learned to create figure paintings of your own.

The general principles used are applicable to most digital painting programs, but the techniques and brushes used in this tutorial are available only to the Painter user. It is recommended that you use Painter 7, 8, or IX. The brushes used are available for download at the publisher's website, www.courseptr.com/downloads. You can use them or create your own to get a unique look.

In this tutorial you begin with a sketch of a person and gradually create a digital painting from the sketch. You can complete this tutorial using either reference materials of your own or using the sketch that is provided in this chapter's folder from the downloads.

Much attention is given to making the digital painting look like a traditional painting, but this tutorial is not about how to use Painter. General questions about using the program are not covered in depth within the tutorial; however, there are some things you must know to follow the tutorial, including:

■ How to create and use layers, including changing the composite method of the layer

■ How to load the brushes downloaded from the publisher's website, www.courseptr.com/ downloads, into your copy of Painter

■ How to import custom palettes

Preliminary Setup

Open Painter and import the custom palette called "Figure Painting." It is available for download at the publisher's website. If you are not able to import the palette or some of the brushes are missing, make sure that you have loaded all of the custom brushes into the Painter Brushes folder inside your copy of Painter. The procedure for importing the palette is as follows:

Note

This procedure works with Painter version 7, 8.1, and IX. If you are using Painter 8 you will need to first install the update for this to work.

1. In the top menu bar, go to the Window Menu and select Custom Palette > Organizer. Figure 5.1 shows where this item is located.

2. The Custom Palette Organizer is displayed. Click the Import button and navigate to the folder where you downloaded the files from the Course website. Select the palette file called "Figure Painting." Figure 5.2 shows the Custom Palette Organizer option box.

3. A new palette is displayed in the Painter window, showing the brushes that will be used in this tutorial. This is a convenient and great time-saving feature of Painter. You can find just the brush you need for any particular project without searching through the myriad palettes and menus. It is a good idea for each project you start to make a custom palette that includes the brushes and the commands you will most often use. Getting into this habit will make your digital painting experience much more pleasant. If you need more in-depth instructions about custom palettes, consult the manual that comes with Painter. You may need to move the Figure Painting custom palette to a convenient space within the Painter window, as shown in Figure 5.3.

The preliminary setup is now done and you are ready to start painting.

Figure 5.1 The palette Organizer menu item.

The Sketch Phase

Open the sketch file that is available from the downloads, scan in a sketch of your own, or create a new canvas that is about 2000 pixels in the largest dimension at 300 dpi. This will provide a decent-sized image to give you a good print of your masterpiece when you are done.

If you create a new image, go ahead and sketch your figure on the canvas using the brush of your choice. A good brush to use for initial sketches is the Fine Tip marker variant in the Felt Pens brush category. Set the color of the marker to a mid value gray, because the strokes you draw will gradually darken as you refine your drawing.

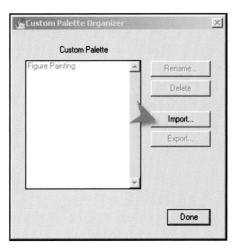

Figure 5.2 The Custom Palette Organizer.

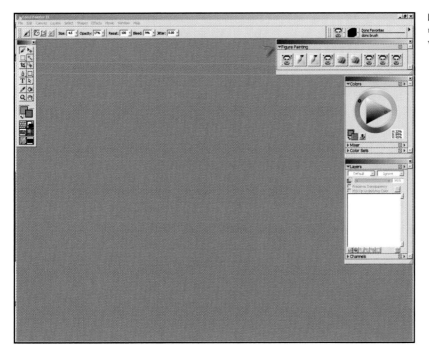

Figure 5.3 The Figure Painting custom palette positioned in the window work space for easy access.

The sketch we will be using in this tutorial was drawn using a photographic reference. At this point, getting a lot of detail in the sketch is not important. Your main chore is to get the position and proportion of the figure sketched on the canvas. You do not want to spend a lot of time with the details because you will be painting over most of your drawing as you go. Remember, this is about painting, not filling in outlines. We received great praise when we were small for staying within the lines of our coloring books, but here the lines are only guides for later work. These guides should always be subject to correction and refinement. One of the biggest errors artists make is getting a very detailed drawing and immediately switching back into coloring-book mode. Figure 5.4 shows the sketch that we will paint.

Copy the entire image using either the Select All menu command or the keyboard shortcut for the Select All command, Ctrl+A. Copy the image using the keyboard shortcut Ctrl+C. Paste the image back into itself using the keyboard shortcut Shift+Crtl+V. In Painter, this keyboard shortcut pastes whatever was selected back into the image in the exact coordinates it was cut/copied from.

Figure 5.4 The sketch we are going to paint.

You now have a new layer that is an exact duplicate of the original sketch. Double-click this layer and name it Sketch. Change the composite method to Gel or Multiply. Doing this will make all of the white on this layer go transparent, leaving only the sketch visible. This is a handy device for checking your sketch against your painting's progress as you cover the original drawing with color. At this time, click the small eye icon next to the layer and hide this layer. We will only turn it on when checking the sketch on top of the painting. We will eventually discard this sketch layer.

Select the canvas layer and create a new layer just above the canvas. Fill this layer with a mid-value grayish-green color. The green color is a good complement for the warmer skin tones that will be painted. Unfortunately, you can no longer see the sketch on the canvas layer, so change the composite method of this green-colored layer to Gel. You will now be able to see the sketch through the green. Drop this green layer onto the canvas and save your image.

Note

Always make a point to save your image whenever you have just made a major change or are about to make a major change. Save with incremental numbered names; for example, file001, file002, file003, and so on. Naming and saving your files this way will make implementing corrections much easier should you make a serious error as you work.

Figure 5.5 shows the sketch with the green layer dropped onto the canvas sketch.

To add a little more interest and color to the drawing, let's add a lighting effect. To do this, go to the Effects Menu and select Surface Control > Apply Lighting. Figure 5.6 shows where this effect is located.

Figure 5.5 The sketch with a green layer dropped over the original drawing.

From the different examples that are displayed, choose the Splashy Color variant and move the lights up slightly in the preview display. Figure 5.7 shows the Apply Lighting palette with all the previews and adjustable sliders. If you need to learn how to move lights, add lights, delete lights, or set any of the other parameters, refer to the Painter manual.

Your image should now look similar to Figure 5.8, with the left side of the image being a more warm green and the right side of the image a more blue-green color. The colors you choose in your own work are strictly your choice.

To give the image slightly more contrast and a bit richer color, select the canvas layer again. Copy the entire layer and paste it back as a new layer exactly in the same position. Change the new layer's composite method to Gel. The image is now much darker but has way too much contrast. Reduce the opacity of this gel layer to around 35 percent. The image is now richer, but not too dark. Save the image. Drop the gel layer onto the canvas and save the image again with a different name. Remember to save your image just before making a major change and then again after a major change. Figure 5.9 shows the image at this point.

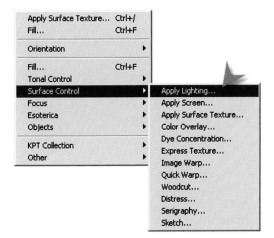

Figure 5.6 The Apply Lighting menu item.

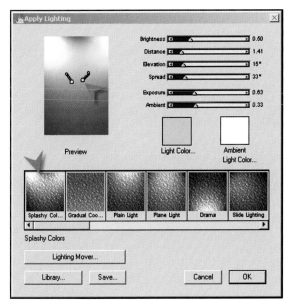

Figure 5.7 The Apply Lighting palette with the Splashy Color variant selected and showing the lights moved up slightly higher in the preview.

Figure 5.8 Our painting with a lighting effect applied.

Starting the Painting

Now our sketch is ready for some real painting. If you have never painted before or have limited experience, here is the secret of good figure painting: *Place the right colors, values, and shapes next to the right colors, values, and shapes.* This is not as hard or complicated as it may sound, so throughout the rest of this tutorial, try to remember this mantra as you work.

Figure 5.9 The painting with both the richness and contrast increased using an additional gel layer.

Approach this painting much as you would approach a traditional oil painting by beginning with some of the darkest colors and also painting some of the lightest colors in the image. One of the first and most important things you should do when you start a painting is to establish your lightest light values and your darkest dark values. Doing this will automatically set the range of values (the lights and darks) that you will be working with. It does not matter if your painting is going to have a very narrow value range or a complete range of values from white to black. Whether the painting is high key (an overall light feeling to the painting) or low key (a darker painting) is completely up to the artist, but it is very important to establish this value range at the beginning of the painting if at all possible and stick to it.

Several other important things to remember as you begin the painting process are to not be concerned with the details and to work with colors that are more intense than you think are necessary.

If you concentrate only on the details, you will tend to work on small individual sections and lose the overall cohesive feeling of the image. Always work from the larger, general shapes to the small details. Paint with a bigger digital brush than you think is necessary. Doing this helps you stay loose. And always remember that you are painting and not filling in the lines.

When painting in traditional media, you almost always want to put your color down more intensely than you think is necessary. As you blend the colors, they will soften and become less intense and hopefully end up in the intensity that is appropriate for your subject matter. The same theory holds for digital painting. Putting the color down more intensely gives you the option to blend and rework the colors a bit more, so you end up with the colors that are the correct intensity and value. Using the image you have prepared up to this point, create a new and empty layer. Name the layer "figure" or something similar to help you keep track of it as you create additional layers throughout the painting process.

Using the Pixel Spray airbrush variant from the Airbrushes library, spray in some of the dark for the hair. This brush is one of Painter's default brushes and has been loaded into the Figure Painting brush palette for your convenience. Don't worry about covering the sketch at this point. This is why you have the sketch on another layer if you need to check your drawing down the line. Switch to the Goodbrush variant in the same palette and begin laying in the colors of the face. Use a larger brush size than you are comfortable with. This particular brush will draw with a fairly small size if you use less pressure on your stylus. If you use more pressure, the size and number of bristles that paint increase. Work from the darks of the face to the lights. Figure 5.10 shows a close-up of the beginning painting so that you can see the individual strokes that the brush leaves.

When you are comfortable with how the painting is coming, save your work. Notice in this figure how little detail is actually painted in the eyes, mouth, and nose of the face.

As you did with the face, continue to paint the arm and chest areas with the Pixel Spray and Goodbrush brushes. Your painting should now look similar to Figure 5.11.

Create two new layers below the figure layer. You can either make the canvas layer active and create the two additional layers which will be automatically below the figure layer or you can create two layers anywhere and drag them below the figure layer in the Layers palette. Name one

Figure 5.10 A close-up of the beginning of painting the face of the figure.

"hair" and the other "background." One of the best things about digital painting is the ability to work on layers and not have to be concerned with the edges of overlapping shapes in the initial block-in of the painting.

Using the airbrush, paint in some darker areas for potential hair. Notice that since this layer is below the figure layer, you do not have to worry about painting over the skin colors you have already established.

On the background layer, begin to experiment with some colors you may want to use in this area. Again, you will notice that since you are painting on the bottom of the three layers, you don't need to worry about painting over the hair or figure.

Do additional painting on the figure layer down through the hand, arm, and back. When painting figures, it is a good idea to paint your strokes across the long axis of the form. This helps build a feeling of roundness. Figure 5.12 shows a close-up of the arm and hand areas with the strokes going across the form. This is particularly apparent in the arm of the figure.

Figure 5.13 shows the entire painting at this point. Notice that some of the background green color on the Canvas layer is showing through the skin tones on the Skin layer. This is a result of the brush strokes not being placed to fill the figure with a solid color. It is a very good idea to let some of the background colors show through into the foreground flesh tones and eventually, some of the flesh tone/foreground colors show here and there in the background.

Additional work is done on the face. Although there is not any actual blending being done with a blending brush at this point in the painting, the subtle buildup of painted strokes begins to appear as if there are blended areas. Most of the colors that are being used in the flesh tone areas are being sampled at this point from within the actual image itself using the eyedropper tool and not being picked from the color wheel. Notice the bright red colors that are being painted in on the borders of the hair and flesh. These bright colors add a lifelike, warm feeling to the image. Figure 5.14 shows a close-up of the face where you can still see the individual strokes of the brush and the subtle buildup of more detail, particularly in the eye and nose.

Figure 5.15 shows the entire painting at this point with additional work in the background layer. It is also important to mention at this point that only two brushes have been used for the entire process. On the right side of the background you can see where some of the flesh tone is painted into the background.

Figure 5.11 The painting showing additional work as we go down the figure.

Figure 5.12 The strokes painted across the form of the figure.

Figure 5.13 The image with three layers. One for the hair, background, and figure.

Continue refining the face and figure using the Goodbrush. Additional work is done on the hair layer. The whole image is still in a very fluid stage, and it is easy to make corrections. Add more hair behind the shadow side of the face, then using the Goodbrush and some of the background color, define the edge of the hair you just painted.

Figure 5.14 Close-up of the face.

The top of the figure's head is really crowding the top of the painting, so now is a good time to correct this before a lot more work goes into the background layer. This is another advantage of working in the digital realm. If you need to crop or expand the image, it is much easier to do digitally than it would be if you were painting in a traditional medium. Cutting or expanding a traditional canvas or panel is, for all practical purposes, impossible. But, if you are painting on the computer you can add and subtract various amounts from any side of the image without fear of ruining your image. Once again though, it cannot be stressed enough that you should save your image before making any radical adjustments such as cropping or adding pixels to your image.

Figure 5.15 The painting with additional work in the face and background.

In this particular painting, I added 200 additional pixels to the top of the image. I did this by making sure the bottom canvas was active and then going to the Canvas menu bar item and selecting Canvas Size. This brings up an options box that lets you add pixels to any of the four sides of the image. Figure 5.16 shows the options box with 200 pixels added to the top of the image.

When you see the pixels added to the canvas, you will notice that they are probably white. The new area may be another color altogether, though, depending on what your paper color was set to. This is not a problem—simply sample some of the green and other colors that you have been painting into the background and paint this area over. You should do this on the background layer, but if you forget to make the background layer active and end up painting on the canvas, don't worry, it really does not make any difference at this point. If you like the size of your new painting, make sure that you save it. You will notice in the tutorial image (see Figure 5.17) that you can tell where the original boundary of the canvas is located by the airbrush spray pattern forming a straight line.

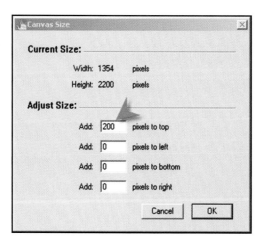

Figure 5.16 The Canvas Size options box.

Up until this point we have not paid any attention to the cloth that the figure is wrapped in. Normally, this would have been painted in roughly earlier in the painting process but because I wanted to spend enough time to develop the painting of the figure and face to a rather finished state, I left this area untouched until now. Normally you would want to develop the entire painting in one gradual process. It is definitely time to begin developing this critical part of the painting. Create a new layer and label it "fabric" or some similar name. Place this layer under the figure layer but above the hair layer. To do this, in the Layers palette click and hold the stylus or mouse button on the layer you want to move, and drag it to the position where you want to locate it. Using some airbrush but mostly Goodbrush, block in the mid value color of the cloth. Although this color looks very purple, it is really mostly a gray color but because of the colors that surround it, it takes on a purplish cast. Remember this as you paint. The way a color looks is often determined not so much by its RGB value but by what colors surround it. Notice also in the background layer some rather freeform, scribbled looking strokes. You can create these fantastic looking strokes using the Nervous Pen. This is one of Painter's default painting tools and is invaluable for making interesting looking textures in backgrounds and such. It is located in the Brush Selector under the Pens category. Figure 5.18 shows a slight close-up of the very first strokes in the cloth and the Nervous Pen strokes in the background. Also notice that some brighter reddish brown colors are being added to the background at this point.

Figure 5.19 shows the whole painting up to this point.

Switch back to the hair layer and add more hair. In this image use the Goodbrush for most of the work. This particular brush makes multiple strokes which imitate hair nicely. Notice that you should get gradually lighter toward the ends of the hair. This is often the effect you will see in dark-haired individuals, because the hair tends to bleach out slightly from exposure to the weather and sun. Do not make the effect too dramatic or the hair will look unnatural. Your strokes should generally follow the direction of the hair. An important thing to remember when painting hair is that even though it is made of many small, individual strands, you should paint it in large masses and shapes. Save painting any individual strands or small groups of strands for the very finishing stages of the painting. Figure 5.20 shows the painting of the large general shape of the hair after painting to change its shape.

Switch to the background layer and use the Pixel Spray airbrush to add more color. The background can be very loose and abstract at this point. Right now the only thing

Figure 5.17 The painting with an additional 200 pixels added to the top of the image.

Figure 5.18 The first strokes in the fabric wrapped around the figure.

Figure 5.19 The whole painting with the fabric blocked in.

we are trying to accomplish is developing a color harmony that works with the figure.

Still working on the background layer, I think that putting the figure in an abstract garden setting might be a good idea. Using the Variable Splatter airbrush, paint in very abstract vegetation forms in the bottom half of the canvas. Accuracy in trying to depict a specific plant is not important. We are trying to achieve a general look. Figure 5.21 shows the lower half of the background now covered with very generalized foliage shapes.

Part of the process and beauty of painting digitally is the ability to make corrections. This step is a perfect example. I decided that the eye as it is painted was a little too large for the face. If I were painting in traditional oils, there would be a whole lot of weeping on my part as I realized that I would need to correct the painting. Not so in the digital universe. You simply draw a selection around the eye, copy the selected area, and paste it back into the image. Make sure that the figure layer is the active layer; otherwise, there is no telling what you will be copying. Figure 5.22 shows a close-up of the original eye. Figure 5.23 shows the eye copied, pasted, and scaled to a more correct proportion. The red arrow in Figure 5.23 shows a line that was part of the original lower eyelid. The scaling is subtle but improves the overall look of the face.

Switch to the fabric layer and develop the folds more. When painting fabric, try to limit the number of values you are using to only three or four. Paint the folds using straight lines. The thinner the fabric, the straighter the lines. If you paint the folds using sweeping curved lines, the chances are that as you blend and rework the painting, these lines that were originally fine and crisp will become soft and droopy. They will imitate wet noodles in their structure.

Things are not working as hoped. The hair is looking lifeless, so it is time to make some dramatic changes. Again, before you make these changes, save your work. Make sure that your hair layer is the active layer and pick the Good-brush.

Figure 5.20 This shows the general block in of the hair as large and un-detailed masses.

Figure 5.21 More work in the lower background.

Figure 5.22 The face before the eye has been scaled.

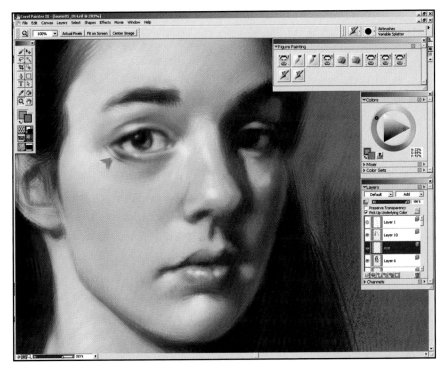

Figure 5.23 The face after the eye has been scaled and positioned. Notice the red arrow showing where the original lower eyelid was in relationship to the new eye.

Selecting colors from the background, begin to paint over the earlier hair shape and develop some curls. Once again, you are not trying to paint individual strands of hair at this point. Select some of the hair color and paint curls back into the background. When you are satisfied with the look of your hair painting, save your work. Figure 5.24 shows some of the curls of the hair being painted using both background and hair color.

Continue working on the figure and fabric. At this point they should be about 85% finished. It is now time to spend some effort in the background. Because one of the goals of this painting is to have an image that imitates oil, switch brushes to a group that uses a feature in Painter called Impasto. Impasto makes it possible to have a brush that not only paints color, but paints to an imitation depth. This effect makes it easier to create an image that has the illusion of a thick, painted surface. Most all of the brushes in Painter give you the option of using an impasto effect. I created custom variants of the brushes that we have been using to paint with the impasto effect. If you want to create your own impasto brushes, refer to the Painter manual. The custom brushes needed for this tutorial are included in the Figure Painting brush palette you are probably already using. If not, these brushes can be found in this chapter's folder on the www.courseptr.com/downloads website.

Figure 5.24 A new design and look for the hair of the figure.

To see what these brushes actually do, look at the image to the left of the figure's shoulder and you'll notice a rather textured surface. As the painting develops more, you will be able to see this effect more and more. Figure 5.25 shows the beginning of the impasto effect painted into the background.

You can do lots of experimenting in the background at this point using the Impasto brushes. Play with the direction of the brush strokes, vary the pressure that you are putting on the stylus, and change the size of the brush. The top-right corner of the painting has a rather bubbling paint effect, which is not attractive at all. The beauty of these brushes is that you can paint out the effect or simply cover it with a different painted effect. Figure 5.26 shows where I have painted various textures using impasto brushes in the background.

The background of the painting is almost finished at this point. We have done the work using the Goodbrush Impasto that is found on the Figure Painting palette. This brush has been used because of its ability to imitate the three-dimensional quality of traditional oil paint. If you are interested in building impasto brushes of your own, please refer to the Painter manual for an in-depth discussion on creating custom brushes. Figure 5.27 is a close-up of the painting to show how the textures and brush strokes have been applied.

Figure 5.25 The very beginning of using the impasto brush in the background of the painting.

Figure 5.26 Impasto paint textures in the background of the painting.

Figure 5.28 shows the entire painting at this stage. Although the top section of the background is looking fairly good, the bottom of the image still needs a lot of work.

Continue to finish the background using the same brush and technique that you used in the top half of the painting. You can apply small touch-ups to paint over various areas of the entire painting to finish any spots that need work.

Figure 5.27 A close-up of the painting showing the strokes used to paint the figure and background.

If you look closely though, you will notice that I left some areas a bit rougher than others. This is intentional because not all areas of a painting should be painted to the same degree of finish. The viewer's eye will be drawn to the areas of greater refinement and subconsciously ignore the less refined areas.

The Finishing Touches

The painting could be considered finished at this point, but I feel there is something missing, so let's add a yellow flower. You can paint the flower any color you choose, but the yellow harmonizes well with the violet and green color theme. Paint the flower on its own layer using the same impasto brushes that you have been using up to this point. Figure 5.29 shows the entire finished painting.

Figure 5.30 shows a close-up of the flower showing the direction of the brush strokes. Notice that there is the feeling of a thicker paint in the lighter areas and thinner paint in the darker areas. This technique imitates the way a traditional oil painting is painted.

Hopefully, you now have a figure painting that you are happy with. Not only do you have a good painting, but you have learned a good method to go about creating a digital painting.

Summary

The human figure is probably the most intensive and difficult of subject matters for an artist to attempt and by default this tutorial was the most intensive of the 2D tutorials presented in this book. Hopefully, you have learned a little more with each tutorial, culminating with and reinforcing the following concepts and techniques to use in your own creations:

- The value of layers when painting and how they can make your life much easier

- Working from the general to the specific in an image

- Working from the dark to light colors and establishing your darkest darks and lightest lights early on

- The use of impasto brushes

Figure 5.28 The top half of the background is finished, but the bottom half needs a lot of work.

Figure 5.29 The finished painting.

Figure 5.30 A close-up of the flower.

Most importantly, hopefully you have learned to have no fear as you paint. Remember that the beauty of working in the digital world is the ability to experiment.

The remainder of the book will now shift to the even more difficult subject of digital 3D art.

6

3D Digital Art

This and the rest of the chapters in this book now move into the realm of 3D digital art. As mentioned in Chapter 1, 3D art has many advantages over other forms of digital art in that the artist creates objects and settings that can be reused or seen from different angles. This gives 3D digital art a distinct advantage over 2D digital art. Because the artist can render a 3D image to 2D, the 3D artist is capable of changing items and angles in the composition without having to repaint the entire scene. All he has to do is to render the scene again to get a new image.

When creating in 3D, the artist is doing more than just creating a picture. In essence, the artist is creating a virtual world or environment. Instead of painting a scene, the artist is more like a theater designer in that he is moving actual objects around. The 3D objects are called models and they are created in 3D modeling programs like Maya. Once created, the models can be used over and over again and they can be modified to create new models.

In a 3D world there is no limit on where the scene can be viewed from. The lighting possibilities are also virtually endless. This flexibility gives the 3D artist a level of creativity that is almost impossible in 2D art. It also brings along with it some problems, the biggest of which is composition.

In 2D art, composition is carefully laid out from the beginning of the painting. In 3D art the artist may find a clever angle, but if he does not pay attention he may find that several elements in the picture have compositional problems like balance or confusing focal points. The 3D artist needs to think of the picture the same way a photographer does when taking a picture. Photographers sometimes spend hours setting up a scene or waiting for just the right moment to shoot a picture. The 3D artist needs to take the same amount of care when setting up a scene.

Get with the Program

The first step in starting with 3D is to understand the 3D program. We are using Maya as the 3D program for this book, and the Personal Learning Edition of Maya is included on the publisher's website (www.courseptr.com/downloads). If you haven't already installed the program on your computer, do so now so you can follow along with the demonstrations in the book.

Maya is a very deep and powerful art creation tool. It is the same tool used by professional motion picture artists to create the amazing 3D creatures and settings in many of the most popular movies. It is also widely used in the video game industry for creating characters and environments.

The first look at the Maya interface can be a little overwhelming. The sheer number of menus and icons seems endless, and it would take volumes of books to explain every feature in Maya. Don't worry right now about learning every feature. The step-by-step instructions in this book are designed to help you understand the features of the program that are needed to create each project. As you work with Maya, you will begin to become accustomed to the features.

Figure 6.1 shows the Maya interface screen as it comes up for the first time.

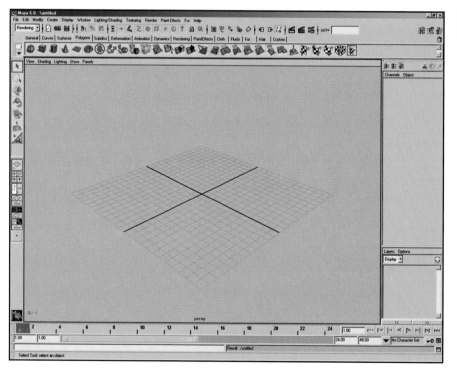

Figure 6.1 The Maya interface screen has many features and options.

The interface screen can be broken down into several component parts to help give clarity to how the program works. Figure 6.2 shows the area of the screen called the Panel.

The Panel is where you build the model. Notice that it has its own menu in the upper left-hand corner. This menu is called the Panel Menu.

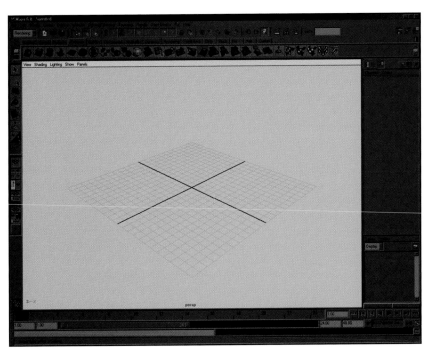

Figure 6.2 The Panel is the work area of the interface.

Figure 6.3 highlights the area to the far left of the screen. This area houses the toolbox and the Quick Layout buttons. The toolbox is in the upper section of the area and it contains model manipulation tools. An icon represents each tool. The lower part of the area has icons that are used to change the view layout of the Panel.

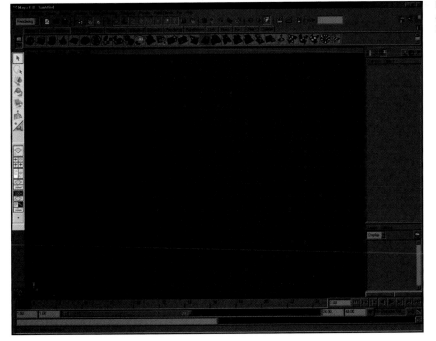

Figure 6.3 The highlighted area contains the toolbox and the Quick Layout buttons.

Figure 6.4 shows where the Main Menu is located. This is where many of Maya's features are located.

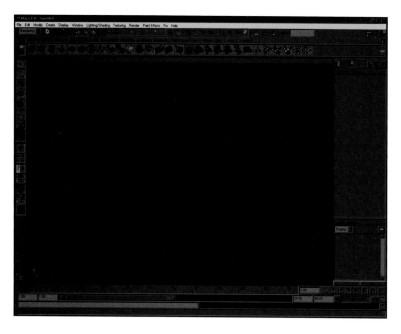

Figure 6.4 Many of Maya's features are located in the Main Menu.

Figure 6.5 shows the Status Line. This line contains many icons. It also contains a selection menu on the far left of the screen. This selection menu changes the Main Menu to configure it to specific functions. The Status Line also contains many common functions. It allows for controlling the selection mask and setting various options. On the far right of the screen are several icons that change the Sidebar. The Sidebar is the area directly to the right of the Panel.

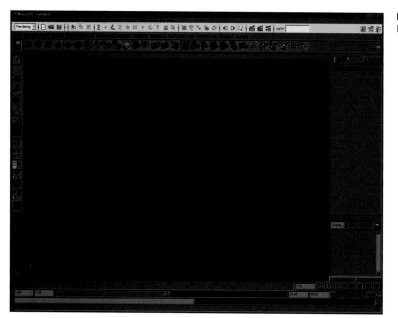

Figure 6.5 The Status Line is directly below the Main Menu.

The area shown in Figure 6.6 directly below the Status Line is called the Shelves. The Shelves contain icons and tabs. Each tab has different icons, and each icon has a different function in Maya. The tabs are used to group functions for specific tasks.

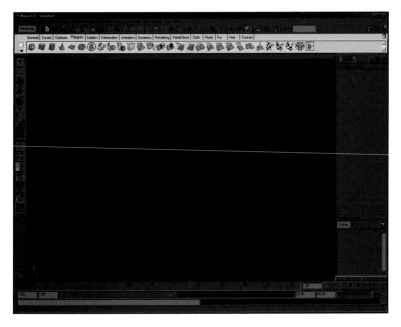

Figure 6.6 The Shelves contain icons that call up specific functions.

Figure 6.7 shows the area of the screen called the Sidebar. This area contains several editor elements and consists of two parts. The top part is the Channel Box, which is used to edit object attributes. The bottom part is the Layer Editor, which is used to edit 3D layers.

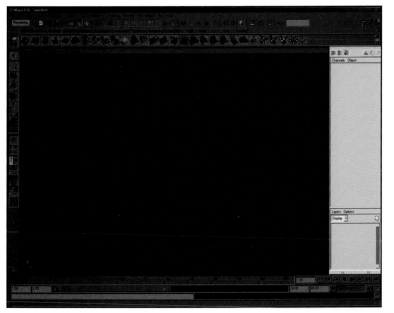

Figure 6.7 The Channel Box and Layer Editor are part of the Sidebar.

Figure 6.8 highlights the lower part of the Maya screen. This is where Maya's animation tools are located. It includes the Time Slider on the upper portion of the highlighted area and the Range Slider on the lower portion of the highlighted area. The right side of the highlighted area contains several tools for playing and viewing animations.

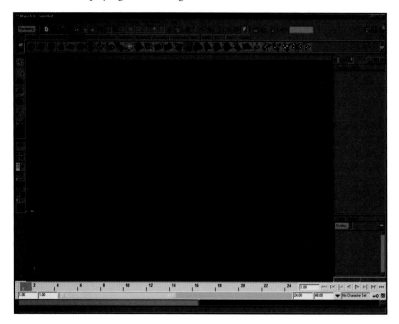

Figure 6.8 Maya's animation tools are located in the lower part of the screen.

At the bottom of the screen shown in Figure 6.9 are three text windows. The one on the upper-left side of the highlighted area is the Command line. This is where special scripts can be entered. The text window directly to the left of the Command line is the area that shows the results of each command. Below the Command line is the Help line. This window is used for help messages.

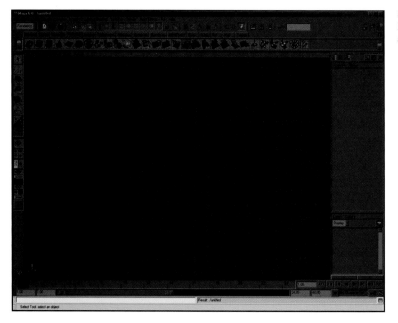

Figure 6.9 The Command and Help lines are located at the bottom of the screen.

See, that wasn't so bad. Now that you know the basic parts of the Maya screen, it's time to put some of that knowledge to work.

Having a Ball

This next part is very basic, so if you have experience with 3D programs you may want to skip this section. If, however, you are new or have not used Maya before, this section will help you get started. In this section you create a simple 3D ball.

1. The first step is to create a polygonal sphere. In Maya's Main Menu, go to Create and then to Polygon Primitive. This brings up a submenu. Find Sphere and select the small box next to it as shown in Figure 6.10. The small box next to any item in Maya means that there is a dialog box associated with the function. Dialog boxes are used to change attributes or settings for the function. The Polygon Sphere Options dialog box appears.

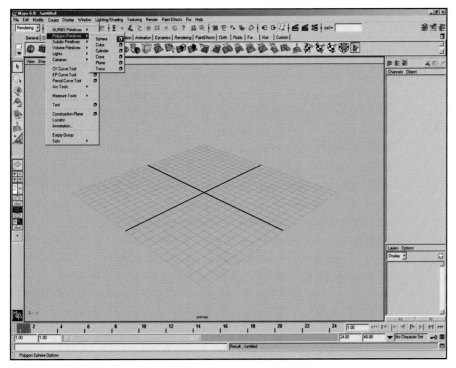

Figure 6.10 Select the dialog box next to Sphere.

2. Change the settings so that the sphere has a Radius of 1 unit. Set the Subdivisions Around Axis to 20 and the Subdivisions Along Height to 20. Set the Axis to Y and check the Texture box. The dialog box should now match Figure 6.11.

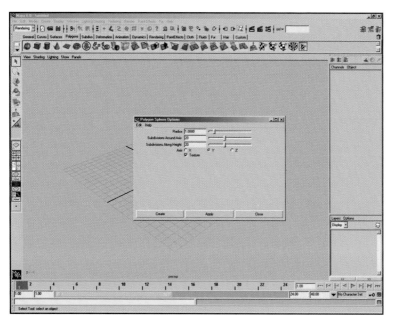

Figure 6.11 The dialog box sets the options for creating a polygonal sphere.

3. Click the Create button to create the sphere. See Figure 6.12.

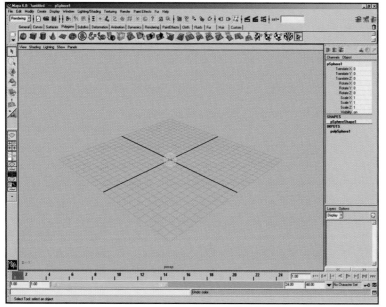

Figure 6.12 The new polygonal object is now in the work area.

4. Press the 6 key on the keyboard to change the View mode to Smooth Shaded. The 4, 5, and 6 keys control the View modes in Maya. The 4 key changes the View mode to Wire Frame; the 5 key changes the View mode to Flat Shaded; and the 6 key changes the View mode to Smooth Shaded. The View modes can also be controlled using the View Menu in the Panel Menu.

5. Zoom into the scene to better see the object. In Maya the view in the Panel can be changed. Zooming into and out of a scene is controlled by the mouse in conjunction with the Alt key on the keyboard. With the Alt key held down, press the right button on the mouse and move the mouse to the right. Moving the mouse to the right zooms into the scene, whereas moving the mouse to the left zooms out of the scene. Figure 6.13 shows the result.

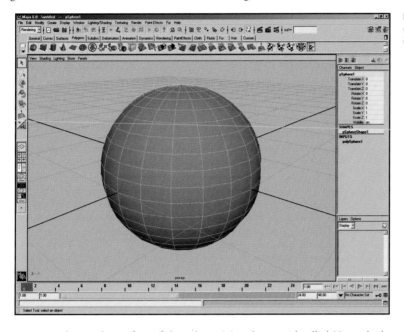

Figure 6.13 Change the View mode to Smooth Shaded and zoom into the scene.

6. The next step is to change the surface of the sphere. Maya has a tool called Hypershade that is used to change the surfaces of objects. You can find Hypershade in the Rendering Editors in the Window Menu as shown in Figure 6.14.

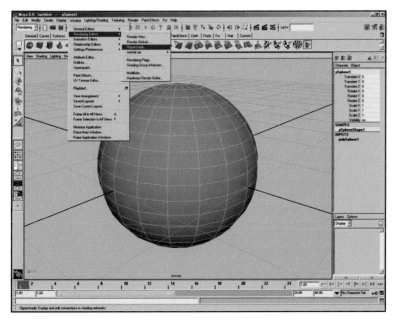

Figure 6.14 Hypershade is one of the Rendering Editors.

7. In Hypershade, go to Create in the menu and select Blinn from the Materials Menu as shown in Figure 6.15.

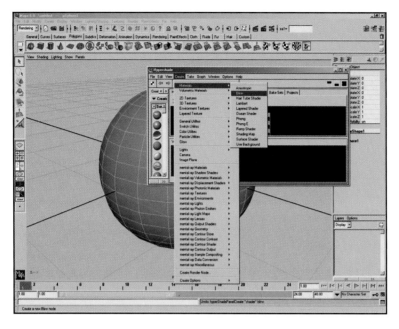

Figure 6.15 Create a Blinn material.

8. To save time in the workflow, Maya uses a system of Marking Menus. Marking Menus are floating menus, and they are called up by pressing the right mouse button. Select the new Blinn material in Hypershade and while holding the cursor over the material press the right mouse button. A menu appears. Move the cursor over Attribute Editor and release the mouse button. The Attribute Editor appears in the Sidebar as shown in Figure 6.16.

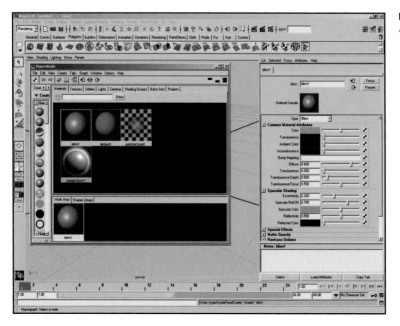

Figure 6.16 Bring up the material's Attribute Editor.

9. There are several attributes in the Attribute Editor for a Blinn material. In this instance the attribute that will be changed is color. Locate Color in the editor and select the checkered icon on its right. This brings up a Create Render Node box as shown in Figure 6.17.

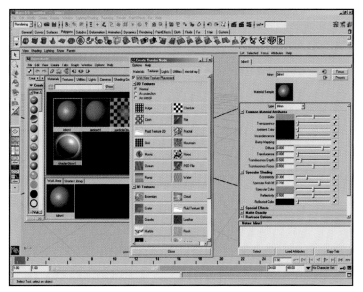

Figure 6.17 Bring up the Create Render Node box.

10. Within the Create Render Node box are many choices for changing the color of a material. Select the Checker icon. The Material in Hypershade now has a checkered pattern.

11. Next apply the material to the sphere. First select the sphere in the Panel and then right-click on the new material in Hypershade to bring up the Marking Menu. In the Marking Menu select Apply Material to Object. The sphere now has a checkered pattern, as shown in Figure 6.18.

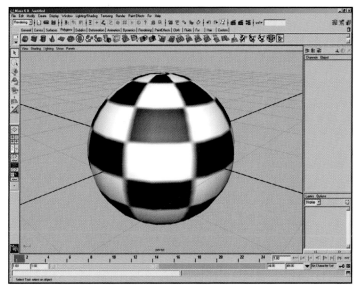

Figure 6.18 Apply the new material to the sphere.

There, you have created your first model in Maya. Aren't you proud of yourself?

Creating 3D Digital Art

This chapter first examines polygon techniques because they are the most basic way to build 3D models. In Chapter 8 we cover some of the other methods of creating models.

The next project is to build a tree. Trees are one of the most challenging subjects for 3D artists because they are organic and don't fit nicely into flat planes. It is easy to build a model of a building or other objects that are based on geometric shapes, but the challenge of creating something more difficult seems appropriate for a book on mastering digital art.

Building a Tree Trunk

Bring up Maya and if the program is not already in Modeling mode change it to Modeling by using the drop-down menu on the left of the screen just below the Main Menu.

1. Click Create in the Main Menu. Select Polygon Primitive > Cylinder and click the small box next to Cylinder to bring up the Create Polygon Cylinder dialog box as shown in Figure 6.19.

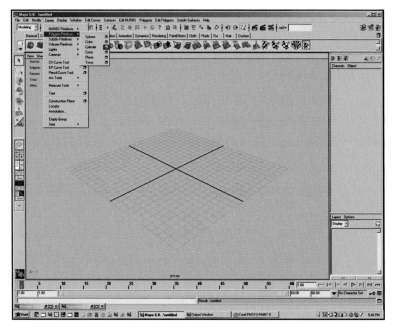

Figure 6.19 Bring up the Create Polygon Cylinder dialog box.

2. The cylinder will be the trunk of the tree. Set the Radius for .1 units and the Height for 8 units so the trunk will be slender and graceful. Polygon cylinders are divided into subdivisions around the axis, along the height on the cap or ends of the cylinder. Sixteen subdivisions around the axis will give the tree trunk a round, smooth surface. Eight subdivisions along the height will give the trunk the flexibility needed to make it look more organic. There is no need for Subdivisions on Cap, so set that number to 1. Make sure the orientation is set to the Y axis and click Apply to create the trunk as shown in Figure 6.20.

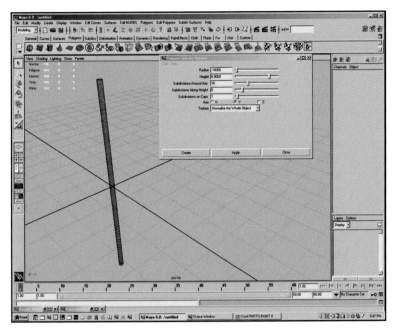

Figure 6.20 Create a slender, round cylinder for the trunk.

3. The cylinder now needs to be positioned so the base is resting at ground level. You can move it manually by choosing the Move Object tool or by using the Channel Box. The Channel Box is the best way to move objects when accuracy is needed. If the Channel Box is not already displayed, click the icon on the far right of the Status Line. Click on the trunk to select it and then in Translate Y in the Channel Box, change the number from 0 to 4 as shown in Figure 6.21. This moves the cylinder 4 units in the positive Y direction.

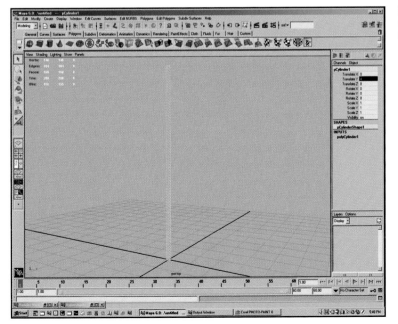

Figure 6.21 Move the cylinder 4 units in the Y direction using the Channel Box.

Note

You may notice a heads-up display of model statistics in the upper-left corner of the screen. The heads-up display is accessed in the Display menu. There you can choose from several options to help you when modeling. To get the display shown in Figure 6.21 select Poly Count.

4. Next, the tree trunk needs to be shaped so that it is narrower at the top and broader at the base. To do this, change the selection mode from Object to Component. Component mode allows for the selection of parts of the object. Change the component type to Vertex by clicking on the cylinder and using the Marking Menu. Press and hold down the right mouse button. The Marking Menu appears around the cursor. Move the cursor toward Vertex and release the mouse button.

5. Zoom into the top of the cylinder and select the top vertices by dragging a box around the top of the cylinder. The screen should now look like Figure 6.22.

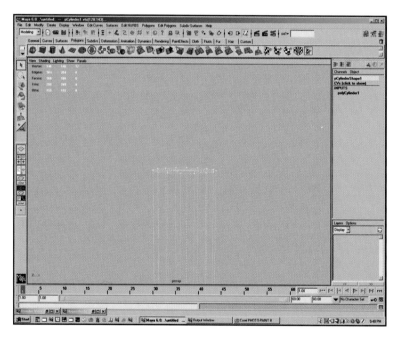

Figure 6.22 Select the top vertices of the cylinder.

6. Scale the top of the cylinder as shown in Figure 6.23 by clicking on the central cube and moving the mouse to the left.

7. Now scale the rest of the vertices of the cylinder to form a tree trunk shape as shown in Figure 6.24.

8. Before going any further with the tree trunk, you need to give the trunk some bark so it looks more like a tree. Maya uses materials to describe surface qualities of an object, and uses the Hypershade tool for creating and editing materials. The Hypershade dialog box is opened by selecting the Windows > Rendering Editors > Hypershade menu command. Maya has a variety of material types or Shaders to choose from, and each type can be modified for the specific surface. Look at the list of material types by selecting Materials in the Create Menu in Hypershade, as shown in Figure 6.25.

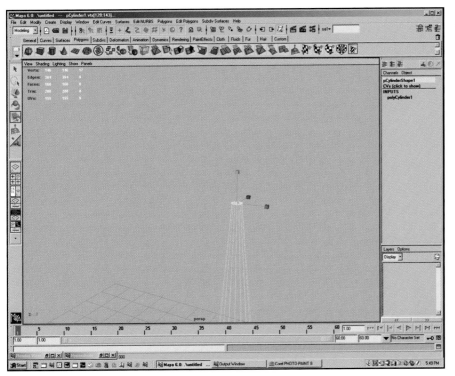

Figure 6.23 Scale the top of the cylinder.

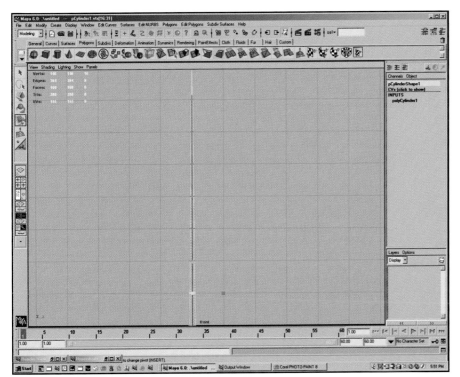

Figure 6.24 Scale the vertices of the cylinder to form the tree trunk.

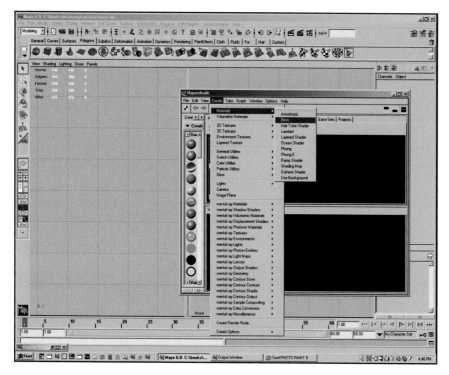

Figure 6.25 Maya supports many material types.

9. For matte surfaces that are not shiny, Lambert materials are good. For surfaces that are shiny, Blinn materials are better. Create a Lambert material by selecting Lambert from the Material Menu. Change the name of the material by right-clicking on the material and selecting Rename from the Marking Menu. Rename the material Bark.

10. Now it is time to add a texture to the material. The texture for the trunk and other textures for this chapter can be downloaded from www.courseptr.com/downloads. It is called bark.bmp. To give a material a texture, bring up the Attribute Editor by first selecting the material in Hypershade and then selecting Attribute Editor from the Marking Menu.

11. The bark.bmp texture needs to be loaded as a Color attribute of the material. Find Color on the first line of attributes in the Attribute Editor. Left-click the checkered icon on the far right-hand side of the editor on the same line as Color. This changes the Attribute Editor to a new box called Create Render Node, from which the bark.bmp file can be loaded. Select the File button.

12. Now the Attribute Editor changes to a new page. Find the file folder and click it to bring up the Load File dialog box. Load the bark.bmp file from the website or use your own texture. The texture is now loaded in the material. Figure 6.26 shows the texture loaded into the material in Hypershade. Hypershade has two windows: the upper window arranges all the materials and the bottom window is the work area. Notice that the texture is attached to the material in the bottom window.

13. Minimize Hypershade and zoom into the lower section of the trunk. Change the selection type to Faces using the Marking Menu.

14. Select the lowest set of faces as shown in Figure 6.27 by choosing the selection tool from the toolbox and dragging a marquee box around them.

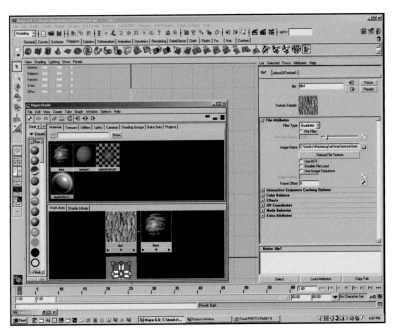

Figure 6.26 The texture is attached to the material.

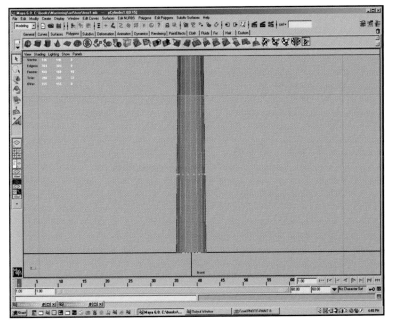

Figure 6.27 Select the lower faces of the trunk.

15. The next step is to project the bark material onto the selected faces of the trunk. Maya supports many projection tools for applying materials to objects. The projection tool needed for the trunk is the Cylindrical Mapping tool. You can find the Cylindrical Mapping tool in the Texture submenu on the Edit Polygon Menu. Click the dialog box icon next to Cylindrical Mapping as shown in Figure 6.28.

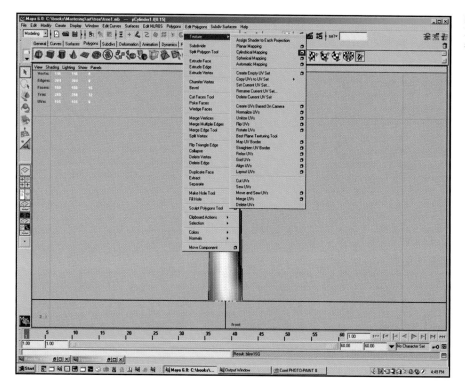

16. The Cylindrical Mapping dialog box allows you to customize the projection. Make sure the two check boxes in the Smart Fit section are checked. The Image Center should be set to .5 for both boxes. Image Rotation should be set at 0. Change the Image Scale to 2 in the first box and 3 in the second box. This will cause the image to repeat in the projection area twice in the horizontal, or U, axis and three times in the vertical, or V, axis. Click the Apply button.

17. Bring up Hypershade again and right-click on the bark material. Select Apply to Selected from the Marking Menu. Minimize Hypershade. The projected bark material should look like Figure 6.29.

18. Repeat the projection process for each section of the trunk, working your way up the trunk to the top.

19. With a material applied to the trunk, it is now ready to be adjusted so it is more natural looking. Change the selection mode to Vertices by using the Marking Menu. Now move the vertices to shape the top of the tree as shown in Figure 6.30. The move tool has several arrows emanating form a central hub. Clicking on any one of these arrows will allow you to move the vertices back and forth in the direction of the arrow. Clicking on the central hub will allow you to move the vertices freely.

Now you have a nice tree trunk with bark and everything. Without its branches, however, it doesn't look much like a tree.

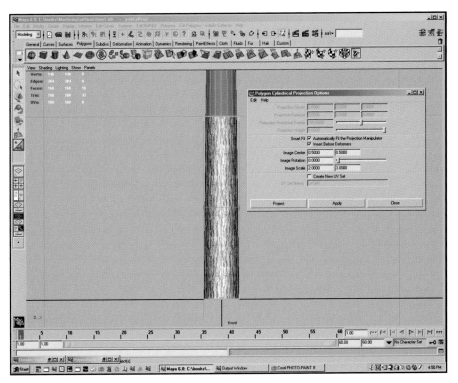

Figure 6.29 The bark material is applied to the bottom of the tree trunk.

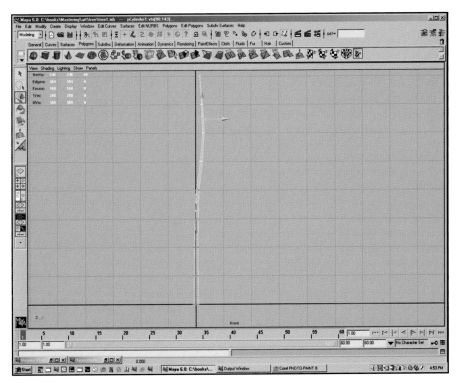

Figure 6.30 Make the trunk look more organic.

Building the Branch

The next part of creating the tree is to create some branches. Rather than creating many individual branches for the tree, you can create one branch and then duplicate it multiple times.

1. Bring up the Create Cylinder dialog box like you did in creating the trunk. Change the settings to match those in Figure 6.31. Click Apply to create the cylinder.

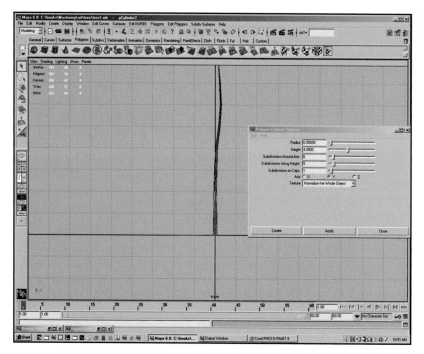

Figure 6.31 Create a new cylinder for the branches.

Hint

The more polygons an object has, the more processing power it takes to display the object. It is always a good idea to use only the number of polygons needed for a project and no more. This will help to keep the program running smoothly without the delays associated with high polygon models. Notice that the number of polygons used to create the branch is much less than those used for the trunk. Fewer polygons are used where fewer polygons are needed.

2. Before moving the branch into its natural position, you need to add materials. Bring up Hypershade again and create two new materials. Rename the first material Bark1 and the second Bark2.

3. The files bark1.bmp and bark2.bmp from the website will now be used. Load these files into the materials as shown in Figure 6.32 the same way you did when building the trunk.

4. You can do this step at any time, but now is as good a time as any. Move the branch cylinder away from the trunk and change the selection mode to Faces. Now select the faces at the top and bottom of the cylinder. These faces are not necessary for the tree and can be deleted. With the faces selected, go to Delete on the Edit menu to remove them, as shown in Figure 6.33.

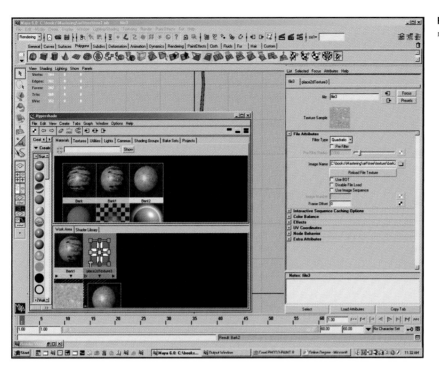

Figure 6.32 Create two new bark materials for the branch.

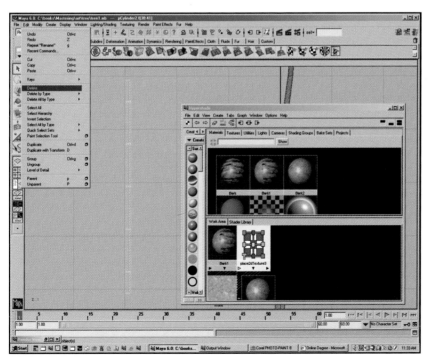

Figure 6.33 Delete the unnecessary faces at the top and bottom of the cylinder.

5. Select the bottom faces of the branch cylinder and apply the bark1 material as shown in Figure 6.34. Make sure the settings are the same as those in the figure.

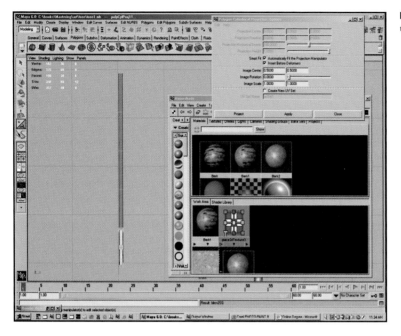

Figure 6.34 Apply bark1 to the bottom of the branch cylinder.

6. Apply the bark2 material to the rest of the branch cylinder.

7. Now scale the vertices of the branch so that the base is larger than the tip, as shown in Figure 6.35.

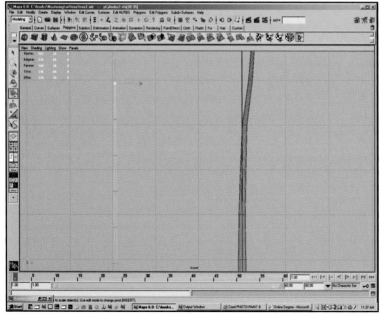

Figure 6.35 Scale the vertices to shape the branch.

8. Select all of the vertices and rotate the branch as shown in Figure 6.36. The Rotate tool is in the toolbox. To use it select one of the circles and move the mouse around the circle. The vertices will pivot around the center of the tool.

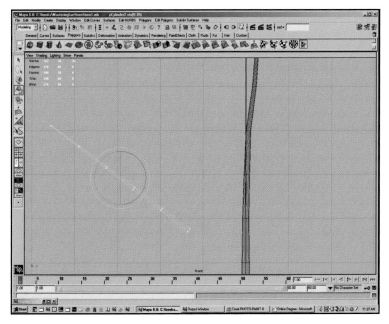

Figure 6.36 Rotate the branch.

9. Now take each individual set of vertices and adjust them to give the branch a curve similar to that shown in Figure 6.37.

10. Change the view to the Top view by selecting Panel > Orthographic > Top from the Panel Menu and the selection mode to Faces.

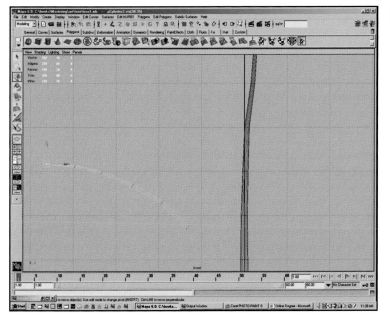

Figure 6.37 Curve the branch to make it look more natural.

11. Select the first three sets of faces from the tip of the branch. These faces will be duplicated to create smaller branches.

12. In the Edit Polygon Menu, find Duplicate Faces and bring up the dialog box. Make sure the settings match those in Figure 6.38.

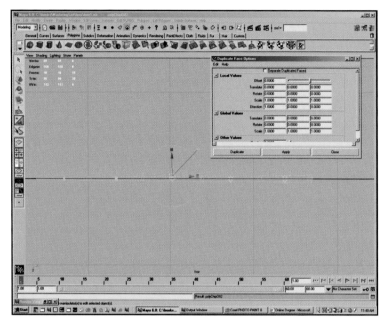

Figure 6.38 Bring up the Duplicate Faces dialog box.

13. Create five smaller branches by clicking Apply on the dialog box. A duplicate is placed directly over the original object. After each duplication, move the duplicate to the side as shown in Figure 6.39.

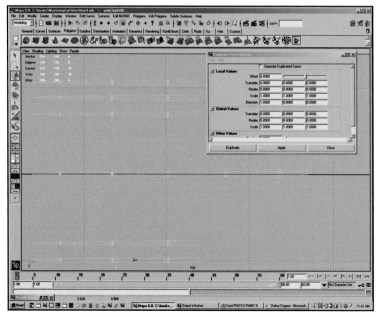

Figure 6.39 Move the duplicate faces to the side of the branch.

14. Change the selection mode to Vertices and move the vertices of the branch as shown in Figure 6.40.

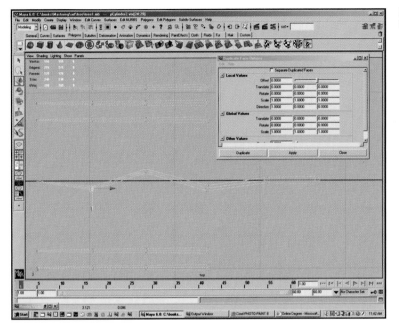

Figure 6.40 Move the vertices of the branch cylinder.

15. The branch is now ready to add the smaller branches to. Select one of the smaller branches and scale it down in size as shown in Figure 6.41.

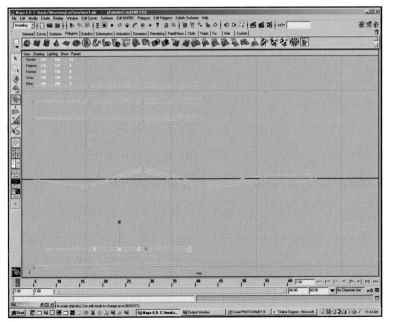

Figure 6.41 Scale one of the smaller branches down in size.

16. Rotate the smaller branch and move the end over the larger branch as shown in Figure 6.42. Move the vertices of the smaller branch as shown in the figure.

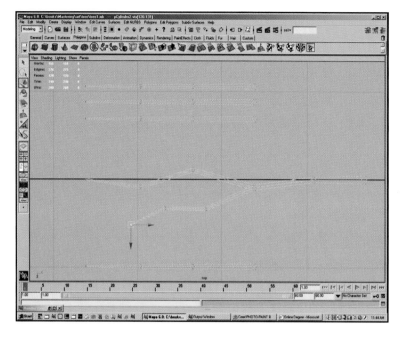

Figure 6.42 Add the smaller branch to the larger branch.

17. Reduce the size of two more smaller branches and add them to the larger branch similar to how they are added in Figure 6.43. Move the vertices of those branches to be more organic looking as well.

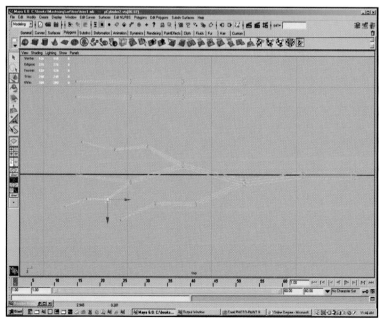

Figure 6.43 Add two smaller branches to the larger branch.

18. The last two branches that we duplicated earlier are too long. Select and delete the faces of the larger end of each branch as shown in Figure 6.44.

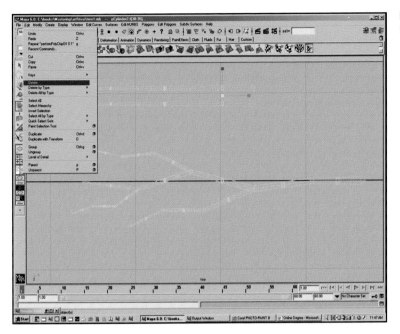

Figure 6.44 Delete the end faces of the two remaining smaller branches.

19. Now scale the two remaining branches down and add them to the larger branch as shown in Figure 6.45. They actually are added to the smaller branches that were added to the larger branch earlier, but they all become a happy branch family.

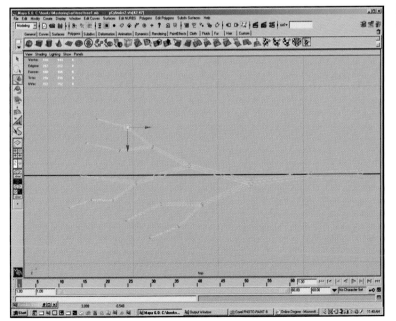

Figure 6.45 Add the two remaining branches to the larger branch.

20. Although it appeared that we attached the branches in the Top view, in the Perspective view we see a much different story. The branches are not connected to each other (see Figure 6.46). The next step is to move the branches to connect to the larger branch from the Perspective view to make sure each branch is attached to the larger main branch.

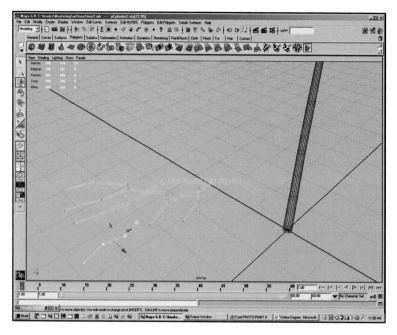

Figure 6.46 Move the smaller branches to connect them to the larger branch.

21. In some cases only the vertices of the larger end of the smaller branches need to be moved to attach them to the larger branch. See Figure 6.47.

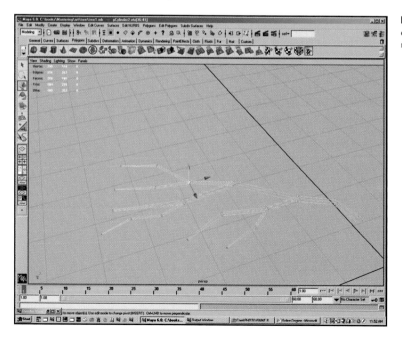

Figure 6.47 For some of the branches only the end vertices need to be moved.

22. Change the render mode to Smooth Shaded by pressing the 6 key on the keyboard. Notice that the branches all seem faceted rather than rounded. This is because there are fewer polygons in the branches than there are in the trunk. See Figure 6.48.

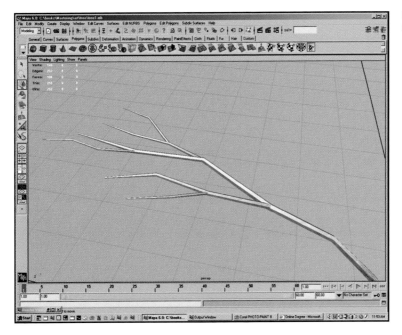

Figure 6.48 The branches appear faceted.

23. The look of the branches can be fixed without adding more polygons to the model by softening the normals of each polygon. Go to the Soften/Harden dialog box in the Normals submenu of the Edit Polygons Menu as shown in Figure 6.49.

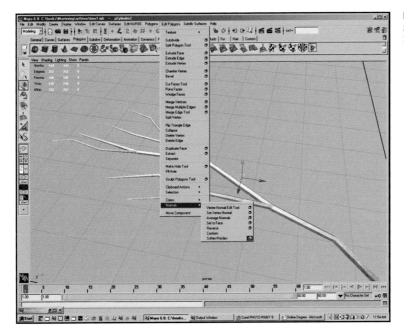

Figure 6.49 You can find Soften/Harden normals in the Normals submenu.

24. The Soften/Harden tool works with edges. Change the selection mode to Edges using the Marking Menu. Set the Angle at 90 and click Apply. Notice that the edges are softened and the branches now look round rather than faceted, as shown in Figure 6.50.

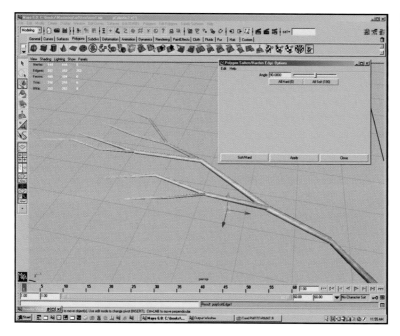

Figure 6.50 The branches now look rounded.

The branch is now finished. Go ahead and attach it to the tree trunk. The branches look good but they seem kind of bare without any leaves. Adding leaves is the next task in creating this tree.

Creating the Leaves

Creating leaves can be a real problem for the 3D artist. Even a small tree can have thousands of leaves. Creating individual leaves as polygons can quickly result in a model with so many polygons that it slows the 3D program to a crawl. In addition, placing individual leaves on a tree can be time-consuming. However, in some instances in which a tree is the central object in a scene, it may be necessary to create and place individual leaves.

Most of the time a tree is a secondary feature in a scene. As such, creating them with a minimum of polygons is usually a good idea. A good way to save on polygons for leaves is to use a texture with a transparent alpha channel.

1. Bring up Hypershade, create a Blinn material, and rename it Leaves.

2. Load leaves.tga into the Color attribute of the material as shown in Figure 6.51. This .tga file is different from the other files because it contains an alpha channel. The alpha channel is what makes the area around the leaves transparent.

3. In the Attribute Editor, click on Leaves. Set the Eccentricity, Specular Roll Off, and Reflectivity to 0. This helps to minimize the planar look of the leaves on the tree.

4. Create a new polygon plane as shown in Figure 6.52. Make sure the settings match those in the figure. The option box is found in Create > Polygon > Primitive > Plane Menu.

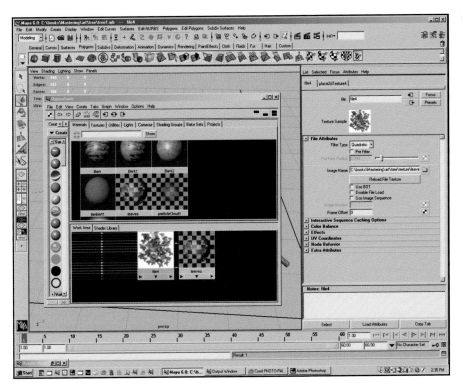

Figure 6.51 Load leaves.tga into the Leaves material.

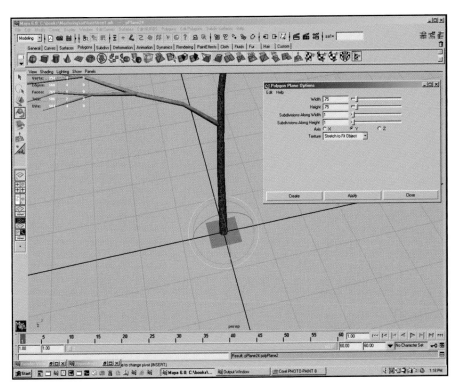

Figure 6.52 Create a new polygon plane.

5. Apply the Leaves material to the new polygon plane as shown in Figure 6.53. Notice that
   the material is transparent.

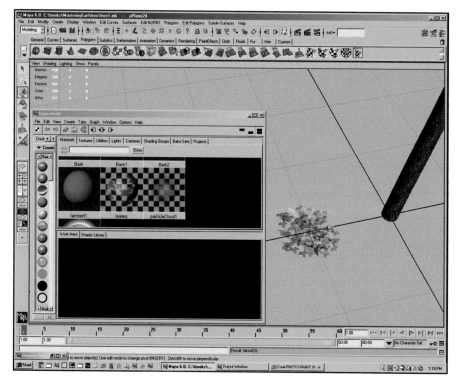

Figure 6.53 Apply the Leaves material to the new polygon plan.

6. Move the pivot point of the leaves object to the edge by where the branch meets the edge
   of the plane. Press the Insert key to adjust the pivot point. The pivot point is the point in
   space that an object rotates around. Press the Insert key again when the pivot is in place.
   Moving the pivot point makes it easier to move and adjust the leaves on the branches.

7. Move the leaves to the branch as shown in Figure 6.54.

8. Duplicate the leaves object by pressing Ctrl+D on the keyboard. Ctrl+D is a shortcut key-
   stroke for the duplicate command used earlier. Move the new leaves object to a different
   location on the branch. Continue duplicating and moving the leaves as shown in Figure
   6.55. Use the Rotate tool to change the position of the leaves so they have a more organic
   look like leaves do in nature.

9. Continue to add foliage to the branches until they seem well covered by leaves, as shown
   in Figure 6.56.

Figure 6.54 Put the leaves on the branch.

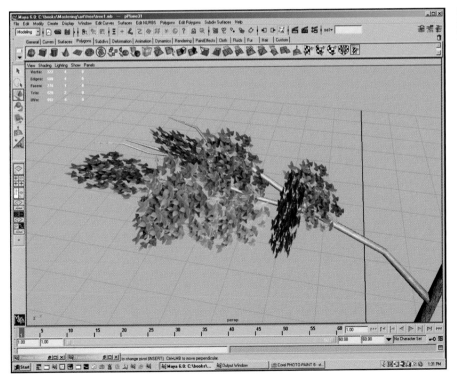

Figure 6.55 Duplicate and move the leaves object to other locations on the branches.

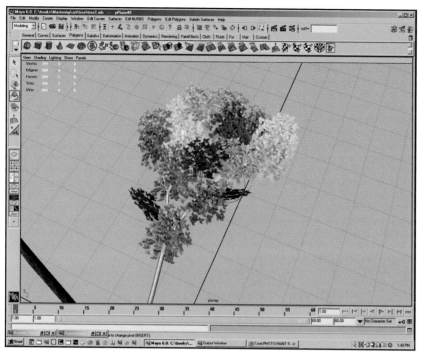

Figure 6.56 Add foliage to all the branches.

10. Select all the leaves and the branches and combine them into one object by going to Combine in the Polygon Menu. See Figure 6.57. This will make it easier to select the entire branch.

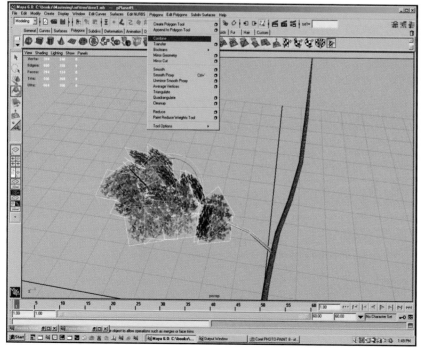

Figure 6.57 Combine the leaves with the branches.

11. Now move the pivot point of the combined object to the end of the branch where it connects to the tree, as shown in Figure 6.58.

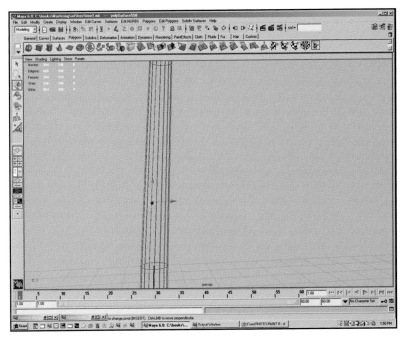

Figure 6.58 Move the pivot point to the end of the branch.

12. Duplicate the branch.

13. Move the new branch up the trunk just above the old branch and rotate it to the right as shown in Figure 6.59.

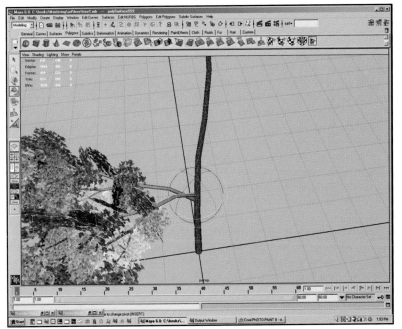

Figure 6.59 Move the new branch up and rotate it to the right.

14. There are many ways to attach branches to a tree trunk, but to make it easier for this first project just continue to duplicate, move, and rotate the branch in a spiral around the tree trunk as shown in Figure 6.60.

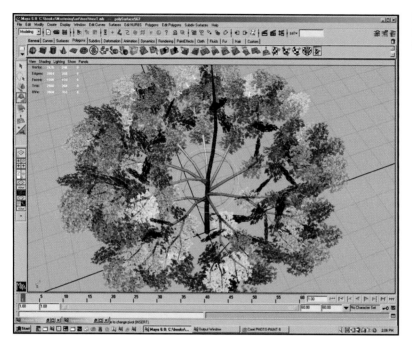

Figure 6.60 Move and rotate the new branches in a spiral around the tree trunk.

15. As the branches near the top of the trunk, the tree should look similar to Figure 6.61.

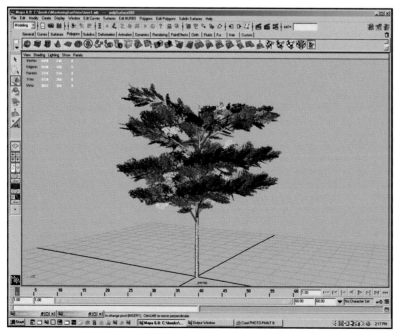

Figure 6.61 Continue adding branches to near the top of the tree trunk.

16. The tree now has plenty of branches, but it looks unnatural. Make the tree look more natural by rotating the branches in different angles. The branches near the top should be rotated up, one or two of them to a near vertical position. Continue rotating the branches until you have a tree that looks similar to the one in Figure 6.62.

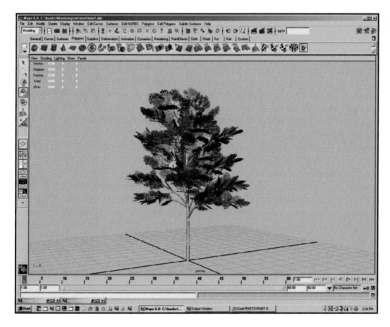

Figure 6.62 Rotate the branches to make the tree seem more natural.

The tree is now finished and you can save it to a directory where you can use it later. This tree is not as refined as one where every individual leaf is modeled, but for most applications it will work well. If you want to better hide the planar nature of the leaves, you can add a few individual leaves here and there.

Summary

You have just finished a couple of exercises in Maya, one very simple and one more complex. You should have at least a beginning knowledge of some of the tools and features of the program. As you continue to go through the next few chapters you will gain an even broader knowledge of the program. Don't be afraid to experiment and try a few models on your own. Ctrl+Z will undo most problems and you can always save your model before you try something really daring.

This chapter was an introduction to 3D model building in Maya. Some of the subjects covered include:

■ An overview of the Maya interface

■ Creating polygon objects from primitives

■ Building and texturing a ball

■ Building and texturing a tree

■ Creating materials

■ Creating a material with transparencies

■ Duplicating repetitive objects

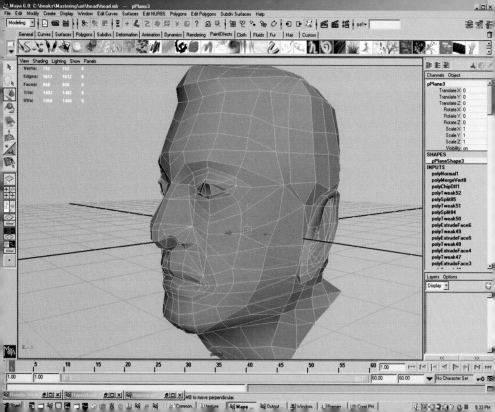

7

Building 3D Models

Building 3D models is the process of creating a virtual 3D representation of a character, an object, or a setting. This chapter and the next explore the process in greater detail. In this chapter the emphasis is on polygonal modeling techniques to help build a stronger understanding of 3D models. Chapter 8 covers more advanced methods of model building like NURBS.

Polygon Modeling Tools

Maya has many tools that are useful for building models with polygons. Understanding these tools will help you to master the techniques of building models with polygons. You should be familiar with some of the tools because they were used in Chapter 6 to create the tree. Now it is time to explain them in greater detail.

Polygon Primitives

A primitive in 3D modeling is a basic geometric shape like a cube, cylinder, or sphere. Many models start with a basic shape and then are modified to create a more complex model. Recall that the tree branches in Chapter 6 started with a cylinder primitive and then were modified.

You can find the Polygon Primitive creation tools on the Create Menu in the Main Menu as shown in Figure 7.1.

The six polygon primitives supported by Maya are Sphere, Cube, Cylinder, Cone, Plane, and Torus. Each has a dialog box for setting the creation options. These options control the size, shape, and number of polygons in the object. Figure 7.2 shows the Polygon Sphere Options dialog box.

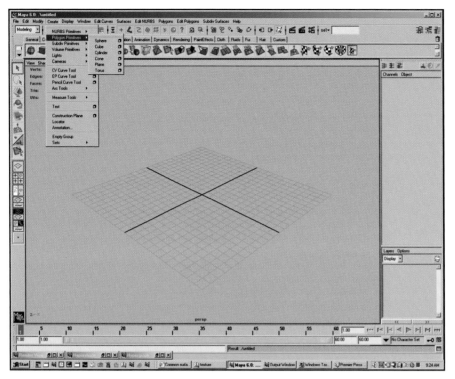

Figure 7.1 Create Polygon Primitive is located in the Create Menu.

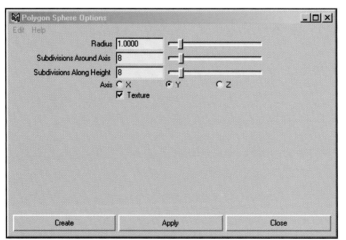

Figure 7.2 The Polygon Sphere Options dialog box.

Each text field and check box in the dialog box controls a different aspect of the object when created. The first option defines the size of the sphere. The number in the box can be set using the slider bar or can be typed directly in the box. The next two options set the number of polygons in the sphere, and they also have slider bars. The next option sets the orientation of the sphere, and the last option sets the texture preference. By default the Texture option is turned on. When texturing is turned on, the object will be created with UVs. UVs are points that provide information for applying textures to surfaces. If the texture preference is turned off the object will be created without UVs. Objects can't have textures without UVs.

Note

Maya remembers the options for dialog boxes. If you want to make several primitives with the same options, you don't need to go back into the dialog box. Just selecting the primitive on the menu or on the Shelf will create a new primitive with the same options as the last one created. This feature in Maya is called *persistence*.

The next primitive is the polygon cube. The Polygon Cube Options are shown in Figure 7.3.

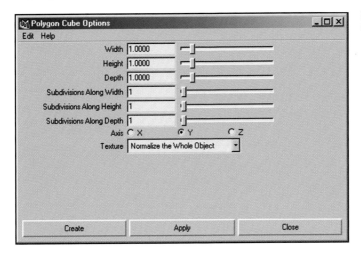

Figure 7.3 The Polygon Cube Options dialog box.

Cubes have a height, width, and depth. The first three boxes of the options box control the size of the cube. The next three boxes control the number of polygons in the cube, and the radio buttons control the axis of the cube. Rather than a check box, the texture options give some choices in how the UVs will be applied to the cube. The default is Normalize the Whole Object. This means that the material is applied to fit once per side of the cube.

Figure 7.4 shows the Polygon Cylinder Options dialog box.

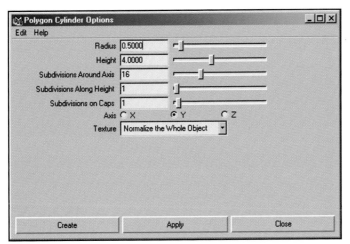

Figure 7.4 The Polygon Cylinder Options dialog box.

Like the sphere, the cylinder has a radius. It also has a height. The first two boxes control the size of the cylinder in its radius and height. The next three boxes control the number of polygons around the axis, height, and cap of the cylinder. The radio buttons control the axis and, like the cube, the Polygon Cylinder Options dialog box has options for applying the UVs.

Figure 7.5 shows the Polygon Cone Options box.

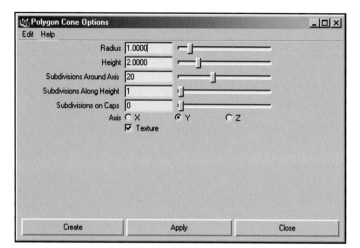

Figure 7.5 The Polygon Cone Options dialog box.

The options for the cylinder and the cone are very similar except for the texture option, which is just a check box.

Figure 7.6 shows the Polygon Plane Options dialog box.

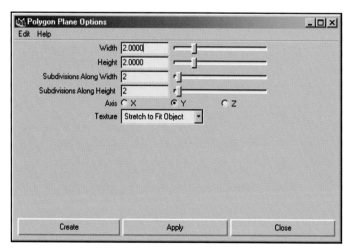

Figure 7.6 The Polygon Plane Options dialog box.

A plane is a flat polygonal object. It only has two directions for size and two directions for polygons. It has an axis like other objects. The default texture mode for a plane is to stretch the material to fit, which means that the texture will be distorted to fit the plane. The other option is to preserve the aspect ratio of the texture. Figure 7.7 shows two planes. The one on the top has the Preserve Aspect Ratio option selected and the one on the bottom has the Stretch to Fit Object option selected.

Torus is the remaining polygon primitive supported by Maya. Figure 7.8 shows its options dialog box.

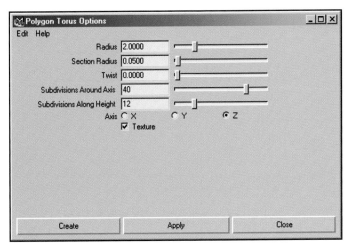

Figure 7.8 The Polygon Torus Options dialog box.

The Polygon Torus Options dialog box is set up similar to the other options boxes. The first three boxes deal with the size of the object. The next two boxes deal with the number of polygons in the object. The radio buttons deal with the object axis and the check box with texture setup.

Menus

Many of the most commonly used tools for polygon modeling are found under the Polygon and Edit Polygon Menus in the Main Menu when set to the Modeling Menu set.

Polygon

It would take a book much larger than this to explain every menu item and function in Maya. This book concentrates on common functions. Figure 7.9 shows the location of the Polygon Menu with the Combine function selected.

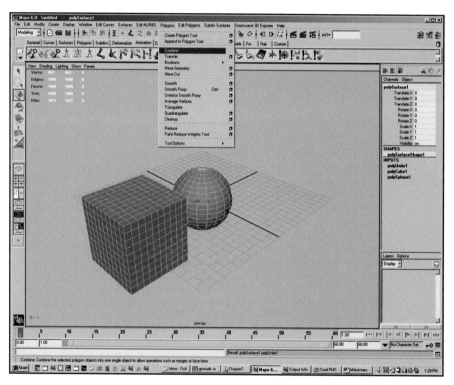

Figure 7.9 The Combine function is in the Polygon Menu.

Combine is a common function. Combine takes all selected objects and combines them into one object. Remember that in the tree model Combine was used to make the branches and leaves all one object.

Another commonly used function in Maya is Mirror Geometry. This function mirrors an object across a plane. It is commonly used for symmetrical models so the modeler only needs to focus on building half the model and then can mirror the model to complete it. A good example is a model of a car. Only half of the car needs to be built. Then using the Mirror Geometry function, the other half is added at the end of the modeling process. Figure 7.10 shows the Mirror Geometry function on the Polygon Menu.

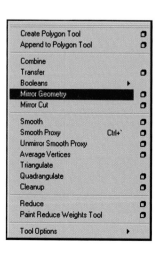

Figure 7.10 Mirror Geometry duplicates an object across a plane.

Smooth adds polygons to an object to reduce the sharp edges of a model. The function averages the angles of the polygons to make the surface of a model more rounded. Modelers often use it because making a simple object is faster than making a complex one. After the basic object is created using just a few polygons, the artist then uses the Smooth function to round the otherwise rough-faceted surface. Figure 7.11 shows the Smooth function on the Polygon Menu.

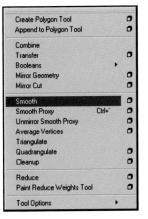

Figure 7.11 The Smooth function adds polygons and smoothes the surface of an object.

Cleanup is used to find and correct problems in a polygonal model. It has a number of options that let the artist define the parameters of a search to detect specific problems. It is similar to a spelling and grammar check in a word processor. Figure 7.12 shows where Cleanup is located on the Polygon Menu.

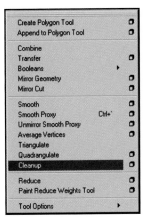

Figure 7.12 Cleanup is used to find and correct problems in a polygonal model.

Edit Polygon

The Edit Polygon Menu has many useful tools and functions used to modify elements of a polygon object. Polygon Menu items are used on polygon objects, where Edit Polygon Menu items are primarily tools for modifying components of an object. When using menu items in the Edit Polygon Menu, the selection mode should generally be a component of a polygon rather than an object. Figure 7.13 shows the Edit Polygon Menu with Texture selected.

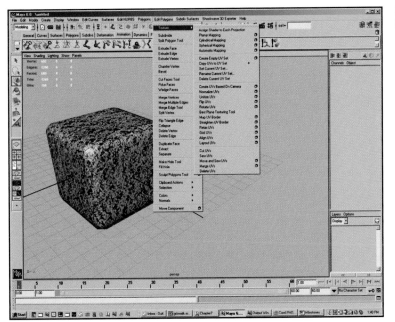

Figure 7.13 Edit Polygon Menu items affect polygon components.

The Texture submenu contains functions for applying and manipulating textures on polygons. These menu items are covered in Chapter 9.

Below Texture on the Edit Polygon Menu is the Subdivide function, as shown in Figure 7.14. Subdivide is used to increase the density of the polygon mesh in selected areas of a model.

Split Polygon is a tool used to divide individual polygons. It is used when specific geometry is needed to complete a model. The tool lets the artist draw in edges to a polygon. Split Polygon is directly below Subdivide on the Edit Polygon Menu, as shown in Figure 7.15.

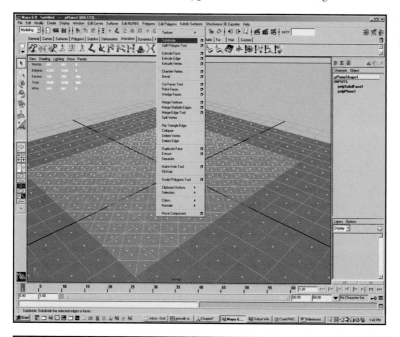

Figure 7.14 Subdivide increases the density of a polygon mesh in a selected area.

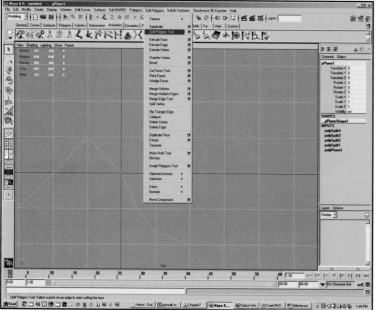

Figure 7.15 The Split Polygon tool is used to divide individual polygons.

Extrude Face is another commonly used tool. It allows the artist to select a number of faces and extrude them. Extrude Face is commonly used to add features to primitive models like arms and legs on characters or to build walls from a floor plan of a room. The Extrude Face function is shown in Figure 7.16.

Extrude Edge is used in model building to extend a plane. It allows the artist to select the edges of a plane or object and extrude new polygons along that edge. It is shown in Figure 7.17.

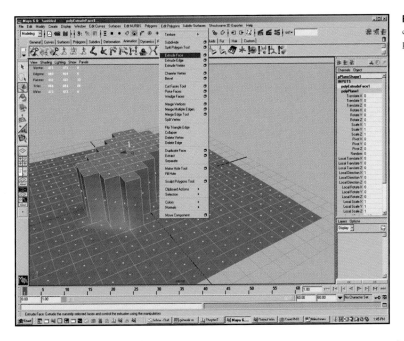

Figure 7.16 Extrude Face is commonly used to add features to primitive models.

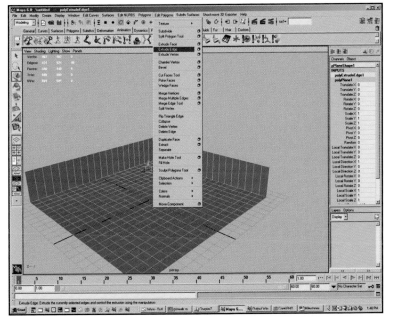

Figure 7.17 Extrude Edge extends a plane or series of planes.

Another common function is Merge Vertices. Merge Vertices is used to combine two or more vertices into a single vertex. Merge Vertices is often used to join two parts of an object or to reduce the number of polygons in an area. It is shown in Figure 7.18.

Duplicate Face makes a copy of a selected set of polygon faces. It is often used to create copies of repetitive polygons such as in building a fence or creating wheels for a car. It is shown in Figure 7.19.

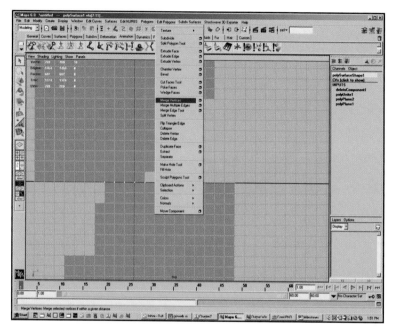

Figure 7.18 Merge Vertices merges two or more vertices into a single vertex.

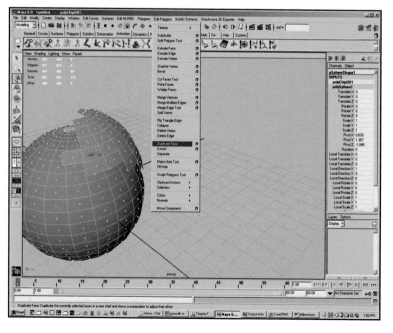

Figure 7.19 Duplicate Face makes a copy of polygon faces.

Extract detaches a selected set of polygons from a model, creating a separate object. It is used for separating model parts like a door on a car or a window in a building. It is shown in Figure 7.20.

Separate is a function used to separate unmerged polygons from each other. For example, in Chapter 6 the Combine function was used to create a single object from several branch and leaves objects. The Separate function could be used to separate the original objects from the combined object. This is useful if modifications are needed to the combined object. Separate is shown in Figure 7.21.

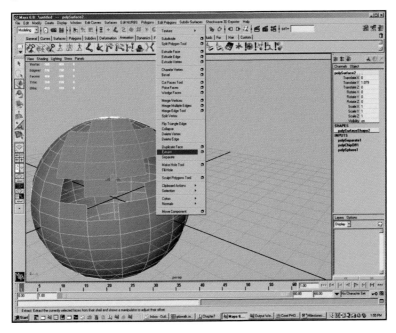

Figure 7.20 Extract detaches from a model.

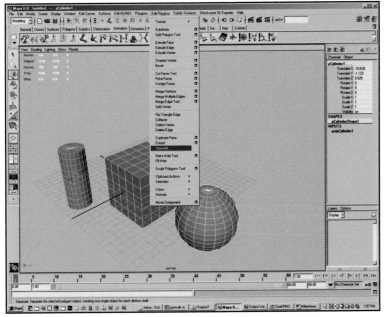

Figure 7.21 Separate polygons from each other.

The Sculpt Polygons tool has many uses but the main use is to interactively move polygons, similar to sculpting clay. This menu item is shown in Figure 7.22.

Selection gives the artist several options for selecting component types of an object. The sub-menu shown in Figure 7.23 shows the available options for selection.

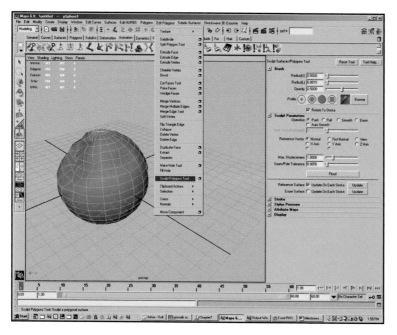

Figure 7.22 The Sculpt Polygons tool shapes polygons similar to sculpting with clay.

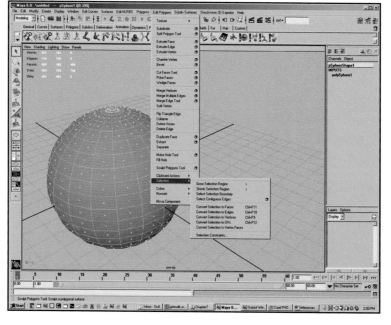

Figure 7.23 Selection gives the artist several options for selecting component types of an object.

A polygon normal indicates the direction a polygon surface is facing. When a texture is applied to a polygon it will appear correctly if the polygon normal is facing the viewer. If the polygon normal is facing away from the viewer, the texture will be reversed. Normals on the Edit Polygon Menu has a submenu of functions for adjusting the direction of the normal on a polygon. It is shown in Figure 7.24.

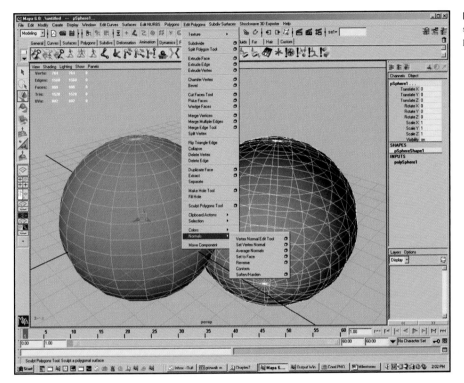

Figure 7.24 The direction a polygon surface is facing is indicated by the polygon normal.

Sidebar Tools and Editors

The Channel Box is located to the far right of the Panel. Figure 7.25 shows the Channel Box for a polygon sphere object. The Channel Box is one of the easiest ways to accurately change attributes of an object.

A very common editor used in Maya is the Attribute Editor. It is located in the side Panel area. Figure 7.26 shows the Attribute Editor for a Lambert material. The Attribute Editor is used to edit attributes of a single node. A node holds specific information about a construct in Maya. For example, in the figure, the Lambert material shown in Hypershade is a node.

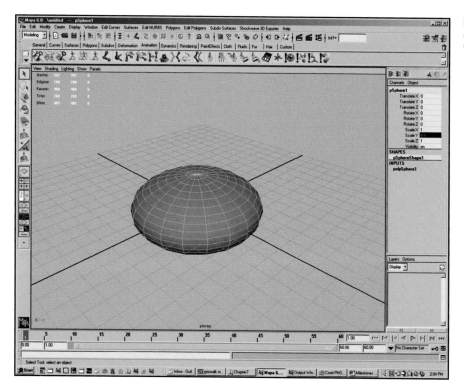

Figure 7.25 You can change the attributes of an object using the Channel Box.

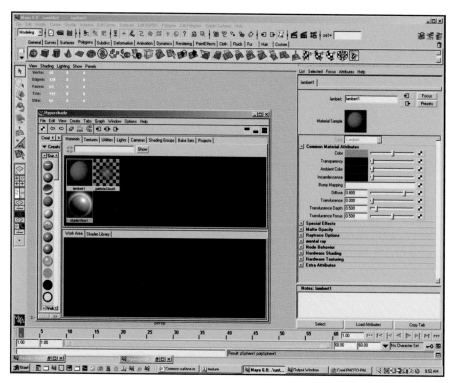

Figure 7.26 The Attribute Editor is a tool for editing attributes of a single node.

Another common element that appears in the sidebar of Maya is the Tool Settings panel. These tools are used for the painting and other applications in Maya. Figure 7.27 shows the Sculpt Surfaces/Polygons tool.

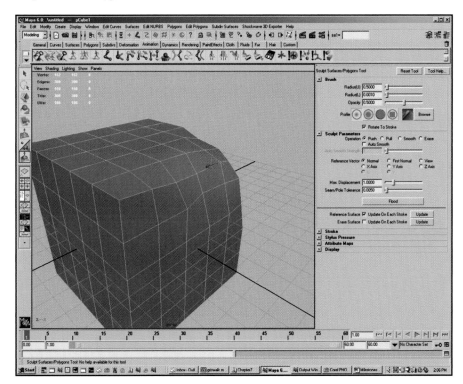

Figure 7.27 The painting tools appear in the sidebar.

These functions and tools are only a few of the many found in Maya, but these will give you a good start. For more information on functions and tools in Maya look at the online help documentation that comes with Maya. It has detailed information on every aspect of the product. It is located in the Help Menu.

Building a Polygon Head

The best way to learn how to master 3D digital art is to practice building models. The next part of this chapter is a demonstration on building a human head with polygons. Following the detailed instructions for building the head will help you to gain a better feel for Maya.

Complex models like human heads are difficult to model without a template of some kind. Figure 7.28 shows a front and side view drawing of a human head. The drawing will be used as a template for the head model.

Preparing the Template

There are two files available for the next exercise, frontguide.BMP and sideguide.BMP. You can find them at www.courseptr.com/downloads. These two files are set up for the drawing to be in the exact center. They are the two template files used in the project.

Figure 7.28 The template for the head model.

1. Create two polygon planes that are 8 units by 8 units. Create the first in the Z axis and the second in the X axis, as shown in Figure 7.29.

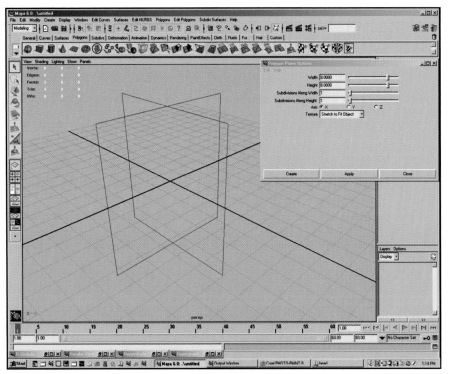

Figure 7.29 Create two single polygon planes.

2. Create two Lambert materials and label them front1 and side1. Load frontguide.BMP into the color of front1 and sideguide.BMP into the color of side1 as shown in Figure 7.30.

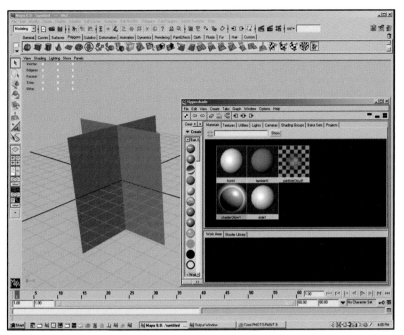

Figure 7.30 Create two materials for the template drawings.

3. Apply front1 material to the plane in the Z axis and side1 material to the plane in the X axis as shown in Figure 7.31.

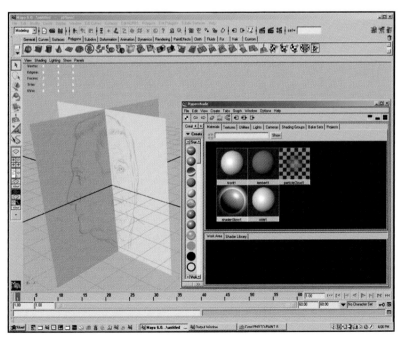

Figure 7.31 Apply the materials to the polygons.

4. Change the shade options of the Panel to Shading, Shading Options, X-Ray in the Panel Menu as shown in Figure 7.32.

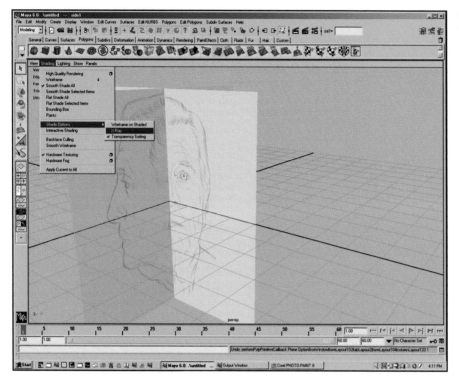

Figure 7.32 Change the shade options of the Panel to X-Ray.

Templates are used as guides to help the artist in modeling complex objects or objects where accuracy is important.

Building the Head

Now that the template is finished, it is time to start constructing the head. Many artists are intimidated by the complexity of constructing a human head but the process is really quite simple and not that hard to follow.

1. Create a polygon plane as shown in Figure 7.33. Make sure the plane options are set to 8 units high by 8 units wide. The subdivisions on the width should be 8 and the subdivisions on the height should be 14. Set the axis to Z.

2. Go to the side view and change the selection mode to Vertex as shown in Figure 7.34.

3. Move the vertices of the plane to follow the contour of the face as shown in Figure 7.35. For now ignore the nose.

4. Go to the front view and select all vertices in the plane. Now scale the plane to the size of the face as shown in Figure 7.36.

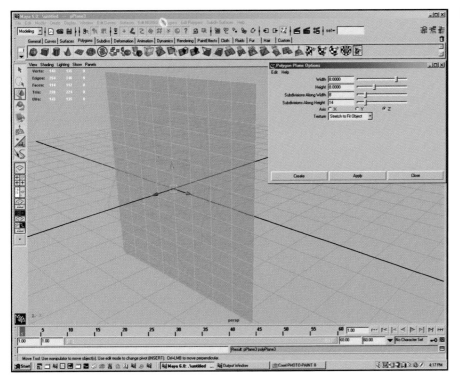

Figure 7.33 Create a polygon plane.

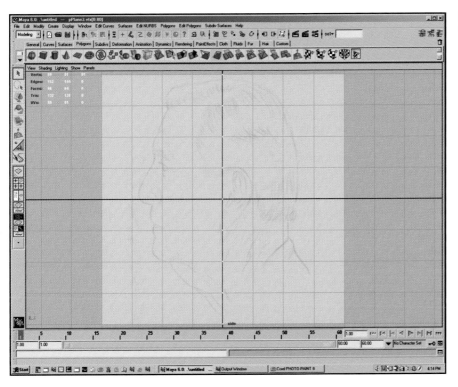

Figure 7.34 Change the Selection mode to Vertex.

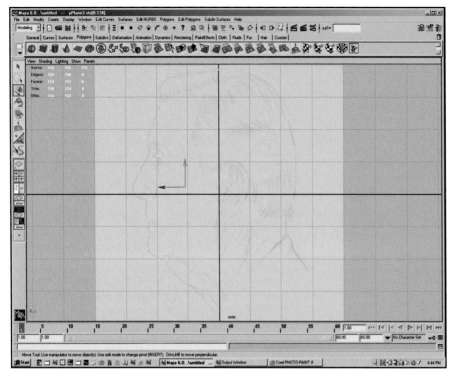

Figure 7.35 Move the vertices of the plane to follow the contour of the face.

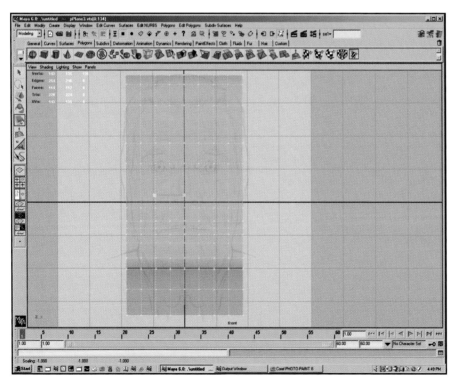

Figure 7.36 Scale the plane to the size of the face.

5. Select each row of vertices on the plane and scale them to the contour of the face as shown in Figure 7.37.

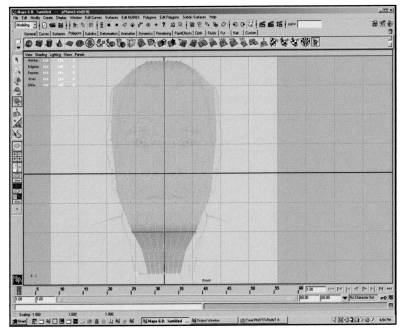

Figure 7.37 Scale each row of vertices to the contour of the face.

6. Change the selection mode to Faces and select all the faces on the left-hand side of the face as shown in Figure 7.38.

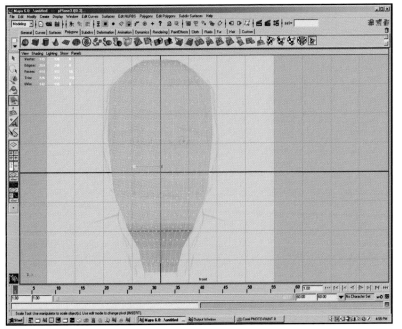

Figure 7.38 Select the faces of the left-hand side of the face.

7. Delete the faces on the left-hand side of the face. Because the face is symmetrical, only half of the face needs to be modeled. The model will be mirrored across the X axis later.

8. Move the vertices of the face to fit the features of the head. Use the Split Polygon tool to add polygons around these features as shown in Figure 7.39. Notice that the polygons around the eye are drawn in concentric rings. This method of creating polygons will help the polygons to deform correctly when the head is animated.

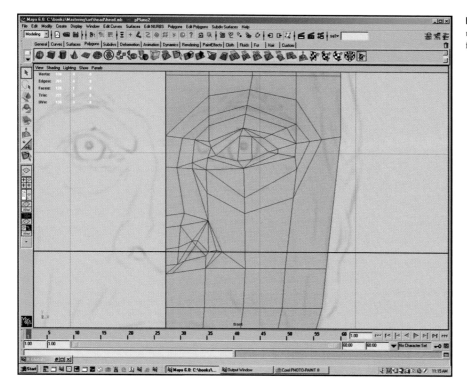

Figure 7.39 Use the Split Polygon tool to draw in new polygons on the face.

9. Continue to draw in new polygons to follow the shape of the face. Figure 7.40 shows a close-up of the mouth area.

10. Continue to split the polygons until all the features are drawn in as shown in Figure 7.41. Make sure that none of the polygons have more than four sides.

11. Now it is time to shape the head from the side. Select all of the vertices on the far right-hand side of the model.

12. Go to the side view and scale the selected vertices in the Z axis until they are lined up evenly with each other as shown in Figure 7.42.

13. Move the scaled vertices to zero in the Z axis as shown in Figure 7.43.

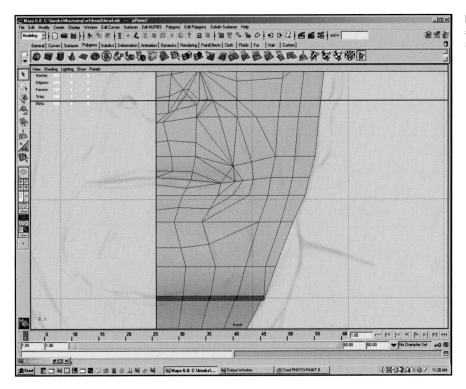

Figure 7.40 Use concentric rings around the mouth when adding the new polygons.

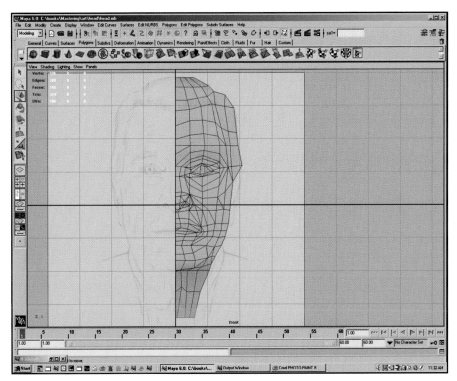

Figure 7.41 Make sure there are no polygons with more than four sides.

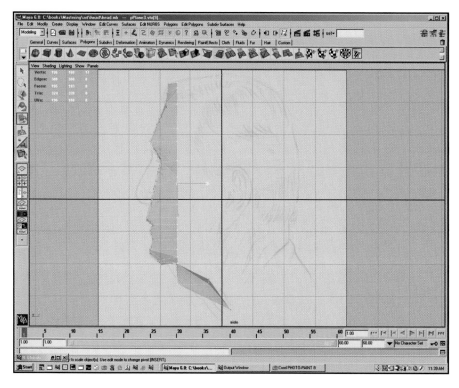

Figure 7.42 Scale the vertices in the Z axis.

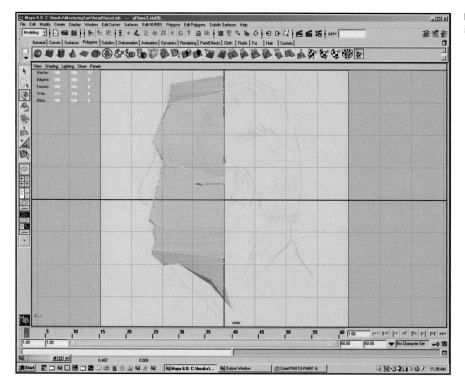

Figure 7.43 Move the vertices to zero in the Z axis.

14. Change to the Perspective view and move the vertices that make up the nose so they follow the contour of the nose as shown in Figure 7.44.

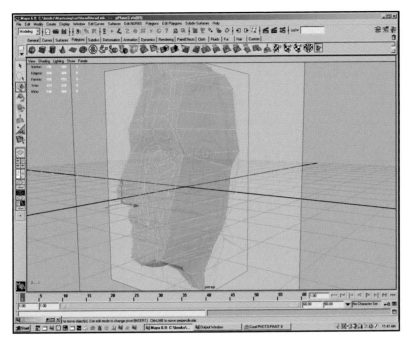

Figure 7.44 Move the vertices to follow the contour of the nose.

15. Move each vertex to sculpt the shape of the face as shown in Figure 7.45. The vertices should only need to be moved in the Z axis. This is probably the trickiest part of the modeling process. Work in the Perspective view and move around the model often to check your work.

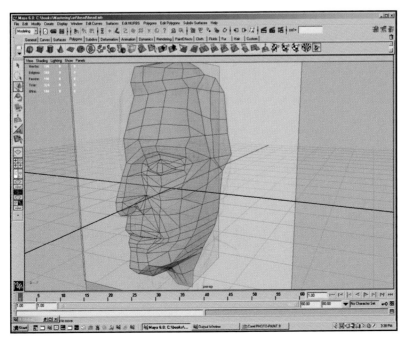

Figure 7.45 Sculpt the face by moving each vertex.

16. They eye will need to be inset. Select the faces that cover the eye as shown in Figure 7.46 and then select Extrude Faces.

Note

Extrude Faces can extrude selected faces individually or as a group. For this project group extrusions are needed. Change the extrusion type by going to Tool Options in the Polygon Menu and selecting Keep Faces Together.

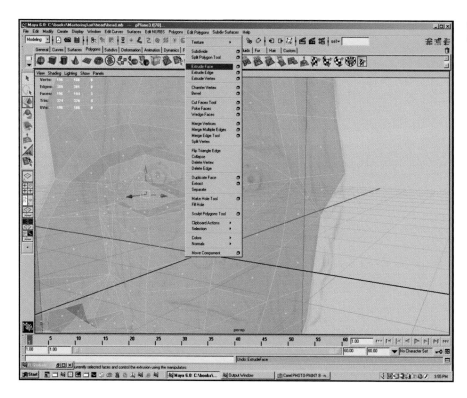

Figure 7.46 Select the faces of the eye.

17. Move the polygons of the eye into the head to create the lip of the eyelids as shown in Figure 7.47.

18. Extrude the nostril of the nose into the head as shown in Figure 7.48.

Shaping the Head

Now that the basic features of the head are in place, the next step will be to refine them so they look right. Because the vertices of the face were moved by hand, it will be difficult to make the face smooth. Maya has a great tool for smoothing rough surfaces interactively: the Sculpt Surface tool.

1. Select the model in Object mode and then select the Sculpt Surface tool as shown in Figure 7.49.

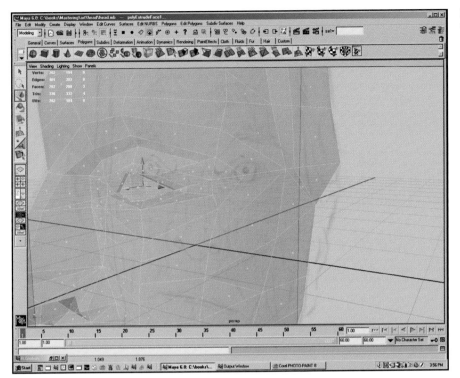

Figure 7.47 Move the polygons of the eye into the head.

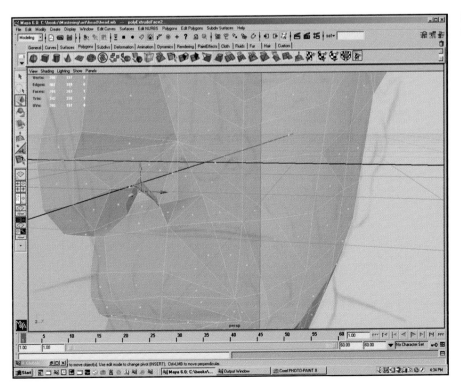

Figure 7.48 Extrude the nostril of the nose.

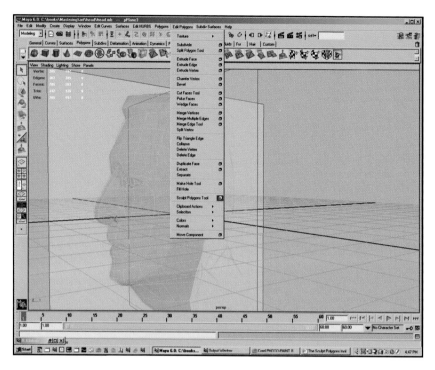

Figure 7.49 The Sculpt
Surface/Polygon tool is used to shape
objects.

2. Set the options on the tool to those in Figure 7.50 and use the tool to smooth the vertices
of the model.

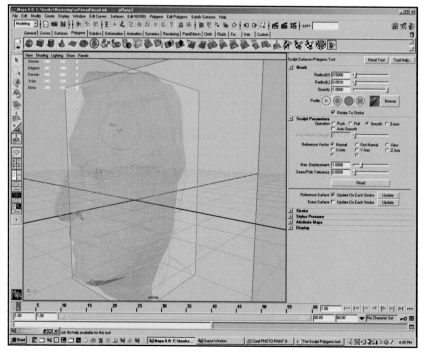

Figure 7.50 Smooth the vertices of
the model with the Sculpt Surface tool.

3. Change the selection mode to Edge using the Marking Menu. Select all the edges along the edge of the model as shown in Figure 7.51.

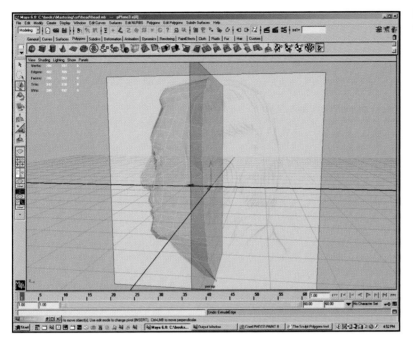

Figure 7.51 Select the edges along the back edge of the model.

4. Extrude the selected edges toward the back of the head several times as shown in Figure 7.52. These extra polygons will be needed to complete the back of the head.

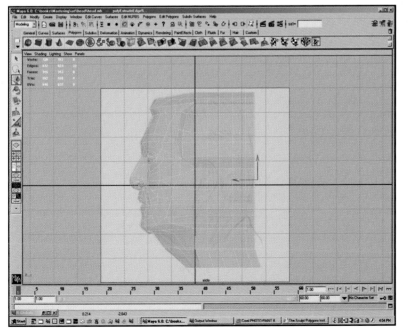

Figure 7.52 Extrude the selected edges toward the back of the head.

5. Use the Move tool to pull the vertices of the extruded geometry in to fit the outline of the head from the side view as shown in Figure 7.53. Try to keep the polygons of similar sizes as shown in the figure.

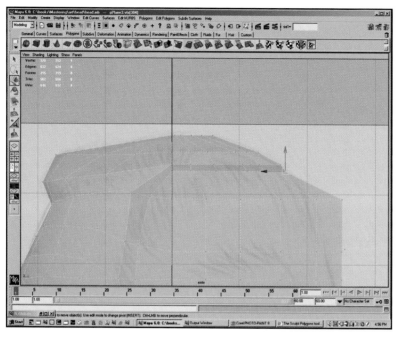

Figure 7.53 Adjust the polygons to fit the template.

6. Continue moving the vertices until the polygons on the back of the head match those shown in Figure 7.54.

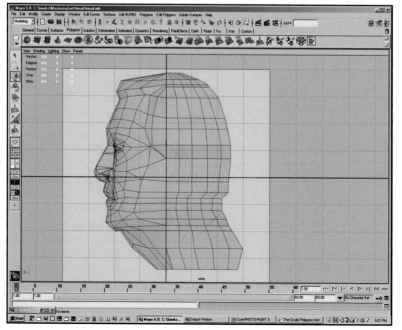

Figure 7.54 Match the polygons of the back of the head to this figure.

7. Select the vertices of the back edge of the model and scale them in the X axis to zero so they all line up with the template in that plane, as shown in Figure 7.55. You may need to use the Move tool to put them in the right place.

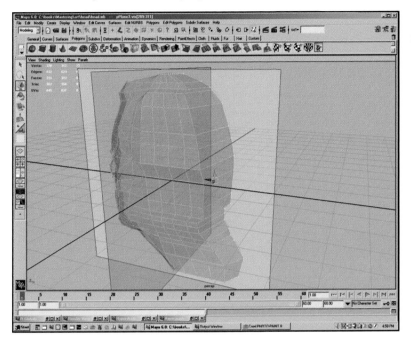

Figure 7.55 Move the vertices of the back edge of the model to zero in the X axis.

8. Use the Sculpt Surface/Polygons tool to smooth and shape the back of the head as shown in Figure 7.56.

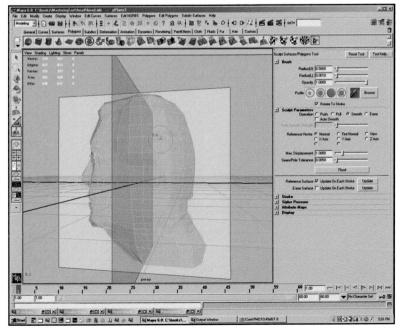

Figure 7.56 Smooth the back of the head.

9. Select the faces of the lower part of the neck as shown in Figure 7.57.

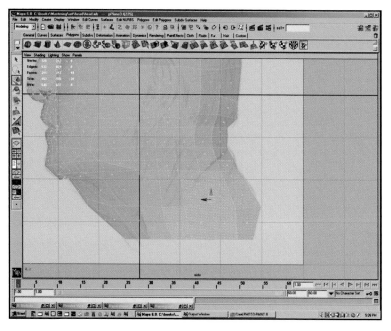

Figure 7.57 Select the polygons of the lower back of the neck.

10. Delete the selected polygons.

11. Use the Snap to Vertex function to snap the jagged vertices to line up with a smooth edge as shown in Figure 7.58. To snap to vertex, select a vertex and then while holding down the Ctrl+V keys, use the Move tool to move the selected vertex over another vertex. The selected vertex will snap to the same position as the nearest vertex.

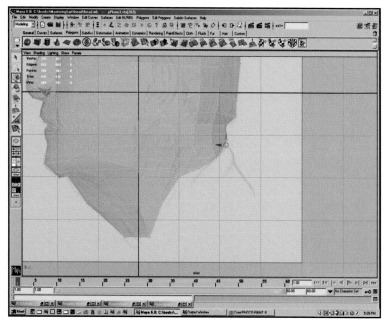

Figure 7.58 Snap the vertices to form a smooth edge.

12. Select all of the vertices along the smoothed edge and merge them as shown in Figure 7.59.

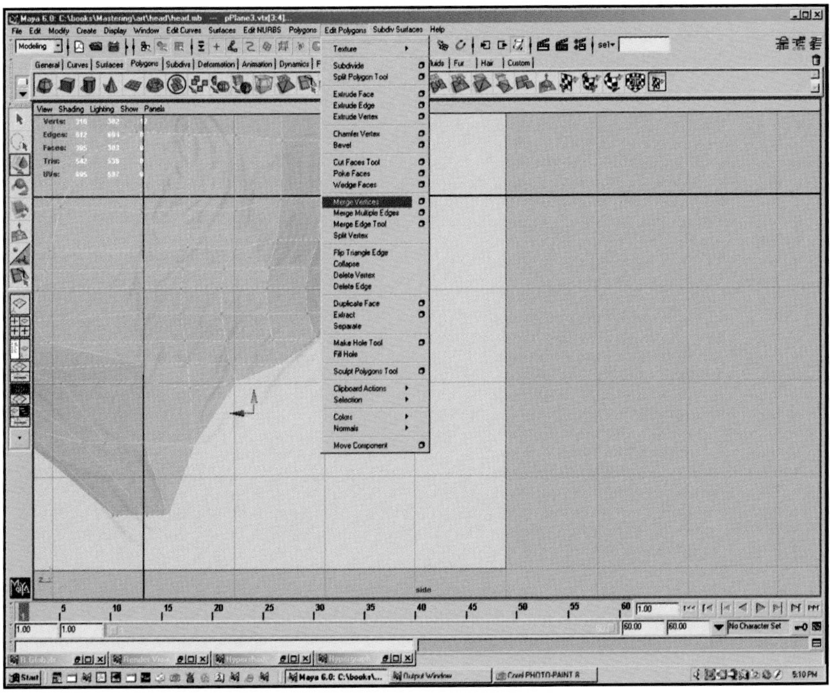

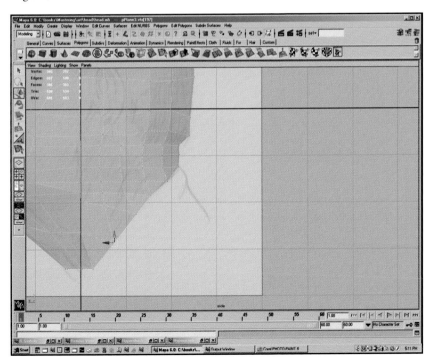

Figure 7.59 Merge vertices of the smoothed edge.

13. Now line up the vertices to fit the contour of the neck as it joins the shoulders as shown in Figure 7.60.

Figure 7.60 Line up the vertices to fit the contour of the neck.

14. Go to the front view and move the vertices to fit the template. Figure 7.61 shows this procedure in progress.

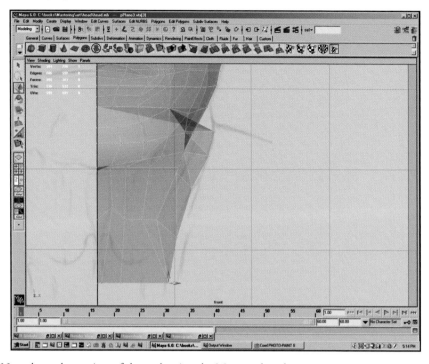

Figure 7.61 Move the neck vertices to fit the template.

15. Now shape the vertices of the neck using the Move tool as shown in Figure 7.62.

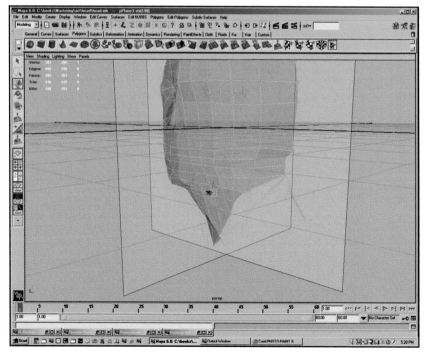

Figure 7.62 Shape the surface of the neck.

16. There are more polygons than needed in the top of the model. Use the Snap to Vertex function to minimize the number of polygons in that area. Merge the vertices to eliminate the extra polygons. The top of the model should look similar to Figure 7.63.

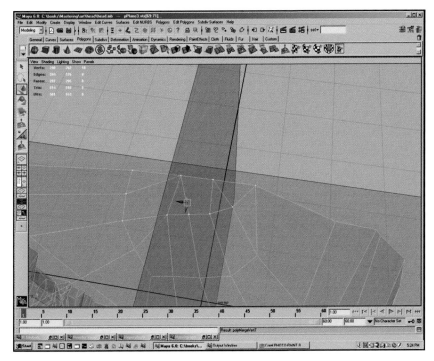

Figure 7.63 Eliminate excess polygons in the top of the model.

17. To mirror the model correctly, every vertex around the edge of the model where it will eventually join with the other half of the head has to be lined up perfectly with zero in the X axis. Use the Snap to Grid function to make sure each vertex along the edge is lined up correctly. Snap to Grid is similar to Snap to Vertex except that it snaps the vertex to a grid rather than another vertex. The function uses the Ctrl+X keys instead of Ctrl+V. When snapping to the grid for this procedure, the vertex only needs to move in the X axis. Moving the vertex in any other axis will cause problems. Be careful to only select the X axis arrow (the red one) when moving the vertex, as shown in Figure 7.64.

Creating the Ear

Now the model is ready for adding the ear. Ears are complex features. To keep the polygon count down on the head, the ear will be simplified.

1. Go to the side view and use the Split Polygon tool to draw in polygons that fit the template, as shown in Figure 7.65.

2. Select the polygons of the ear as shown in Figure 7.66.

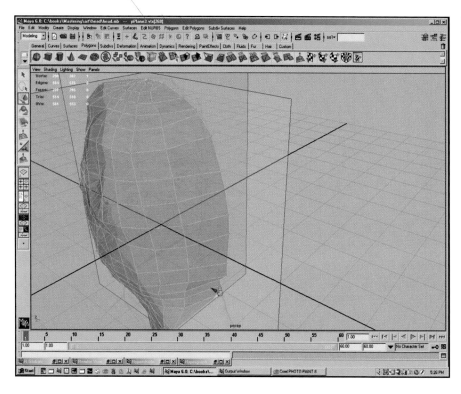

Figure 7.64 Use Snap to Grid to line up the vertices with zero in the X axis.

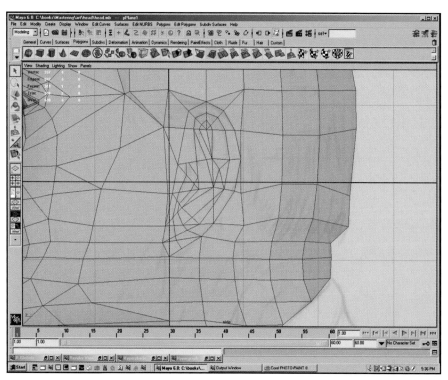

Figure 7.65 Split the polygons of the ear to fit the template.

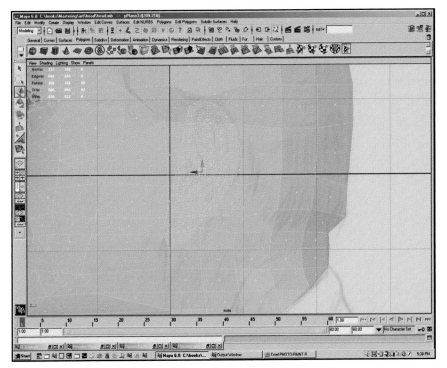

Figure 7.66 Select the polygons of the ear.

3. Change to the front view and extrude the polygons outward as shown in Figure 7.67.

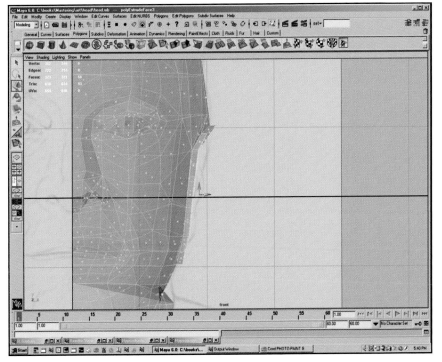

Figure 7.67 Extrude the faces of the ear.

4. Extrude the ear again as shown in Figure 7.68.

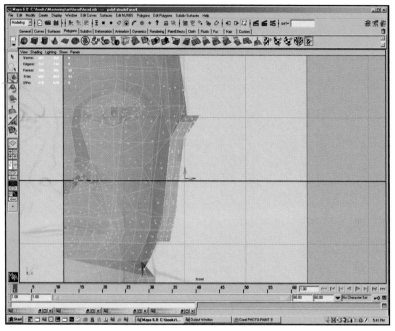

Figure 7.68 Extrude the ear again.

5. Select the faces along the back inner section of faces and extrude them inward using the Scale tool as shown in Figure 7.69.

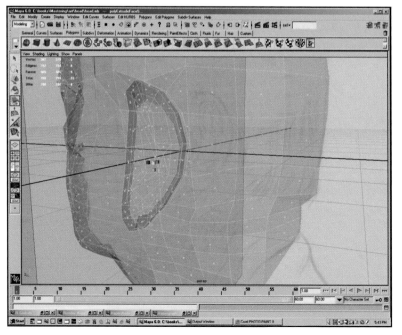

Figure 7.69 Extrude the polygons on the back of the ear.

6. The extruded polygons need to be reduced to better match the back of the ear and not use too many polygons. This may be a little tricky to see in Figure 7.70, but take the outside vertex of the extruded polygon at the top of the ear and snap it to the inside vertex as shown.

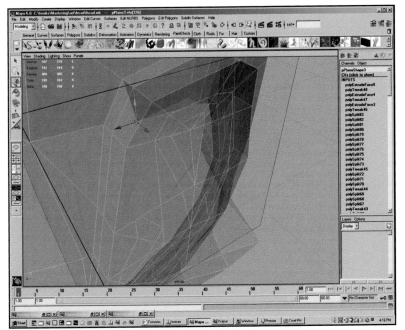

Figure 7.70 Merge the vertex of the extruded polygon.

7. Now continue through the rest of the polygons all along the back of the ear as shown in Figure 7.71 until all vertices have been merged.

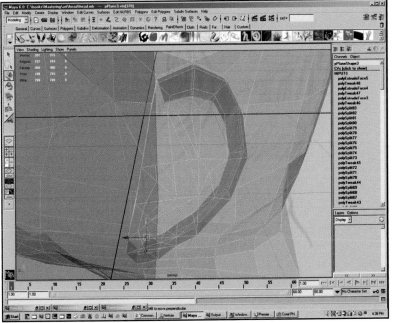

Figure 7.71 Merge the vertices along the back of the ear.

8. Take the inner vertex at the top of the ear and snap it down to the lower vertex as shown in Figure 7.72.

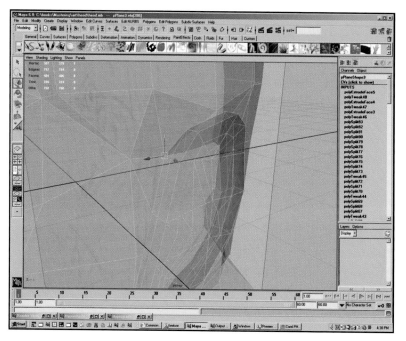

Figure 7.72 Snap the inner vertex at the top of the ear down to the lower vertex.

9. Snap the inner vertex at the bottom of the ear up to the higher vertex as shown in Figure 7.73, forming the lobe of the ear.

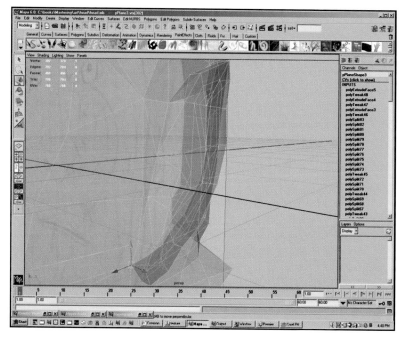

Figure 7.73 Create the ear lobe by snapping the inner vertex up to the next vertex.

10. The front part of the ear needs to slope up from the side of the face. Select the vertices of the front part of the ear and merge them with the vertices of the face as shown in Figure 7.74.

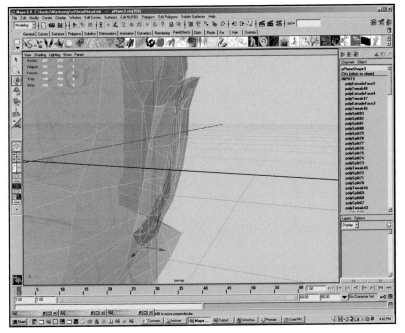

Figure 7.74 Merge the vertices of the front of the ear to the side of the face.

11. Select the inner faces of the ear as shown in Figure 7.75.

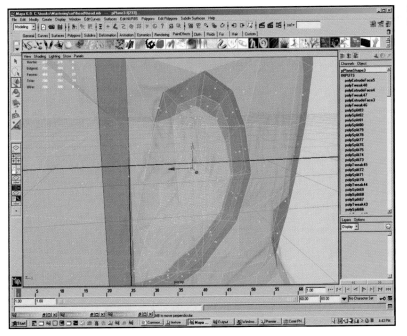

Figure 7.75 Select the inner faces of the ear.

12. Extrude the face toward the head to shape the inside of the ear as shown in Figure 7.76.

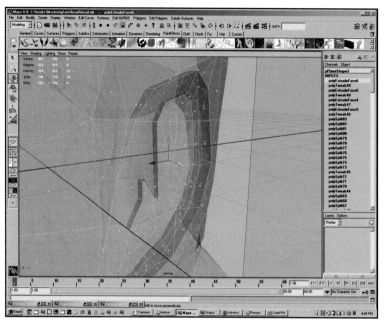

Figure 7.76 Extrude the faces toward the head.

13. Now using a process of moving vertices, shape the surface of the ear to a more natural look as shown in Figure 7.77. Some of the vertices along the bottom of the extruded polygons will need to be merged.

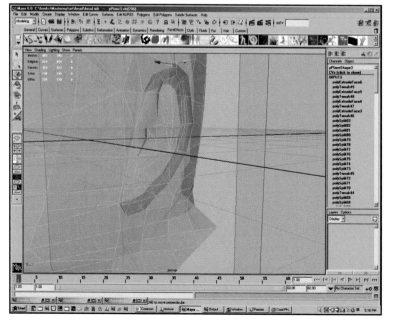

Figure 7.77 Shape the ear to a more natural look.

The modeling of the head should now be finished. Take a look at the head from as many angles as possible in the Perspective view to check the shape.

Finishing the Head

The head should be ready to mirror. Before mirroring it is always wise to save the head model. Saving the head at this point will make it easier to create new heads or adjust this head because only the polygons on half the head will need to be adjusted.

1. Change the selection mode to Object and select the head in the front view.

2. Bring up the Mirror Geometry dialog box under the Polygon Menu as shown in Figure 7.78.

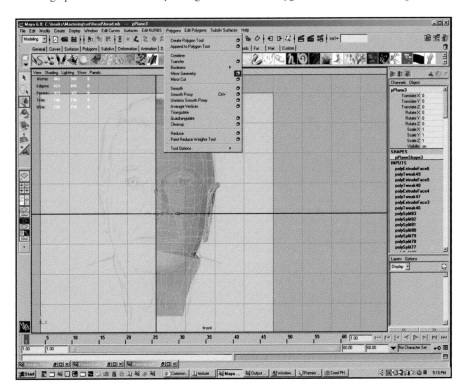

Figure 7.78 Bring up the Mirror Geometry dialog box found in the Polygon Menu.

3. Set the model to mirror across the negative X direction and check the Merge With The Original check box. Also set the model to Merge Vertices. Merging with the original will weld the mirrored geometry with the original geometry. Click the Apply button. The model should now look like Figure 7.79.

4. The templates are no longer needed. Hide them by first selecting each object and then selecting Hide Selection under Hide in the Display Menu as shown in Figure 7.80.

5. Now select X-Ray in the Shading Options submenu of the Shading Menu in the Panel as shown in Figure 7.81 to change the model back to a non-transparent view.

Figure 7.82 shows the finished modeled head. This model only uses 858 faces, which is a good number if the head is to be used in a real-time application like a video game.

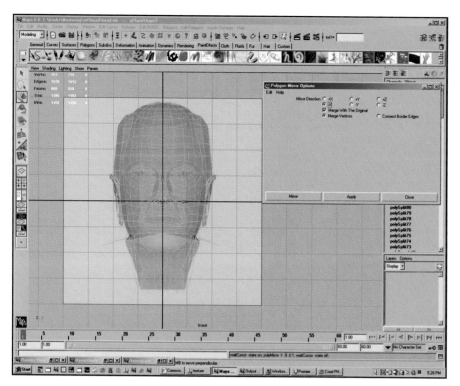

Figure 7.79 Mirror the model across the negative X direction.

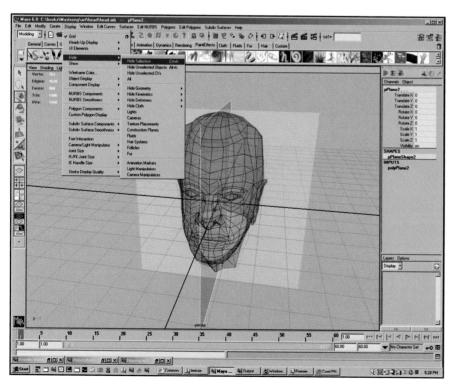

Figure 7.80 Hide the templates.

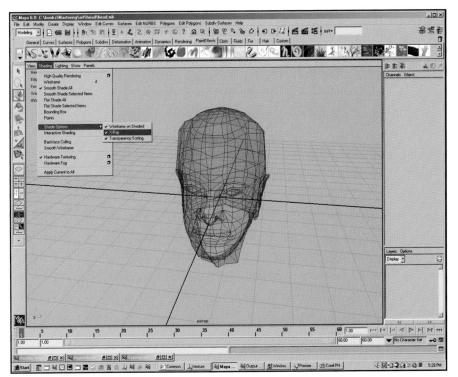

Figure 7.81 Change to Shading Options of the Panel.

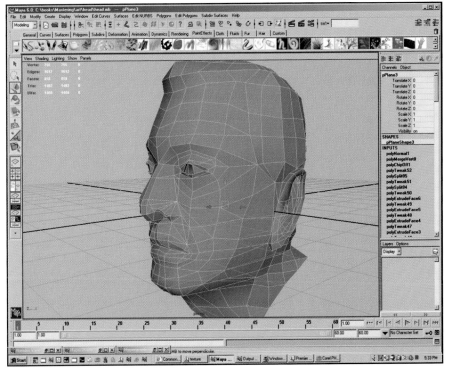

Figure 7.82 The finished model of the head.

Summary

This chapter covered several polygon modeling techniques. If you have followed along with the instructions in this chapter, you should have a nice looking low polygon head. You should also have a much better understanding of many of the common tools and functions in Maya. This chapter covered the following tools and functions:

- Polygon Primitive creation
- Polygon Menu items
- Edit Polygon Menu items
- Sidebar items

Many of these tools and functions were then used in creating the model. The demonstration for creating a human head was started by the creation of a template from a drawing of the front and side views. The model was created starting with a simple polygon plane and modified to the shape of the head. Features were drawn in by using the Split Polygon tool. In addition, the Extrude Polygon and Extrude Edge functions were used to modify the model and complete the formation of the facial features. Finally the model was mirrored to finish a symmetrical model.

Try modeling a few more objects using the polygon modeling techniques shown in this chapter. Build some simple objects such as buildings or mechanical devices. Also try some more complex models such as a car or a body for the head you just created.

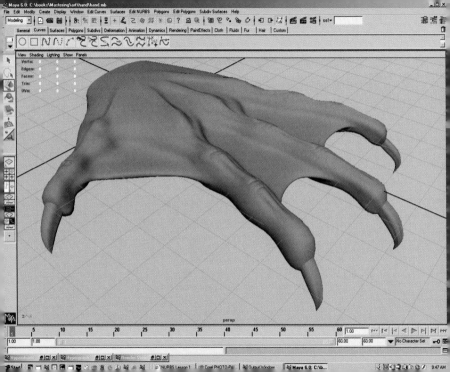

8

Advanced Modeling Techniques

In addition to polygon modeling, several other methods of creating digital 3D models exist. This chapter deals primarily with two of these methods: NURBS and Subdivision Surfaces. Each of these two methods of modeling has advantages for building complex models depending on the type of model constructed. NURBS modeling tends to work very well for smooth rounded shapes. Subdivision Surfaces is very good for modeling forms that have both rounded surfaces and creases.

NURBS Modeling

NURBS models use curves instead of flat planes to describe a 3D surface. The use of curves gives a NURBS model a smooth finish rather than the facets found in polygon models.

Maya has several tools specifically for NURBS modeling. These tools are found primarily in the Edit Curves, Surfaces, and Edit NURBS Menus of the Modeling Menu set.

Like polygons, NURBS models can start with a primitive shape; however, a more common way to build NURBS models is to start with a curve. In the following example, curves and primitives are used to build a trophy cup. The cup will be created using a CV curve and the handles will be built from a cylinder primitive.

Using Curves

The first step to creating a model from a curve is to create a curve. The most common method of creating a curve is to use Maya's CV Curve tool. This tool is found in the Create Menu of Maya's Main Menu as shown in Figure 8.1.

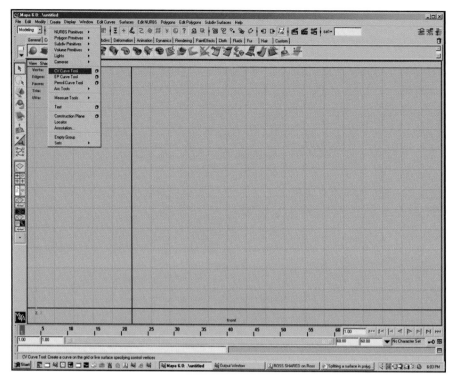

Figure 8.1 The CV Curve is found in the Create Menu.

CV stands for control vertice. Control vertices are similar to vertices on a polygon model except that they are not on the model, but rather influence the model or curve. In a way it is like working with a fairly stiff rope. If the rope is laid out on the ground and one part is moved, it affects either side for quite a ways.

1. Select CV Curve Tool from the Create Menu.

2. In the front view, click the left mouse button with the CV Curve tool four times as shown in Figure 8.2. Hold down the Ctrl+B keys for the first click to snap the first CV to the grid as shown.

Note

Notice that the CVs are not on the curve but rather to the side of the curve. To see how a CV affects a curve, select CV number 3 and drag it to a different position. Watch how moving the CV changes the curve. Select Undo from the Edit Menu to return the CV to its original position.

3. Create two more CVs as shown in Figure 8.3 to form the inside of the trophy cup.

4. Place the next CV as shown in Figure 8.4. Notice how the curve, shown in white in the figure, curves back on itself. The white color shows the area or segments that are influenced by the CV.

5. Continue to place new CVs to create the outer line of the cup as shown in Figure 8.5.

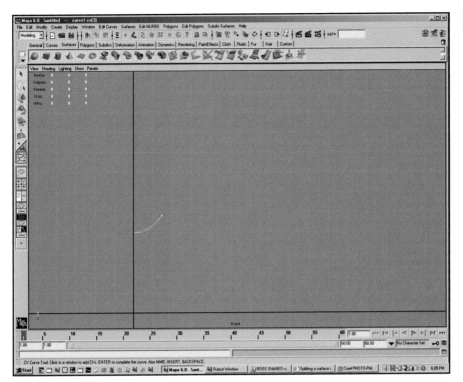

Figure 8.2 Use the CV Curve tool to create a curve.

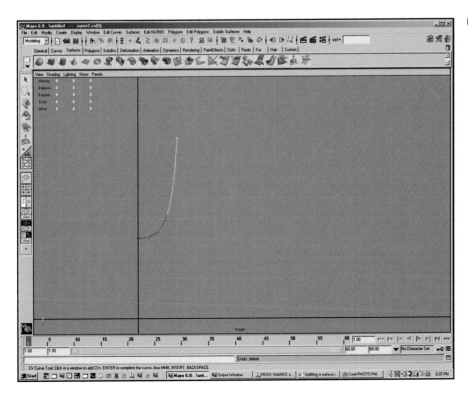

Figure 8.3 Create two more CVs.

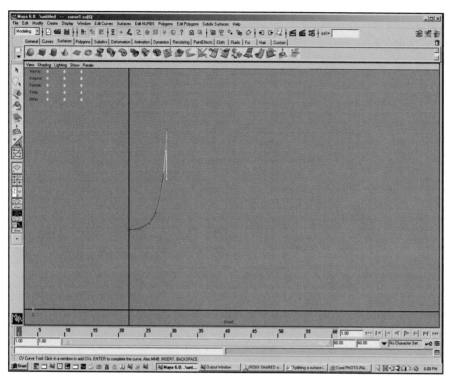

Figure 8.4 The next CV forms the upper lip of the cup.

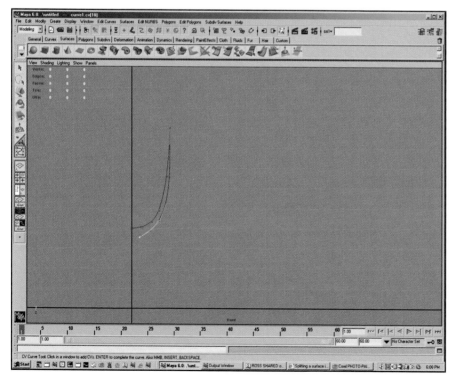

Figure 8.5 Create the outer line of the cup.

6. Continue to place new CVs to create the stem of the cup as shown in Figure 8.6. At the highlighted point at the end of the curve shown in the figure, place three CVs directly on top of each other. This will create a sharp or hard corner in the curve.

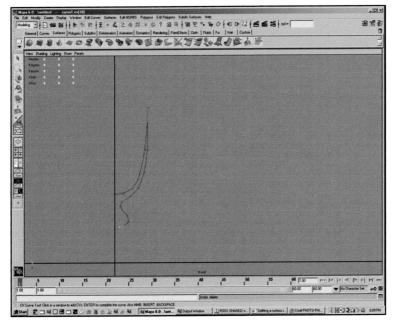

Figure 8.6 Start creating the stem of the cup.

7. Finish placing CVs until the cup resembles the curve in Figure 8.7. Place three CVs at the base of the cup to form a sharp corner. Press the Ctrl+X keys to place the last CV on the grid. Press Enter on the keyboard to exit the tool.

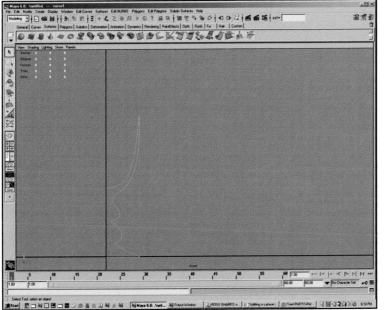

Figure 8.7 Finish placing the CVs to form the curve of the cup.

8. Right-click on the curve to bring up the Marking Menu and select Control Vertice. Make sure the cursor is directly over the curve or the wrong menu will appear. The curve should now resemble the one shown in Figure 8.8. The light blue line is the curve and the magenta dots are the CVs.

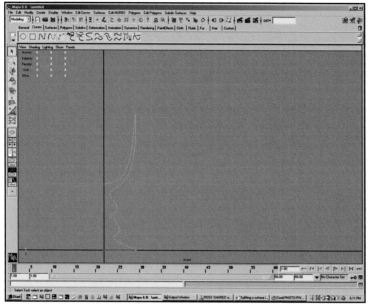

Figure 8.8 The magenta dots are the CVs.

9. Select the last CV in the curve and pull it upward using the Move tool, as shown in Figure 8.9. Be sure to only move the CV upward. Any move right or left will cause problems with the model. The easiest way to avoid problems with the move is to click only the upward arrow when moving the CV.

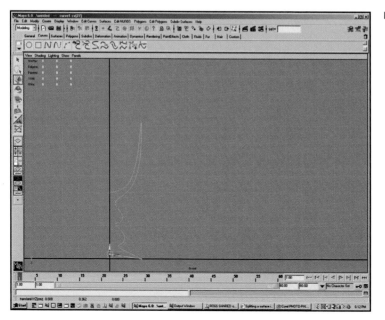

Figure 8.9 Move the last CV upward.

10. Adjust the CVs of the stem to give that area a more symmetrical look as shown in Figure 8.10.

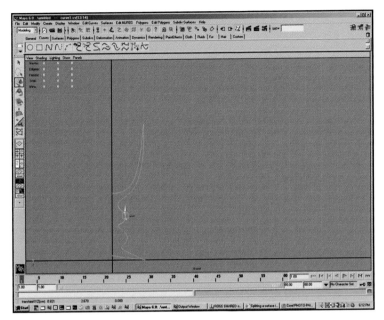

Figure 8.10 Fix any problems with the shape of the curve.

11. The curve should now form half the silhouette of a cup as if it were cut right down the middle. It is now ready to be revolved into a full 3D model. Change the selection mode to Object by pressing the F8 key.

12. In the Main Menu go to Surface and select the dialog box next to Revolve as shown in Figure 8.11.

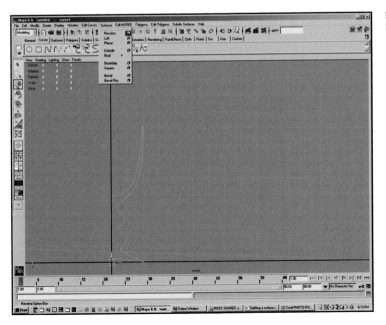

Figure 8.11 Select the Revolve dialog box.

13. Set the options of the Revolve Options dialog box to those shown in Figure 8.12. Make sure the Y axis is selected. Click the Apply button to revolve the curve. The model should now look similar to the one shown in the figure.

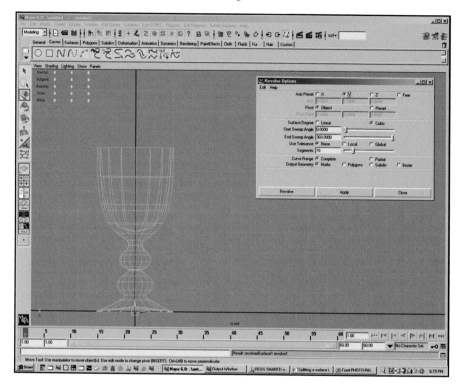

Figure 8.12 Revolve the curve to create a 3D model of the cup.

There, now you have a nice little model of a cup using just one CV curve. The trophy cup is now ready for some handles. The handles will be built from NURBS primitives.

Building with NURBS Primitives

NURBS primitives are similar to polygon primitives in many ways. Figure 8.13 shows the menu for creating NURBS primitives. Notice that in addition to the primitives available to the polygons there are two more choices, Square and Circle. The square and circle primitives are curves rather than 3D models.

1. The first step in creating handles for the trophy cup is to create a NURBS cylinder. Bring up the Cylinder Options box as shown in Figure 8.13.

2. Set the options for the cylinder to those shown in Figure 8.14. Notice that there are several more options for NURBS cylinders than there were for polygon cylinders. For now just set the options as shown. Click on the Apply button.

3. Move the cylinder to the side of the cup as shown in Figure 8.15.

4. Go to the top view and zoom in on the cylinder. Use the Scale tool to change the shape of the cylinder to an oval as shown in Figure 8.16.

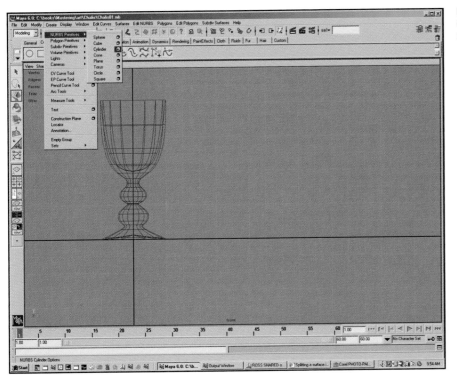

Figure 8.13 Select the Cylinder Options dialog box from the NURBS Primitive Menu.

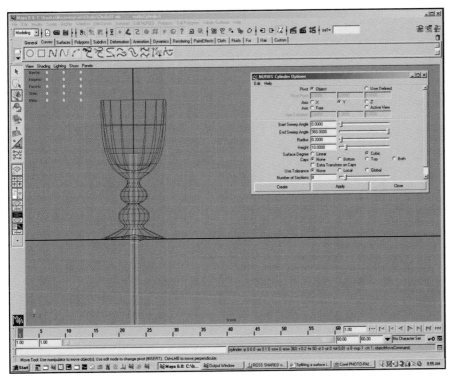

Figure 8.14 Set the options for the cylinder.

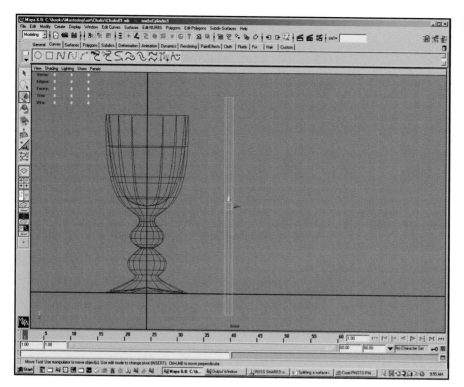

Figure 8.15 Move the cylinder to the side of the trophy cup.

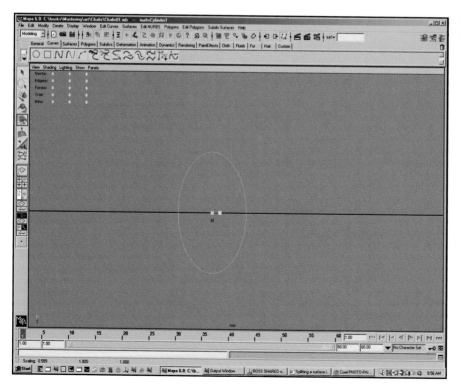

Figure 8.16 Scale the cylinder to an oval from the top view.

5. To create a good handle for the trophy cup, the cylinder needs to have more isoparms. An *isoparm* is a line that follows the shape of the surface either vertically or horizontally. Go back to the Front view. To add an isoparm, select the top isoparm of the cylinder model and drag it down as shown in Figure 8.17.

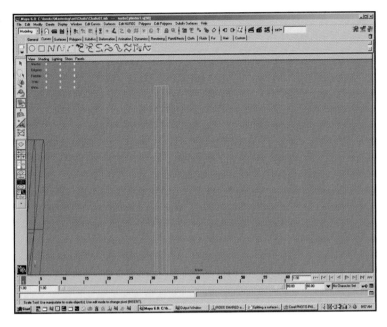

Figure 8.17 Drag an isoparm down the cylinder.

6. Hold the Shift key while dragging additional isoparms down the cylinder until there are seven, as shown in Figure 8.18. The dotted lines are markers.

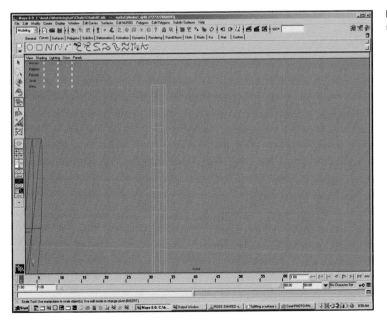

Figure 8.18 Drag more isoparm markers down the cylinder.

7. In the Edit NURBS Menu, select Insert Isoparms to change the markers to isoparms as shown in Figure 8.19.

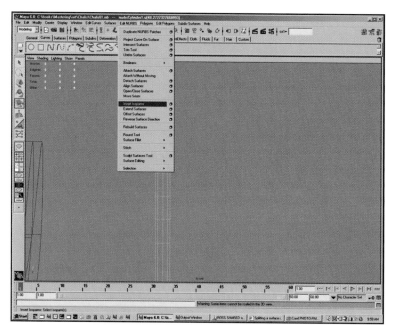

Figure 8.19 Insert Isoparms.

8. Change the selection mode to Control Vertex by right-clicking on the cylinder and using the Marking Menu.

9. Select the top two rows of CVs and scale them as shown in Figure 8.20.

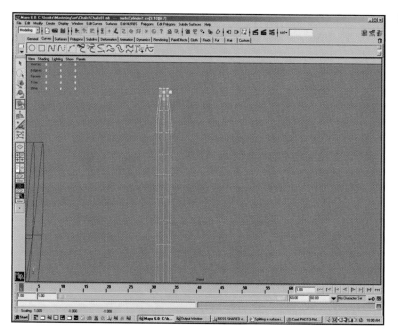

Figure 8.20 Scale the top CVs.

10. Change to the Rotate tool and rotate the CVs as shown in Figure 8.21.

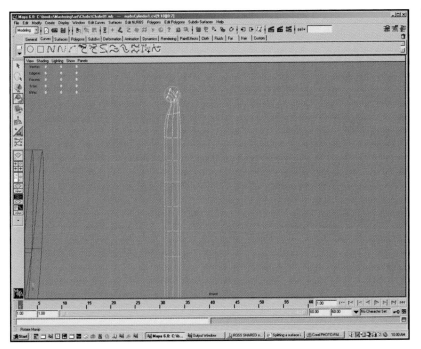

Figure 8.21 Rotate the CVs.

11. Change back to the Move tool and move the rotated CVs to the left as shown in Figure 8.22.

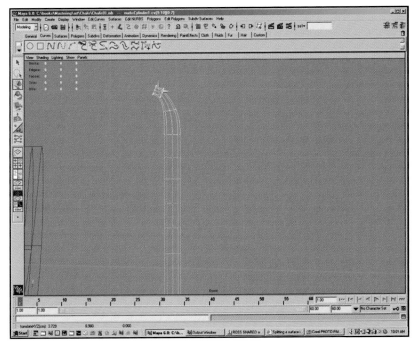

Figure 8.22 Move the rotated CVs to the left.

12. Continue to rotate and move the CVs, moving down a row at a time to form the curl of the handle as shown in Figure 8.23.

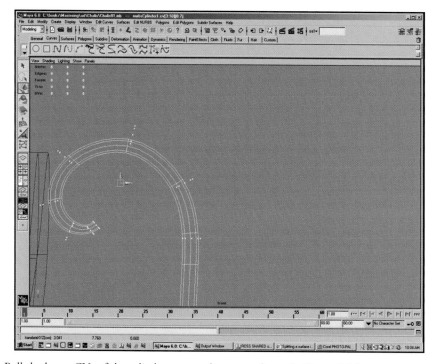

Figure 8.23 Form the curl of the handle by rotating and moving the CVs of the cylinder.

13. Pull the lower CVs of the cylinder next to the cup as shown in Figure 8.24.

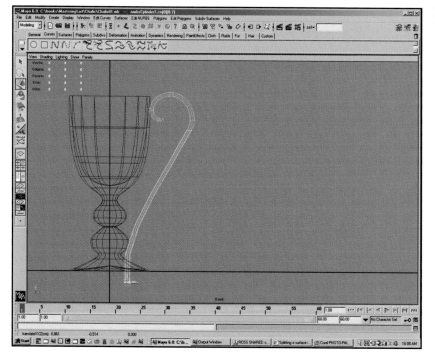

Figure 8.24 Move the lower part of the cylinder next to the cup.

14. Mark nine new isoparms on the lower part of the cylinder as shown in Figure 8.25.

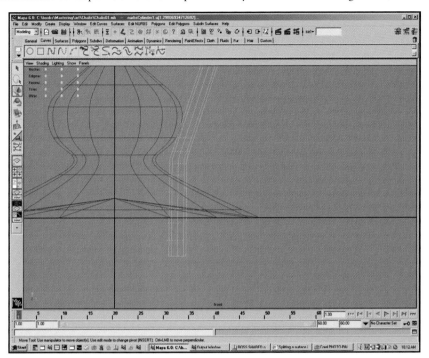

Figure 8.25 Mark the lower cylinder for more isoparms.

15. Insert the isoparms in the same way as at the top of the cylinder. The cylinder should now look similar to Figure 8.26.

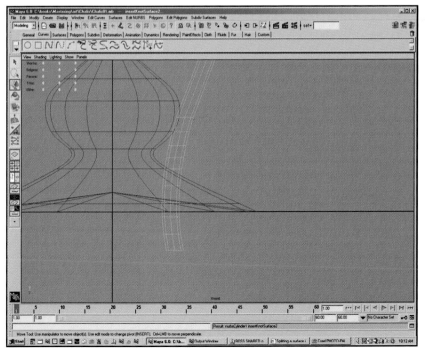

Figure 8.26 Insert the new isoparms.

16. Scale, rotate, and move the rows of CVs to form the curl of the lower part of the cup handle as shown in Figure 8.27.

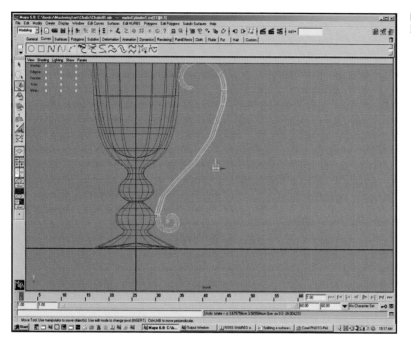

Figure 8.27 Create the curl of the lower part of the cup handle.

17. Move the CVs of the handle to create a better transition from the top to the bottom as shown in Figure 8.28.

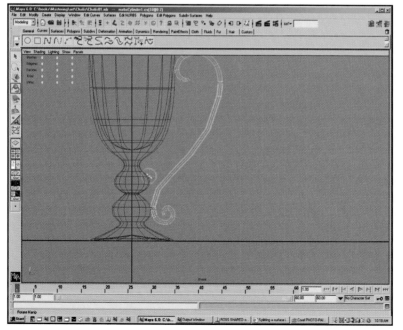

Figure 8.28 Adjust the CVs of the handle.

18. In the Edit Menu, select Duplicate to create a duplicate version of the cup handle as shown in Figure 8.29. Duplicating places a new object directly over the current object.

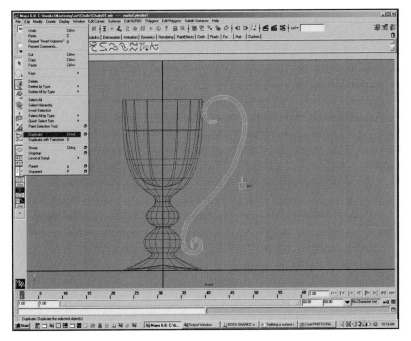

Figure 8.29 Duplicate the handle.

19. Rotate the duplicate 180 degrees in the Y axis as shown in Figure 8.30 using the Channel Box.

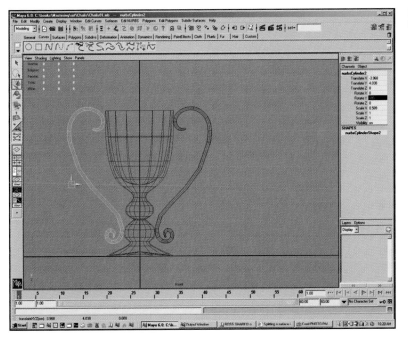

Figure 8.30 Rotate the duplicate handle in the Y axis.

The trophy cup is now modeled. The model may look a little segmented or rough, but it really isn't. It is just the display mode. Press the 2 and then the 3 keys to see higher resolutions of display. With the 3 key pressed the model should look similar to Figure 8.31.

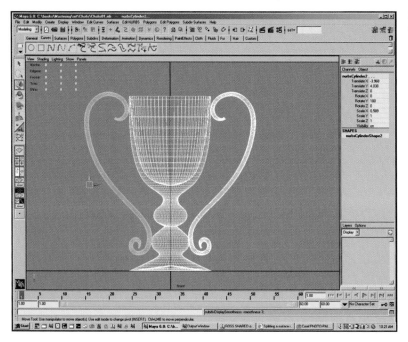

Figure 8.31 Set the display mode for a higher-resolution image.

Creating rounded objects like the trophy cup using NURBS modeling techniques is much easier than trying to create it in polygons. It is possible to get the same results using polygon modeling techniques, but it may not be as easy.

Subdivision Surfaces

Subdivision Surfaces modeling is an advanced modeling method used in creating models that have high surface detail. It can be used to create simple objects but it is more useful for complex models.

Creating models with Subdivision Surfaces is a little like creating a model with both polygons and NURBS at the same time. In the following example, a model of a clawed hand will be built. The process of building the hand will show many advantages of creating models using subdivision surfaces. The basic model will be created from a simple polygon cube in Polygon Proxy mode. After the basic shape of the model is finished, Standard mode will be used to refine the detail in the model. These two modes will be explained during the course of the project.

Polygon Proxy Mode

One of the biggest advantages to using Subdivision Surfaces is the Polygon Proxy mode. This mode is designed to give the artist access to the polygon modeling tools while creating a smooth rounded surface. It also allows the artist to start the model using polygons and then switch over to Subdivision Surfaces and back again later as needed.

1. Create a polygon cube as shown in Figure 8.32. This cube will be the basis for developing the clawed hand.

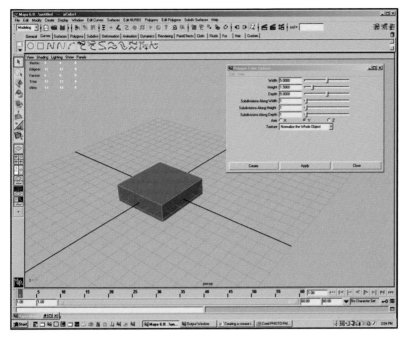

Figure 8.32 Create a polygon cube.

2. Open the dialog box for converting polygons to Subdivision Surfaces as shown in Figure 8.33. It is located under Modify > Convert > Polygons to Subdiv.

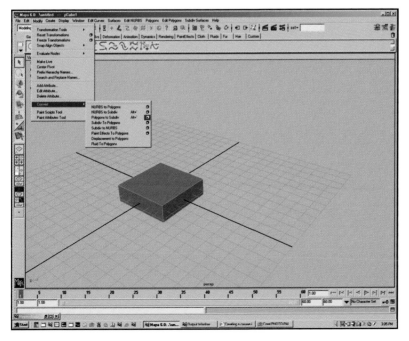

Figure 8.33 The conversion function to change polygon objects to Subdivision Surfaces is in the Modify Menu.

3. Set the options in the Convert To Subdiv Options box to those shown in Figure 8.34 and click Apply to convert the model.

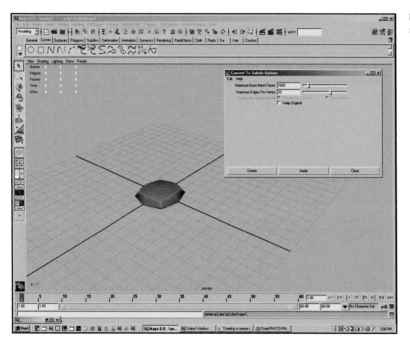

Figure 8.34 Convert the model to subdivision surfaces.

4. Now set the model to Polygon Proxy Mode. The function is located in the Subdiv Surfaces Menu, as shown in Figure 8.35.

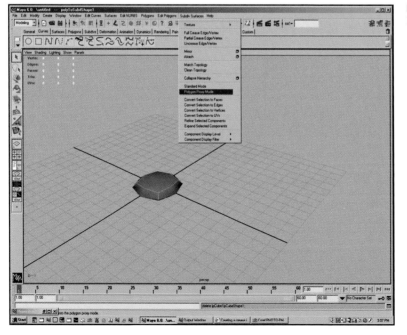

Figure 8.35 Set the model to Polygon Proxy Mode.

5. The model should now have a wire-frame cube around it of the same dimensions as the original polygon cube. This box controls the look and shape of the Subdivision Surfaces model. Swing around to the right side of the model in Perspective view and use the Split Polygon tool from the Edit Polygons Menu to draw in four vertical lines as shown in Figure 8.36. These lines will be used to define the fingers of the hand.

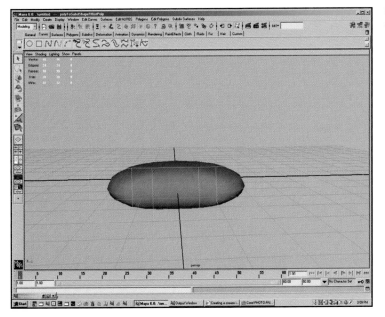

Figure 8.36 Split the polygons of the right side of the cube.

6. Now between two sets of the vertical edges, split the polygons horizontally as shown in Figure 8.37. These polygons will be used to form webbing between the fingers.

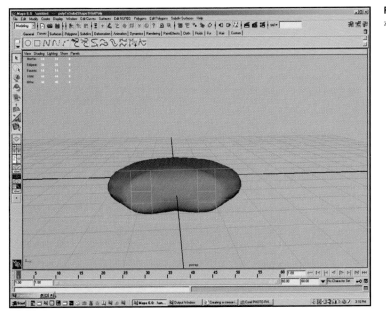

Figure 8.37 Split the polygons horizontally.

7. Change the selection mode to Faces.

8. Select the faces shown in Figure 8.38.

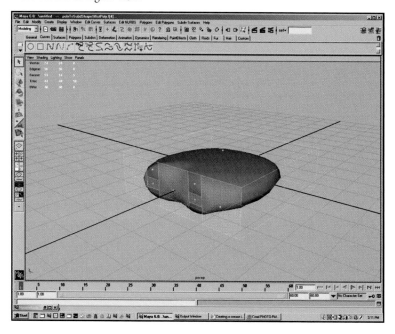

Figure 8.38 Select the polygon faces for the fingers.

9. The clawed hand will only have three fingers, in keeping with the standard for cartoon characters. Extrude the faces of the selected polygons. Extrude Faces is found in the Edit Polygons Menu. Move the extruded faces in the X direction as shown in Figure 8.39. Notice how the subdivision surface model follows the polygon proxy.

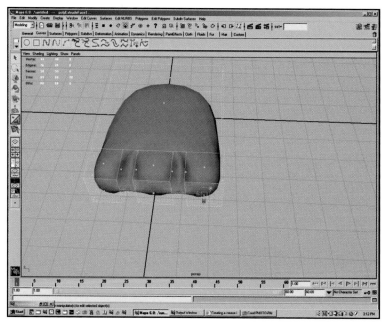

Figure 8.39 Extrude the fingers of the hand.

10. The fingers should not all be the same length. This first extrusion will place the first knuckles. Select the polygon for each finger and move it in the X direction to take into account the differing lengths of the fingers, as shown in Figure 8.40.

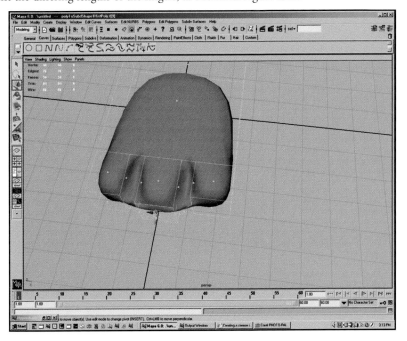

Figure 8.40 Adjust the lengths of the fingers.

11. Now reselect the polygons of the fingers and webbing and extrude them again as shown in Figure 8.41.

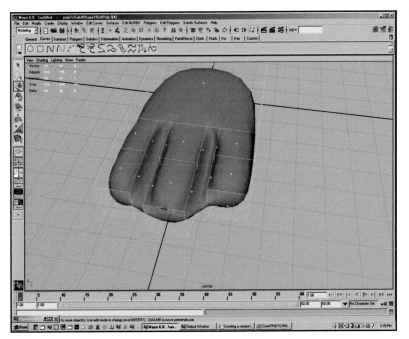

Figure 8.41 Extrude the fingers again.

12. Adjust the fingers as needed for placement of the second knuckles so that the center finger's knuckle extends farther than the other two.

13. Extrude the fingers again, except this time don't include the webbing.

14. Adjust the ends of the fingers as shown in Figure 8.42.

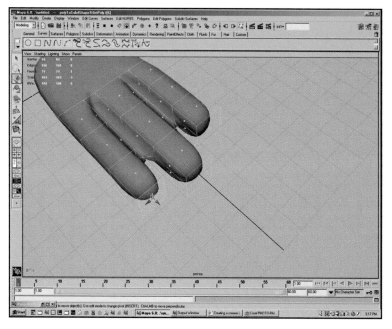

Figure 8.42 Adjust the ends of the fingers.

15. Each finger will now need a clawed end. Select one of the fingers and extrude the end polygon. Rotate the extruded polygon and move it down as shown in Figure 8.43.

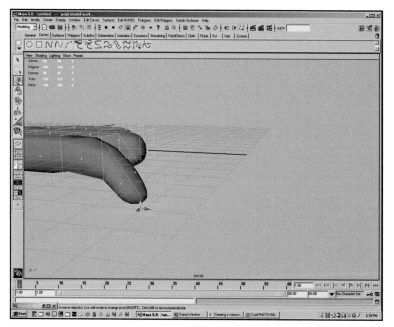

Figure 8.43 Extrude the claw of the finger.

16. It doesn't look much like a claw now, but it will before the project is done. Use the Scale tool to bring the claw to a point as shown in Figure 8.44.

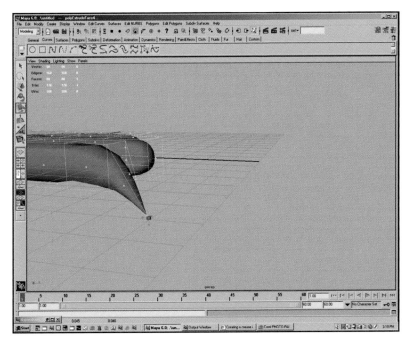

Figure 8.44 Give the claw a point by scaling the polygon.

17. Repeat the process for the claw on each of the remaining fingers. The model should now look similar to Figure 8.45.

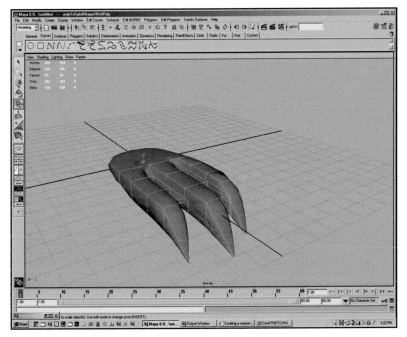

Figure 8.45 Create claws for the other fingers.

18. Next, the hand needs a thumb. Split the polygons of the front of the model as shown in Figure 8.46.

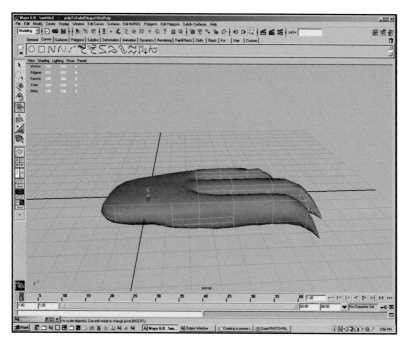

Figure 8.46 Split the polygons of the front of the model to create the thumb.

19. Extrude the newly split faces as shown in Figure 8.47.

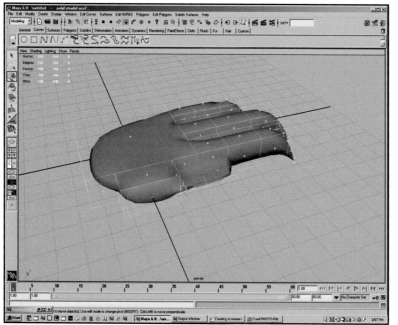

Figure 8.47 Extrude the thumb to the first knuckle.

20. Use the Scale tool to pull the vertices together tapering the thumb from the hand as shown in Figure 8.48.

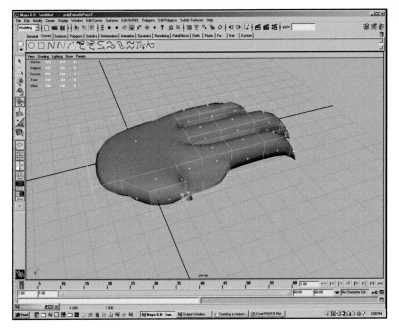

Figure 8.48 Scale the thumb.

21. Extrude the faces of the thumb a second time to the second knuckle of the thumb. Taper the thumb again.

22. Select the faces of the webbing and adjust them so they have better taper between the thumb and the fingers, as shown in Figure 8.49.

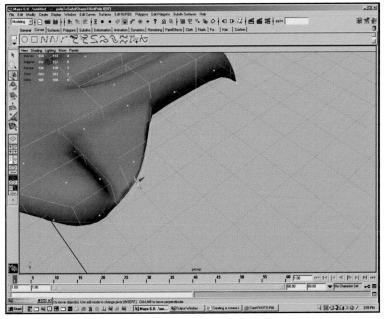

Figure 8.49 Adjust the shape of the webbing between the thumb and the fingers.

23. Extrude the thumb face one more time.

24. Now give the thumb a claw as shown in Figure 8.50.

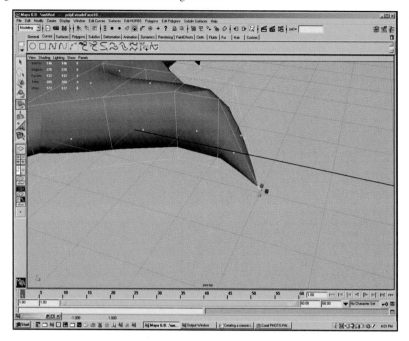

Figure 8.50 Give the thumb a claw as well.

25. Change the polygon proxy to Vertex selection mode using the Marking Menu.

26. Use the Scale tool to refine the shape of the fingers as shown in Figure 8.51. Each finger should taper from the base to the end.

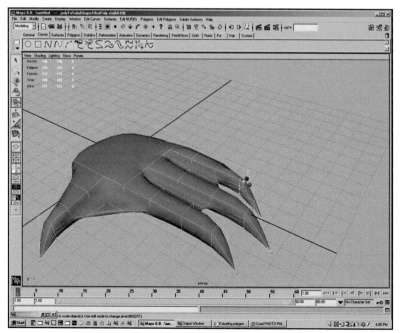

Figure 8.51 Refine the shape of the fingers.

27. Select the face at the base of the hand as shown in Figure 8.52.

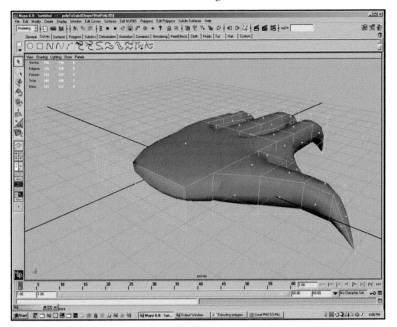

Figure 8.52 Select the face at the base of the hand.

28. Delete the face. This will open up the base of the hand as shown in Figure 8.53. Opening the base of the hand will allow the hand to connect to an arm.

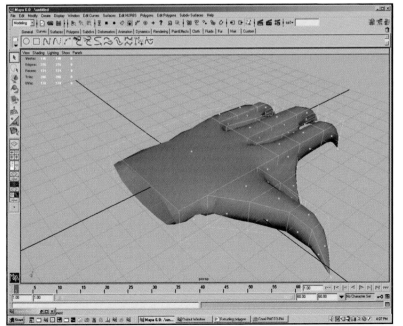

Figure 8.53 Delete the face at the base of the hand.

Using Polygon Proxy mode, the hand is quickly constructed. It lacks refinement but the basic shape is in place. From here on out the model will be completed in Standard mode.

Standard Mode Modeling

To convert the model to Standard mode, it first has to be changed to Object Selection mode. Once it is in Object Selection mode, change to Standard mode by selecting it in the Subdiv Surfaces Menu as shown in Figure 8.54.

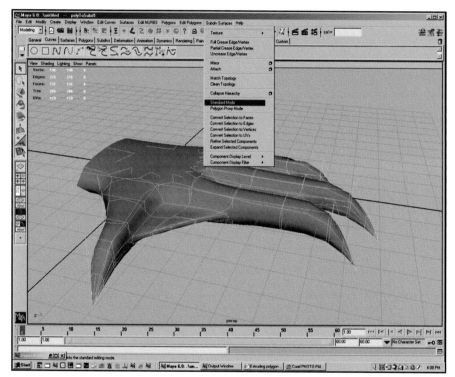

Figure 8.54 Change the model to Standard mode.

Now the model is ready for modeling using standard subdivision surface tools and options.

1. Change the selection mode to Vertex using the Marking Menu. Notice that instead of magenta dots, the number 0 marks the vertices, as shown in Figure 8.55.

2. Subdivision Surfaces have several levels of resolution. Zero is the lowest level. This level is good for making larger changes to the model. Smaller refinements need to have higher resolutions. Change the resolution of the model to 1 by using the Marking Menu and selecting Finer just above Vertex. The change in resolution is only on those areas selected.

3. Select the vertices around one of the fingers between the joints as shown in Figure 8.56. Use the Scale tool to reduce the circumference of the finger.

4. Continue to reduce the circumference of the fingers and the thumb between the joints.

5. Select the vertices around the base of the hand and scale them to look more natural, as shown in Figure 8.57.

6. Now that most of the major adjustments have been made, it is time to move on and add detail to the hand. Move in close to the tip of the thumb. Select the vertices of the claw and use the Rotate tool to adjust the claw to look more natural, as shown in Figure 8.58.

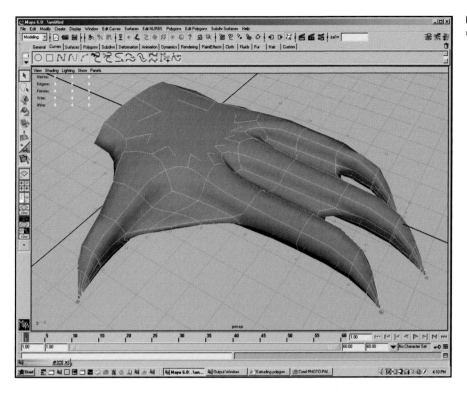

Figure 8.55 Change the selection mode to Vertex.

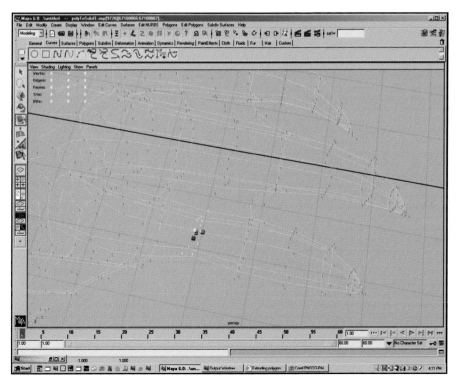

Figure 8.56 Reduce the circumference of the finger between the joints.

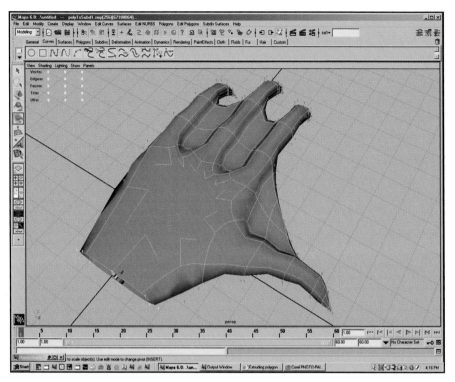

Figure 8.57 Scale the base of the hand.

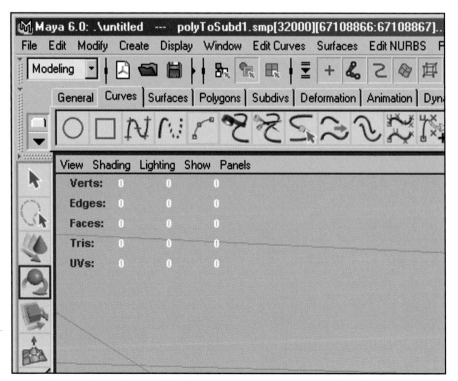

Figure 8.58 Adjust the vertices in the claw.

7. Rotate the remaining vertices of the claw until they match the shape of Figure 8.59.

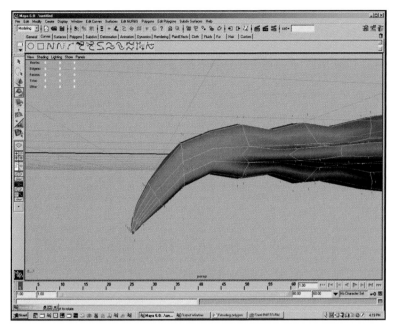

Figure 8.59 The claw should curl downward at the end.

8. Change the selection mode to Edges.

9. Select all of the edges of the claw and the end of the thumb.

10. Refine the surfaces to level 2 by selecting Finer in the Marking Menu. The model should now look similar to Figure 8.60.

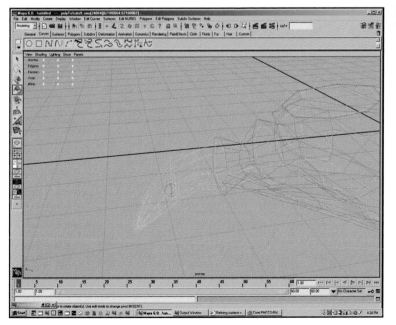

Figure 8.60 Refine the surface resolution.

11. The surface needs to crease where the claw extends from the end of the thumb. The
Subdivision Surfaces Menu has a tool for creating creases in models. Select the edges of
the model as shown in Figure 8.61 in white. Make sure only the edges around the claw
are selected and none of the edges that run the length of the claw.

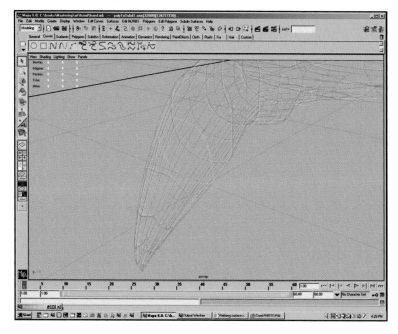

Figure 8.61 Select the edges where the claw extends from the end of the thumb.

12. With the edges selected, go to Full Crease Edge/Vertex in the Subdiv Surfaces Menu as
shown in Figure 8.62.

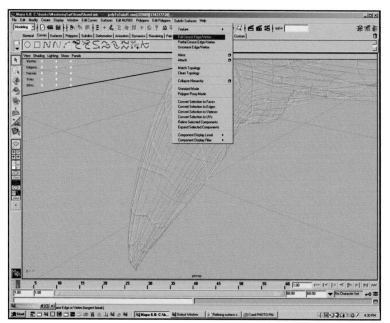

Figure 8.62 Crease the edges of the claw.

13. The selected edges will change to a dotted line. Scale the edges inward and move them toward the end of the thumb as shown in Figure 8.63.

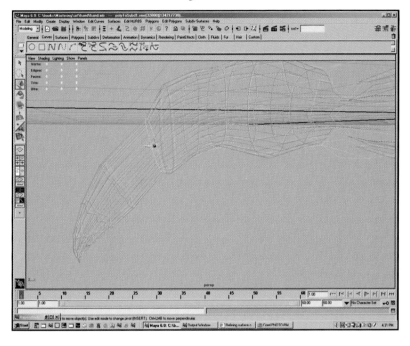

Figure 8.63 Scale the edges and move them closer to the end of the thumb.

14. Now change the selection mode to Vertex.

15. Use the Scale, Rotate, and Move tools to refine the shape of the thumb as shown in Figure 8.64.

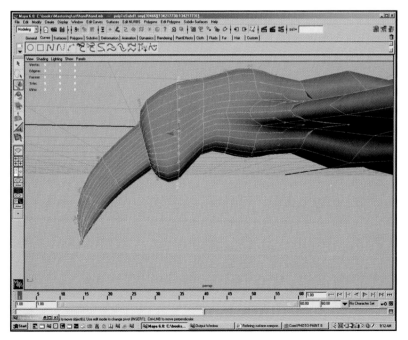

Figure 8.64 Refine the shape of the thumb.

16. It is time to refine the shape of the rest of the thumb. Go back to level 1 by selecting Courser from the Marking Menu, located just below Vertex.

17. Select the vertices between the base of the thumb and the end of the thumb.

18. Select Subdiv Surfaces/Refine Selected Components. This should increase the resolution of the selected area to 2 as shown in Figure 8.65. Each vertex will be designated by the number 2.

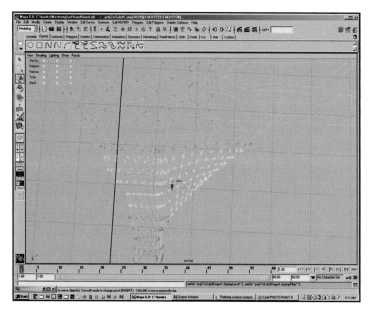

Figure 8.65 Refine the resolution of the remaining surfaces of the thumb.

19. The surfaces of the model need to be refined even more in a few areas to add detail to the top of the thumb. Change the selection mode to Faces and select the faces between the second and third joint of the thumb, as shown in Figure 8.66.

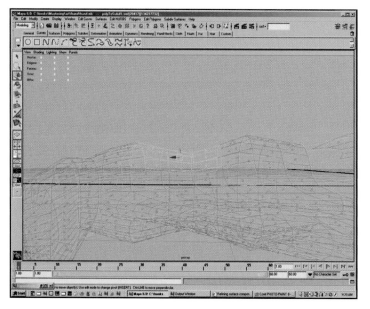

Figure 8.66 Select the faces between the second and third joint of the thumb.

20. Now go back to Vertex selection mode and move the vertices of the area between the joints to create a defined tendon between the joints as shown in Figure 8.67.

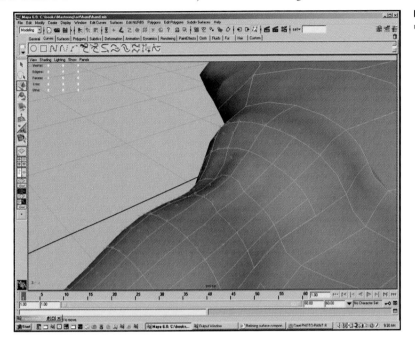

Figure 8.67 Define the tendon along the top of the thumb.

21. Repeat the process to define the tendon between the third joint and the end of the thumb as shown in Figure 8.68.

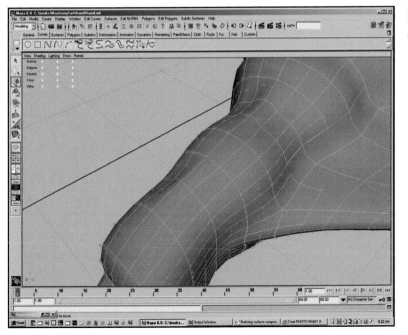

Figure 8.68 Define the tendon between the third joint and the end of the thumb.

22. Refine the surface resolution of the knuckles of the thumb to level 4 as shown in Figure 8.69.

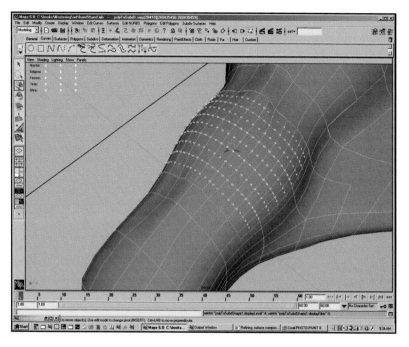

Figure 8.69 Refine the surface resolution of the knuckles.

23. Change the selection mode to Edges and select the line of edges shown in Figure 8.70. These edges will be used to simulate the creases that form at the top of the joints.

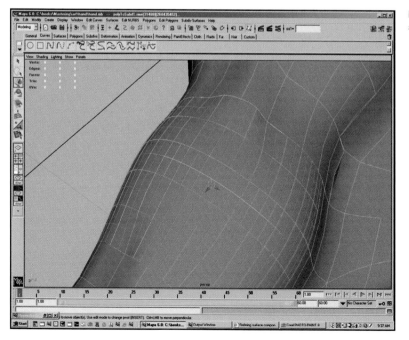

Figure 8.70 Select a line of edges along the top of the knuckle.

24. Crease the edges as before in step 12 and use the Scale tool to first flatten the curve of the edges, and then move the edges downward as shown in Figure 8.71.

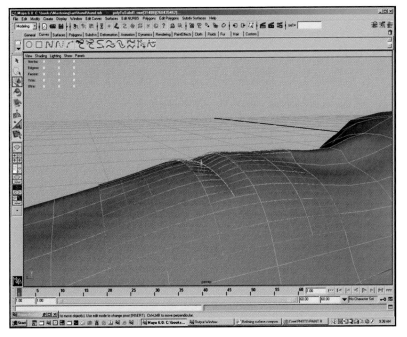

Figure 8.71 Move the creased edges down.

25. Change the selection mode back to Vertex and scale the vertices on ether side of the crease together as shown in Figure 8.72.

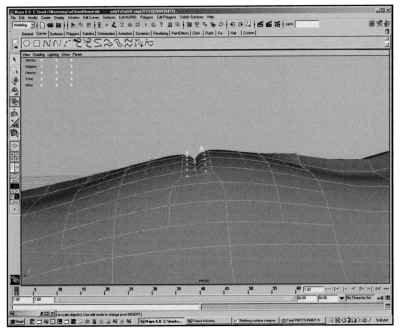

Figure 8.72 Pull in the vertices on either side of the crease.

Note

Currently the thumb is at a 90 degree angle from the hand. Even though this is not a natural position for the thumb, it makes it easier to perform operations like scaling components in one direction as shown here. If the thumb were at its natural position, the scale function would have been more difficult. After the thumb is finished it will be an easy process to move the thumb into its natural position.

26. Now crease and adjust the two lines of edges on either side of the original crease, as shown in Figure 8.73. These two creases do not go as deep as the center crease.

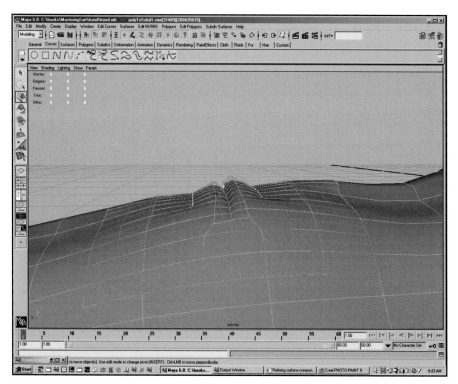

Figure 8.73 Make two more creases.

27. Scale the vertices to either side of the crease as shown in Figure 8.74.

28. Now select individual rows of vertices perpendicular to the creases and move them along the length of the thumb to give the area a more organic look. The results should be similar to Figure 8.75.

29. Add a crease underneath the knuckle as shown in Figure 8.76.

30. The process of adding tendons and creases to the fingers is the same as it is for the thumb. Move over to the fingers and modify them in the same way as the thumb, first creating the claw and then defining the surface qualities of the finger.

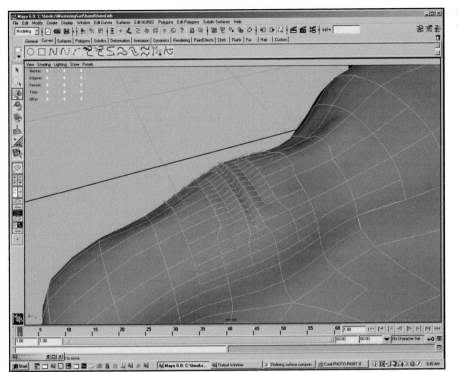

Figure 8.74 Scale the vertices on either side of the creases.

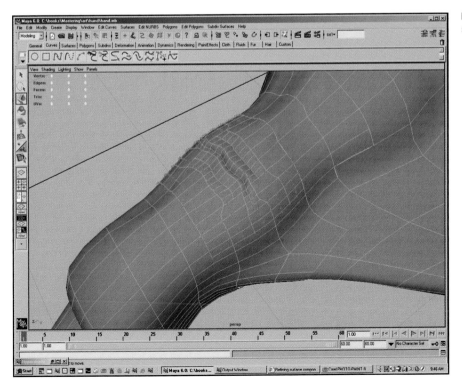

Figure 8.75 Move the vertices to make the creases seem more organic.

Hint

Working with complex models can become confusing at times because of the number of lines in the wire frame. A good way to isolate an area is to limit the parts of the model displayed. In the Panel Menu is a function called View Selected. This function allows for the elimination of elements from the view area, making it possible to focus only on those areas that the artist is working on at the time. Figure 8.77 shows how to use the function. First select the faces that will be worked on and then select View Selected from the menu as shown.

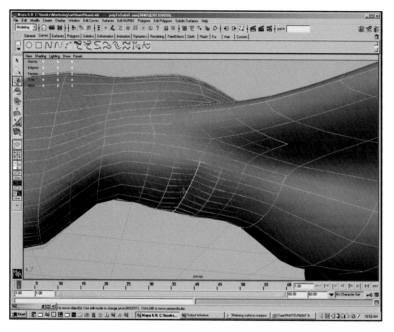

Figure 8.76 Add a crease underneath the knuckle.

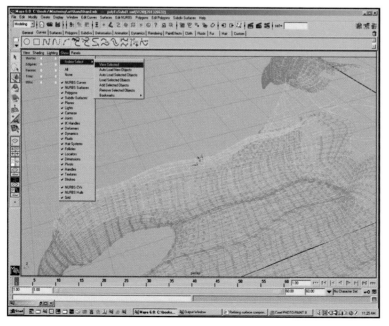

Figure 8.77 Use the View Selected function to isolate areas of the model.

Figure 8.78 shows the fingers after the refinements have taken place.

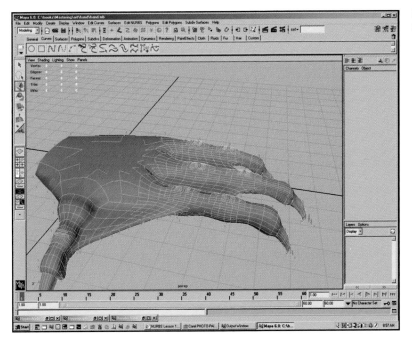

Figure 8.78 Add surface definition to the remaining fingers.

31. Next, move on to the palm and back of the hand. First, increase the surface resolution of that area as shown in Figure 8.79.

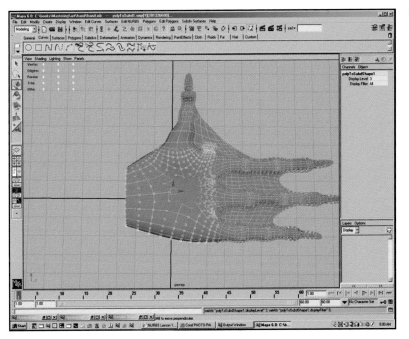

Figure 8.79 Increase the surface resolution of the hand.

32. Turn the hand over and add some creases to the palm of the hand as shown in Figure 8.80.

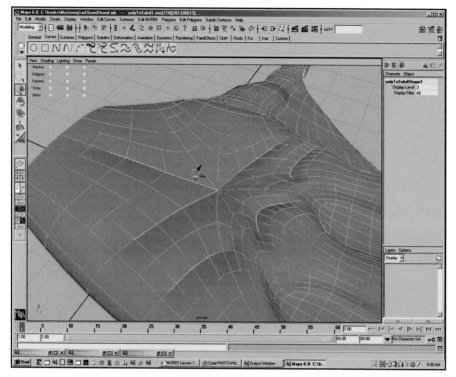

Figure 8.80 Add creases to the palm of the hand.

33. After creasing the palm, move the edges of the creases to look more natural for the surface of the palm.

34. Turn the hand over to view the top. Change the surface resolution to 1 using the Marking Menu.

35. Select the vertex in the center of the hand and pull it toward the base of the hand as shown in Figure 8.81. Notice how moving the vertex smoothly adjusts the surrounding vertices. The area of influence in modeling can be adjusted by changing the surface resolution. This is a big advantage for modeling in Subdivision Surfaces over other modeling methods.

36. Increase the surface resolution to 3.

37. Select the vertices around the base knuckles of the fingers and move them upward in the Y direction to define the knuckle ridges in those areas, as shown in Figure 8.82.

38. Define the tendons that run from the base knuckles to the wrist area as shown in Figure 8.83.

39. Now add the base knuckle of the thumb as shown in Figure 8.84.

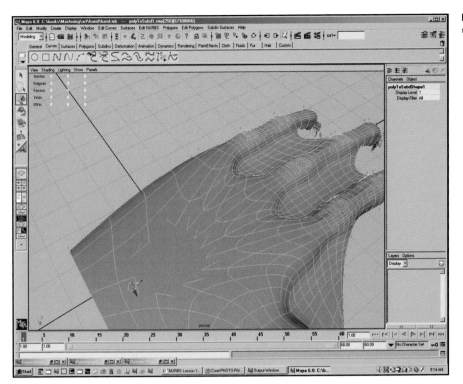

Figure 8.81 Move the center vertex to the base of the hand.

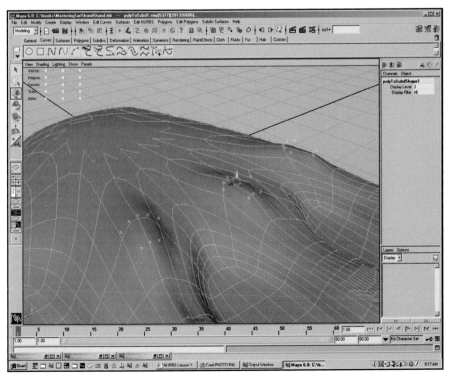

Figure 8.82 Define the base knuckles of the fingers.

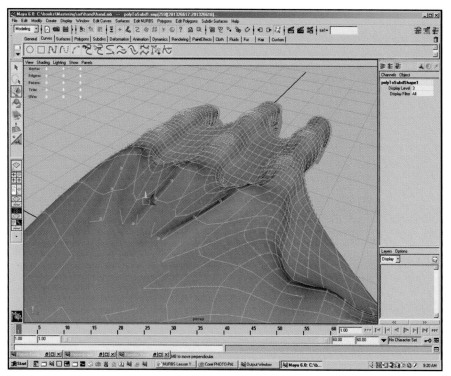

Figure 8.83 Define the tendons on the back of the hand.

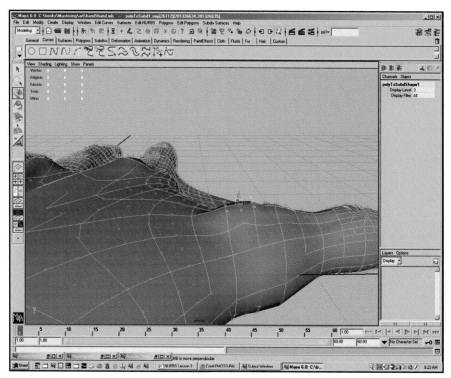

Figure 8.84 Define the base knuckle of the thumb.

40. Define the thumb tendon in the same way that the finger tendons were defined, as shown in Figure 8.85.

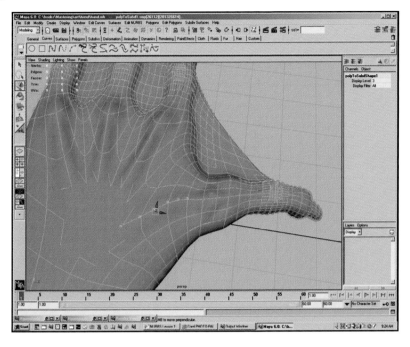

Figure 8.85 Add the thumb tendon.

41. The thumb tendon has a slight curve across the top of the hand. Move the individual vertices to make the tendon stretch in a straight line from the knuckle to the wrist area by moving the vertices along the line of the tendon, as shown in Figure 8.86.

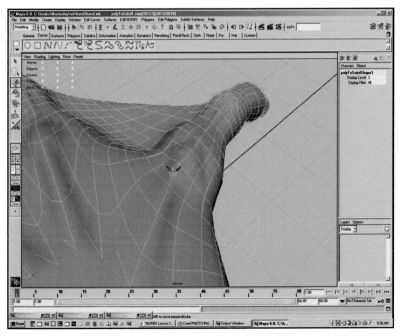

Figure 8.86 Straighten the line of the thumb tendon.

42. Now that most of the surface detail is completed, the thumb can be adjusted to a more natural position.

43. Change the surface resolution to 1.

44. Select the vertices near the base of the thumb toward the base of the hand and move them to form a more natural thumb muscle, as shown in Figure 8.87.

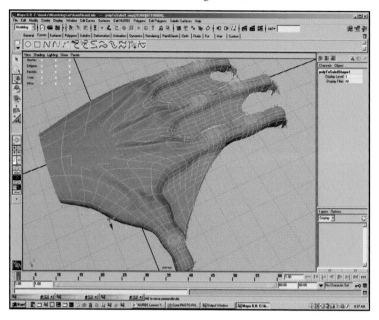

Figure 8.87 Reshape the muscle of the thumb.

45. Select the vertices of the thumb and using the Rotate and Move tools put the thumb into a more natural position, as shown in Figure 8.88.

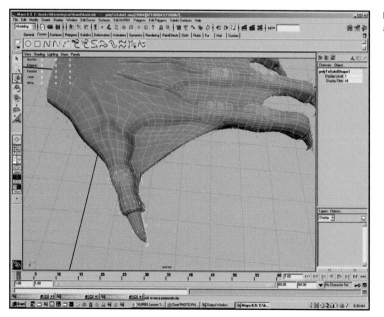

Figure 8.88 Put the thumb into a more natural position.

46. Rotate the fingers to a more natural position as well, as shown in Figure 8.89.

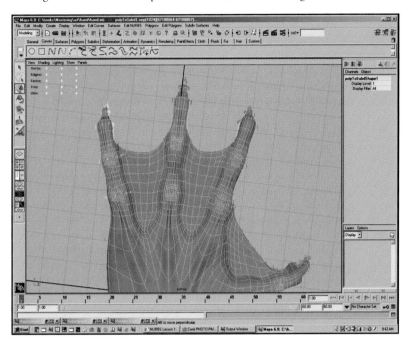

Figure 8.89 Put the fingers into a more natural position as well.

Figure 8.90 shows the finished clawed hand.

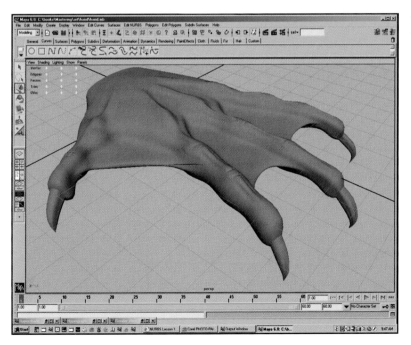

Figure 8.90 The finished clawed hand.

Using subdivision surfaces, it was relatively easy to complete a complex model with lots of surface detail. Subdivision Surfaces is one of the best modeling methods for complex organic shapes.

Summary

This chapter covered two modeling methods for creating 3D digital models: NURBS modeling and Subdivision Surfaces modeling. Both modeling methods have advantages depending on the type of model being built.

NURBS modeling is useful in creating smooth rounded surface models. The chapter covered:

- Building NURBS models using curves and primitives
- CVs and how they are used to modify model shape
- Revolving curves to create a model
- Inserting Isoparms and resolution to a NURBS model

NURBS modeling tools were used in the example of the trophy cup model, but a number were not. Experiment with the many NURBS tools; a better understanding of the tools will increase your ability to create models using NURBS.

This chapter covered many modeling techniques, but it was not an exhaustive manual for all the tools and functions in Maya. If you followed the examples in this chapter, you should have a good foundation for creating models using the two methods mentioned. For additional information on the tools and functions not covered in this chapter, refer to the Help files in Maya.

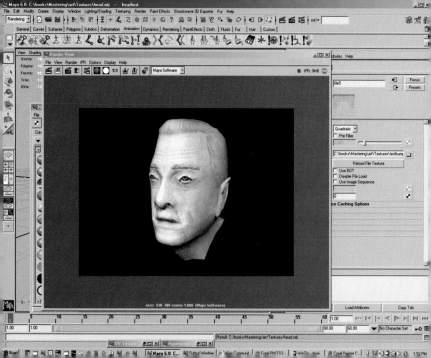

9

Texturing 3D Models

A 3D model needs to have much more than just well-built geometry to be a convincing depiction. The last two chapters focused on building models. This chapter looks at how to get the surface of the model to look right. A gray head is okay if the model is of a statue made from gray material, but to get the head to look like a real human head, the model needs to have a surface that looks like human skin, hair, eyes, and so forth.

Surface Qualities

To get the 3D model's surface to look correct, a texture is applied. Textures are 2D images that are applied to a 3D model to give the model surface detail. In the real world, every surface has a texture. Sometimes it may only be a color and other times it may be very complex, like the bark of a tree. Take a quick look around and study some of the many textures you see in everyday life. You will notice on close examination that every surface has some qualities that can fit into a few specific categories:

- Color
- Saturation
- Value
- Roughness
- Transparency
- Reflectivity
- Luminance

Each one of these qualities or attributes is part of what gives the surface the look that is inherent in the materials it is made of. For example, the hard gray of a sidewalk is very different than the spiky look of the lawn right next to it. The metallic sheen of a kitchen appliance has a very different look than a weathered fence post.

Color

One of the most noticeable characteristics of any surface is its color. The world is filled with color. People often refer to an object by its color; for example, they may refer to a red car or a blue sweater. Some colors have emotional ties—a person who is on a lucky streak is red-hot and a person who is depressed is blue. We even assign temperatures to colors—red, yellow, and orange are considered warm colors, whereas purple, blue, and green are thought of as cool colors. Artists can use these elements of color to their advantage by coordinating the colors they use in a 3D scene with the emotion they wish the viewer to feel.

Light and Color

The light that our eyes process so that we can see the world around us is called the visible band of light. All colors discernable by the human eye are part of this band. A rainbow is a good example of the visible band of light. Rainbows form when light bounces off water particles in the air, and because each color has its own unique characteristics, based on the color's wavelength some colors bounce in one direction and some bounce in another direction, forming bands of pure color. These bands of color are always in the same order, with red at one end and violet or purple at the other end. All the rest of the colors fall in between those two colors.

White light contains the full spectrum of colors. White objects reflect a balanced spectrum of light. Gray and black objects also reflect a balanced spectrum of light—the difference between white and black is how much of the light is reflected. A black object absorbs most if not all of the light hitting it, whereas a white object reflects most if not all of the light hitting it. Try placing a black object and a white object under a lamp. After a few minutes, feel the two objects. The black object will be warmer because it is absorbing the light energy.

Colors that are not black, white, or gray reflect an unbalanced spectrum of light. A red object, for example, reflects red light and absorbs the other colors of light. A red light only emits part of the full spectrum of light. That is why it is difficult to see color in a room that is lit by a strong colored light like at a concert or nightclub.

Saturation

Color saturation is the intensity and purity of a color. When a color is fully saturated, it contains color. The color is not grayed or tinted; it is the pure color at its full strength. Reducing saturation causes the color to gray. Fully saturated colors are not common in nature.

Value

Value is a measurement of light or dark. Much of what we see is defined by value. All colors have a value. Colors like red and blue tend to have dark values, whereas a color like yellow tends to have a lighter value. A black-and-white photograph is a good example of a value picture.

Roughness

Every surface in real life has some degree of roughness. Some surfaces, such as glass or polished metal, have such a low degree of roughness that it can only be seen in a microscope. Other surfaces, such as a rock wall or gravel, have obvious roughness. The rougher a surface is the more it refracts light. *Refraction* is the scattering of light when it hits an uneven surface.

Transparency

Not all surfaces in nature are opaque, meaning that light does not pass through it. Some surfaces are transparent. A transparent surface is one that allows some amount of light to pass through it, making it possible to see through the surface. Clear glass, for example, allows almost all light to pass through it, which gives it a high degree of transparency.

Reflectivity

Many surfaces reflect light. Reflection is related to refraction. In both cases the light bounces off a surface, but whereas refraction spreads the light in many directions, a reflective surface bounces the light in the same direction. A mirror is a reflective surface. Other surfaces such as standing water, chrome finishes on a car, and the human eye have high degrees of reflectivity.

Luminance

Luminance is the brightness of an object. For example, a lightbulb has a high degree of luminance when the light is turned on and no luminance when it is turned off. High luminance not only affects the object, but also objects that are around it because it is emitting light on them.

3D Surfaces

Because surfaces are so important, 3D modeling programs offer a number of techniques that artists can use to create believable surfaces on their models. These include colors, filters, texture maps, bump maps, and many others. This book doesn't cover all of the methods used to create surfaces on 3D models, but it gives enough information to get you started.

Applying Color to a Surface

2. The new Blinn material will app

upper window; the new Blinn material is the box on the upper left surrounded by a yellow highlight. The other three boxes contain default materials used by Maya. Bring up the Attribute Editor to see how the material can be modified. With the Blinn material selected, select Attribute Editor from the Window Menu as shown in Figure 9.4.

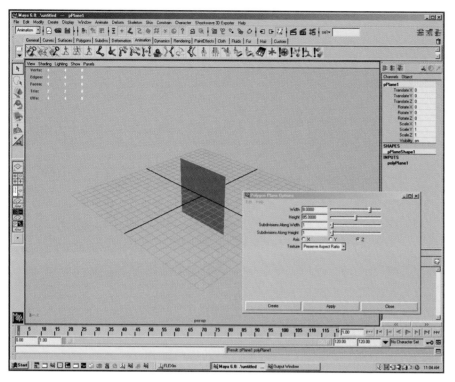

Figure 9.1 Create a single polygon plane.

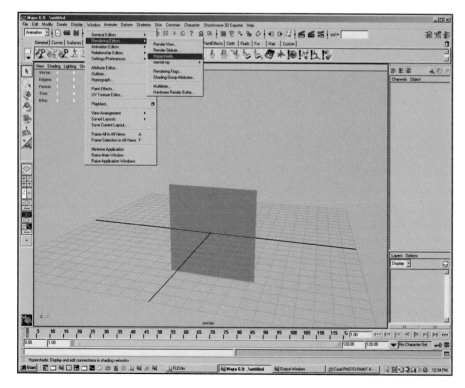

Figure 9.2 Hypershade is located in the Window Menu.

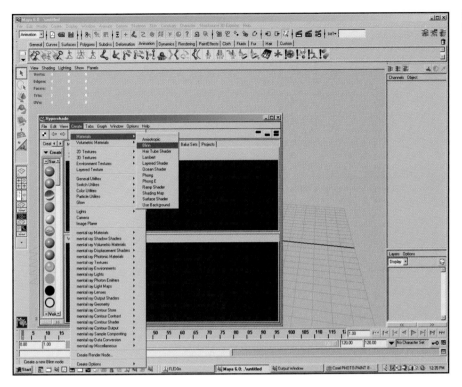

Figure 9.3 Create a Blinn material in Hypershade.

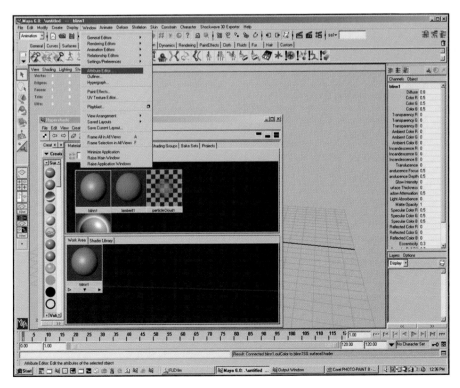

Figure 9.4 Select Attribute Editor from the Window Menu.

3. The Attribute Editor appears on the right side of the screen. It has the material name and a sample ball with the material similar to the one in Hypershade at the top. Below these are the attribute editing options. Look them over to become familiar with them. They are broken into groups with the first two groups—Common Material Attributes and Specular Shading—open. For now just concern yourself with color. It is the first attribute in the Common Material Attributes group. Click the swatch next to the word Color.

4. The Color Chooser appears in a new window. The Color Chooser has a color pallet area and a value scale for selecting colors. It also has several other controls below the pallet for fine color manipulation. The small circle on the pallet is the current color, and the bar on the value scale is the current value. Move both of these selectors to a golden color, as shown in Figure 9.5.

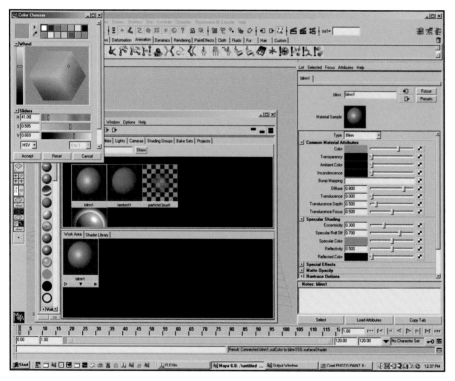

Figure 9.5 Select a gold color.

5. The sample ball in the Attribute Editor and in Hypershade changes to a golden color. Move Hypershade to see the Panel and the polygon. Select the polygon and then right-click the golden ball in Hypershade to bring up the Marking Menu. Move the cursor to select Apply Material to Selection. The golden-colored material is now applied to the polygon, as shown in Figure 9.6. Make sure smooth shading is on by pressing the 6 key.

6. Although lighting and rendering are covered in Chapter 10, the next few steps cover some basic lighting and rendering techniques to show how the materials in this chapter will look when rendered. Go to the Create Menu and select the Directional Light dialog box as shown in Figure 9.7.

7. Set the options as shown in Figure 9.8 and click the Apply button to create a new light in the scene.

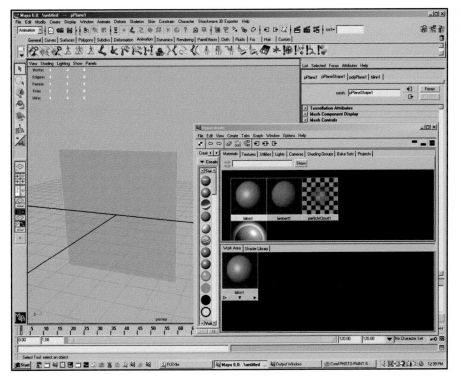

Figure 9.6 Apply the material to the polygon.

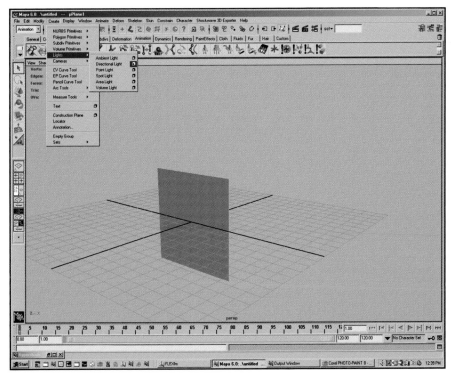

Figure 9.7 Bring up the Directional Light dialog box.

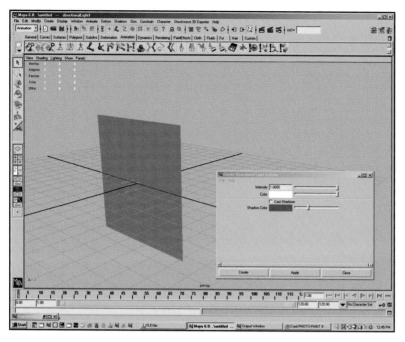

Figure 9.8 Create a new light.

8. The easiest way to position lights in the scene is to use the Show Manipulator tool. It is the bottom tool in the Tool Box. When the tool is selected the light will have a move manipulator on it and a move manipulator on a target. Both the light and the target can be moved independently with these manipulators. Move the light and target as shown in Figure 9.9.

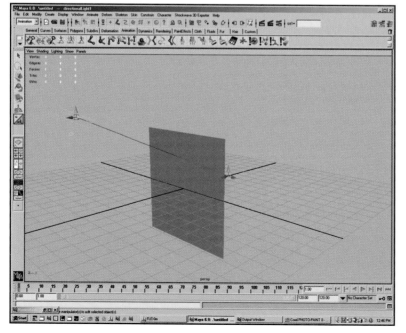

Figure 9.9 Move the light to illuminate the polygon.

9. Now bring up the Ambient Light dialog box as shown in Figure 9.10. It is located just above Directional Light.

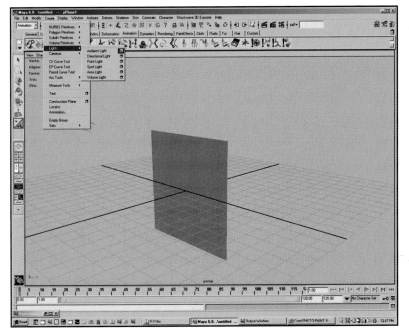

Figure 9.10 Ambient Light is located just above Directional Light.

10. Like materials, lights can have colors as well. Click the swatch next to Color to bring up the Color Chooser and select a light blue color, as shown in Figure 9.11. Change the Intensity to .5 as shown in the figure and click Apply to create the light.

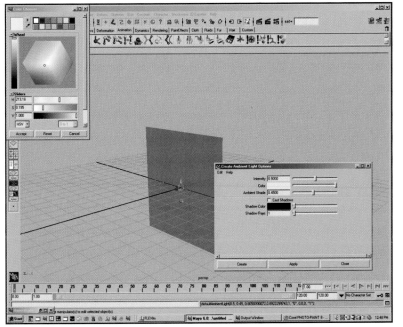

Figure 9.11 Create an ambient light for the scene.

11. Move the ambient light as shown in Figure 9.12. The ambient light like the directional light has a target. Both targets appear in the same location.

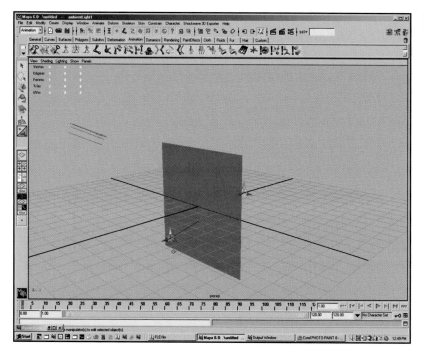

Figure 9.12 Position the ambient light in the scene.

12. Change the menu set to Rendering, as shown in Figure 9.13 from the drop-down list.

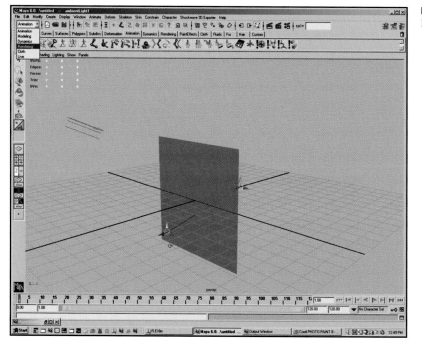

Figure 9.13 Change the menu set to Rendering.

13. Select Render Current Frame from the Render Menu. A Render View window appears and the polygon renders within the window, similar to Figure 9.14.

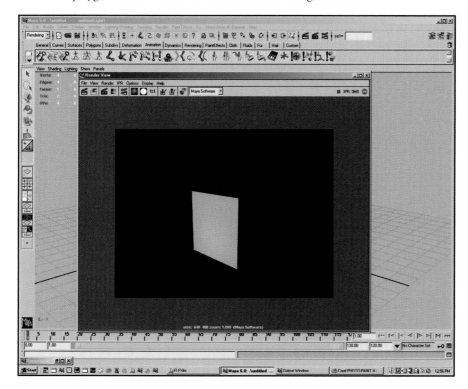

Figure 9.14 Render the polygon.

The rendered polygon does not look much different from the one in the scene window. That is because it is a single flat surface and a solid color. Solid colors work great when an object has only one continuous color; however, that seldom happens in real life. Most objects have variations in color, even if they are only slight variations. Flat colors are boring and not much fun, so let's move on to some more advanced material attributes. Minimize the Render View window.

Shapes and Patterns

Most objects in real life have a pattern of some kind on their surface. If you look at the skin on the back of your hand, you will notice a fine network of pores and hair follicles. You may also notice veins and tendons. A single color will not work well for flesh tones.

In this next section patterns will be added to the material.

1. Hide the golden polygon. You will use it later. Select the polygon and then select Hide Selection from the Display Menu as shown in Figure 9.15.

2. Create a polygon sphere as shown in Figure 9.16.

3. Now apply the golden material to the sphere, as shown in Figure 9.17.

4. Bring up the Render View window again and select Current (Persp) from the Render Menu as shown in Figure 9.18.

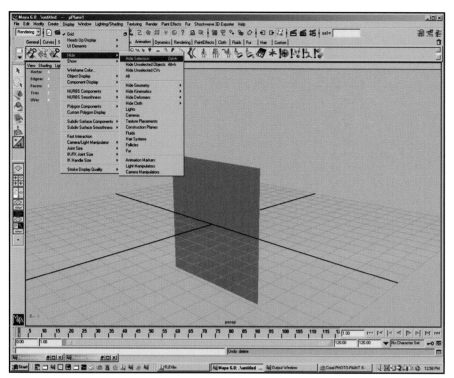

Figure 9.15 Hide the golden polygon.

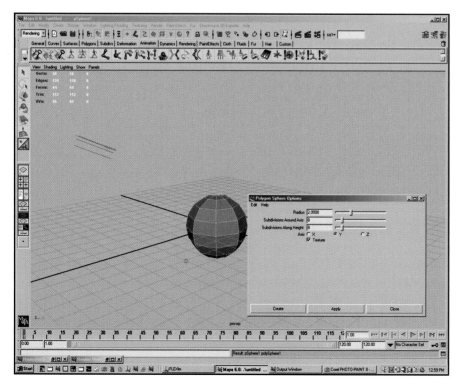

Figure 9.16 Create a polygon sphere.

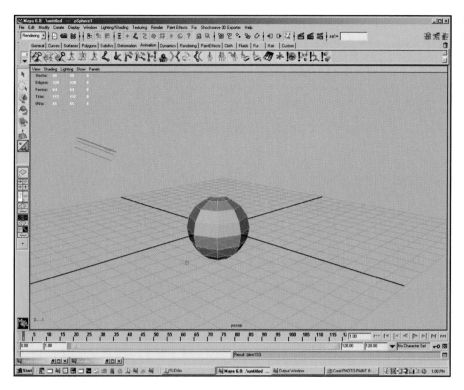

Figure 9.17 Apply the golden material to the sphere.

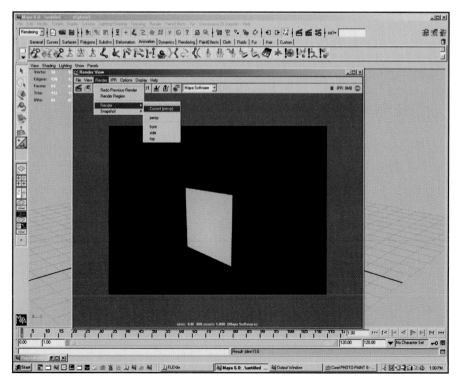

Figure 9.18 Select Render > Current (persp) from the Render Menu.

5. The sphere will render in the window, as shown in Figure 9.19. Notice that the lighting on the sphere comes from only one side, so it has no light except for the ambient light on the dark side. This type of single source lighting works well for scenes in outer space, but it does not show very well how we see things in life. Minimize the Render View window.

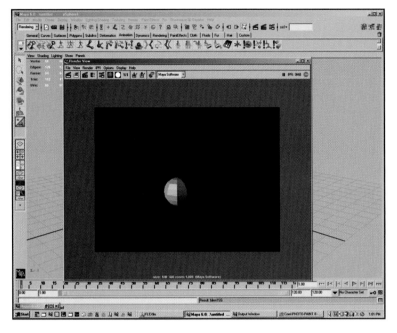

Figure 9.19 The lighting is primarily from one source giving harsh shadow areas.

6. Create another directional light with an intensity of 0.6 and the color and other settings shown in Figure 9.20. Position the light behind the sphere as shown.

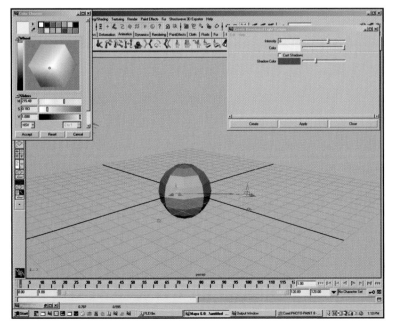

Figure 9.20 Position the new light behind the sphere.

7. Now bring up the Render View window once more and render the scene again. Notice that the lighting on the sphere looks more natural, as shown in Figure 9.21.

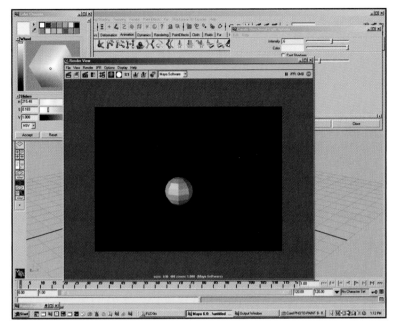

Figure 9.21 The lighting is more natural.

8. Now get rid of the facets in the sphere. Go back to the Modeling Menu set. Select the sphere and bring up the Soften/Harden dialog box from the Edit Polygons Menu as shown in Figure 9.22.

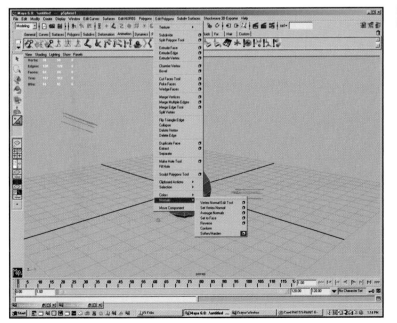

Figure 9.22 Find Soften/Harden in the Edit Polygons Menu.

9. Set the option to All Soft (180) or type in 180 in the Angle text box and click Apply to give the sphere a no-faceted look, as shown in Figure 9.23.

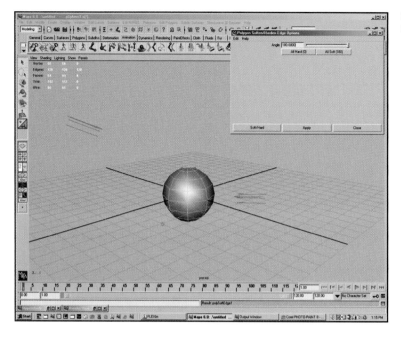

Figure 9.23 Set the option to All Soft.

10. Render again and see the results. It should look like Figure 9.24.

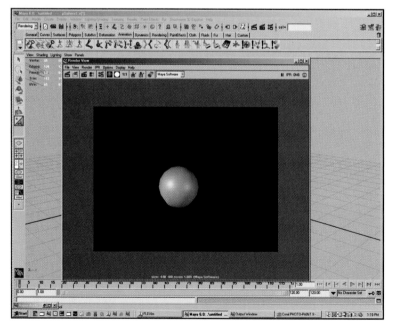

Figure 9.24 Render the sphere again with the softened edges.

11. Now change the material on the sphere. Bring up Hypershade and select the golden material.

12. Bring up the Attribute Editor as shown in Figure 9.25.

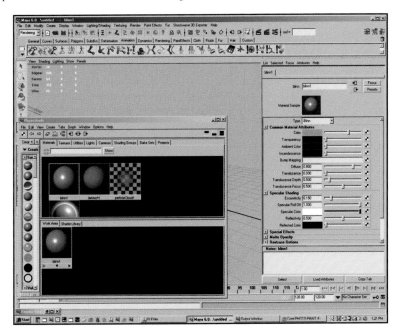

Figure 9.25 Bring up the Attribute Editor for the golden material.

13. Instead of clicking the color swatch next to Color, click the checkered icon to the right of the slider bar. This brings up the Create Render Node window, as shown in Figure 9.26.

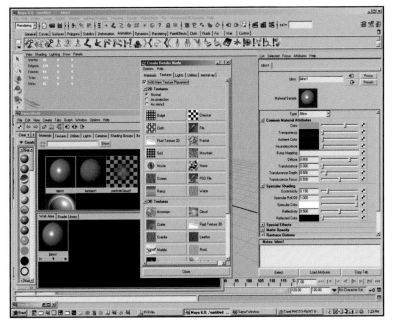

Figure 9.26 Bring up the Create Render Node window.

14. Click the icon labeled Noise. This will add noise to the material. Noise is a random-pattern material.

15. Render the sphere again to see the difference the noise material makes. The sphere now looks a little like a marble, as shown in Figure 9.27.

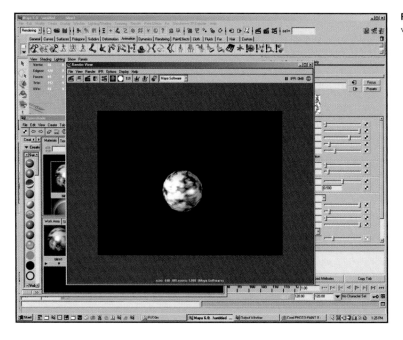

Figure 9.27 Render the sphere again with the noise material.

16. Minimize the Render View window and go back to the Attribute Editor. Click the material in Hypershade to reset the editor to the material, if needed.

17. Scroll down the editor to the Color Balance field in the noise node, as shown in Figure 9.28.

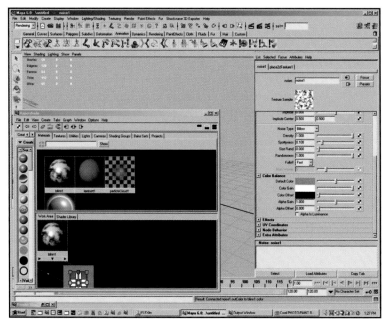

Figure 9.28 Find the Color Balance field in the Attribute Editor.

18. Click the color swatches to change the colors to light, medium, and dark orange using the Color Chooser, as shown in Figure 9.29. This will change the colors used in the noise material.

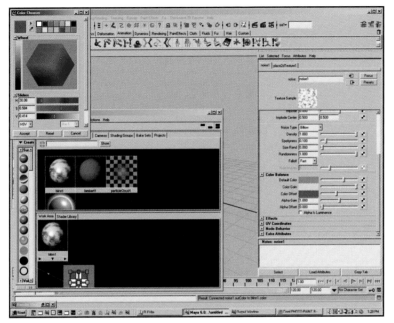

Figure 9.29 Change the material color.

19. Now render the sphere again with the new colors. The new render should look like Figure 9.30.

Figure 9.30 Render the sphere again with the new colors.

20. Minimize the Render View window and experiment with adjusting some of the sliders in the Attribute Editor. Notice how the material changes in the sample window and in Hypershade. This shows how easy it is to change the look of a material.

21. Adjust the sliders in the Attribute Editor in Ratio, Frequency Ratio, Depth Map, Time, and Frequency as shown in Figure 9.31 to get a fine texture in the material.

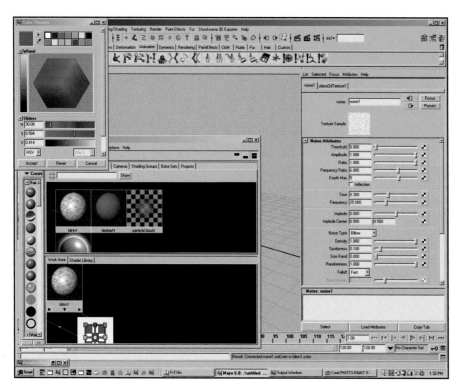

Figure 9.31 Change the texture to a fine pattern.

Noise is just one of many possibilities within Maya for creating textures. But what if the texture needs to show specific detail instead of just a pattern? That is where texture maps come in.

Texture Maps

A texture map is a bitmap picture that is applied to a 3D model. Texture maps can be applied in a number of ways, the most common texture map is color. Texture maps can be any size; however, some computer systems have limits on memory size and complex texture maps can easily go over memory limits, especially for real-time applications. A good rule of thumb is to use as small a map as possible when building models for real-time applications like video games.

Many systems have optimum sizes for texture maps. These sizes are generally a power of 2. For example, 8×8, 16×16, 32×32, 64×64, 128×128, 256×256, 512×512, and 1024×1024 are common texture sizes as measured in pixels. The reason these sizes are common is that they fit together better in system memory.

The next exercise shows how to add a texture map to an object and some ways to modify the texture map in the Attribute Editor.

1. In Maya, minimize Hypershade and close the Attribute Editor.

2. Go to Show Last Hidden in the Display Menu, as shown in Figure 9.32. (This step pre-supposes that these exercises have been completed in one session. If you are starting from a saved file in Maya, you will have to bring up Hypergraph and find the original polygon. It will be the grayed rectangle. Select it and then select Show Selected from the Display Menu.)

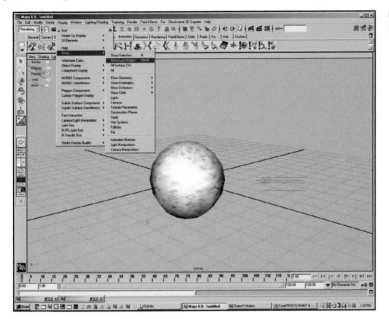

Figure 9.32 Select Show Last Hidden from the Display Menu.

3. Create a new Blinn material in Hypershade. With the new material highlighted by a yellow box bring up the Attribute Editor as shown in Figure 9.33.

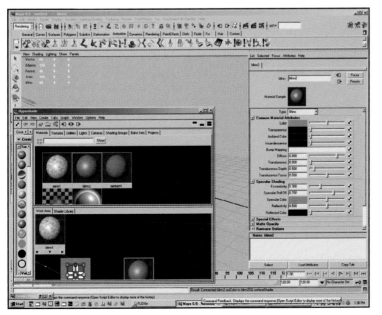

Figure 9.33 Create a new Blinn material.

4. Click the checkered icon to the right of the Color slider bar to bring up the Create Render Node window, as shown in Figure 9.34.

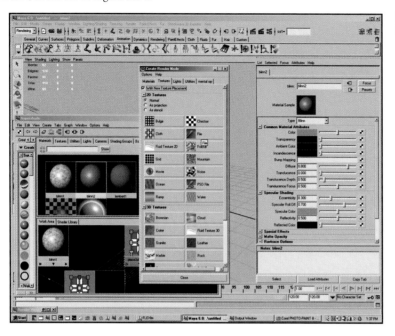

Figure 9.34 Bring up the Create Render Node window.

5. Find the icon button labeled File and click it.

6. The Attribute Editor will change to a new set of controls. Select the icon that looks like a file folder to bring up a file browser, as shown in Figure 9.35.

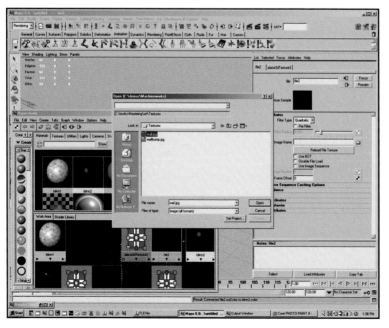

Figure 9.35 Bring up the file browser and find the wall.bmp file.

7. The file wall.bmp is one of the files available online at www.courseptr.com/downloads. Select the wall.bmp file and click Open to load the texture map into the material.

8. Apply the new material to the single polygon plane. The scene should now look like Figure 9.36.

Figure 9.36 Apply the new wall material to the single polygon plane.

9. Move the sphere so that it is behind the polygon plane, as shown in Figure 9.37.

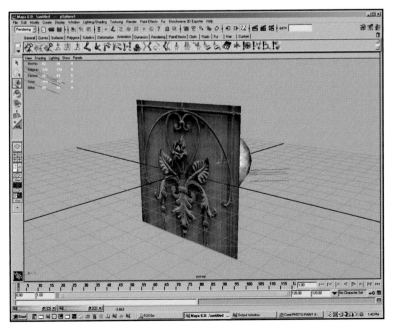

Figure 9.37 Move the sphere.

10. Render the scene as before. Notice in Figure 9.38 how much difference a nice texture map can make on a simple flat polygon. The texture looks good, but it can still be adjusted.

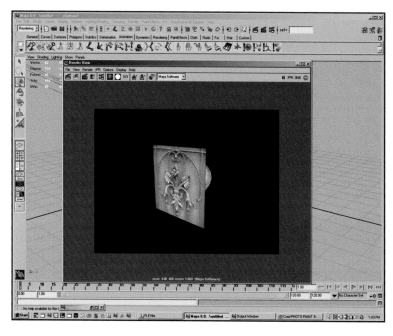

Figure 9.38 Render the scene again with the new material.

11. In the Attribute Editor, click the checkered icon to the right of the Bump text box. Then select the file from the Create Render Node box.

12. A new tab labeled Bump2D1 appears, as shown in Figure 9.39. Click the icon to the right of the Bump Value slider bar. The icon has a box with an arrow pointing in.

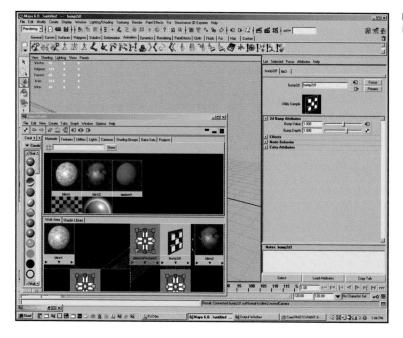

Figure 9.39 Go to the Bump2D1 tab in the Attribute Editor.

13. Clicking the icon brings up a new tab in the Attribute Editor that has a place to load texture map images, as shown in Figure 9.40. Click the file folder icon next to Image Name to bring up a browser and select the wallbump.bmp file. Wallbump.bmp can be found at www.courseptr.com/downloads.

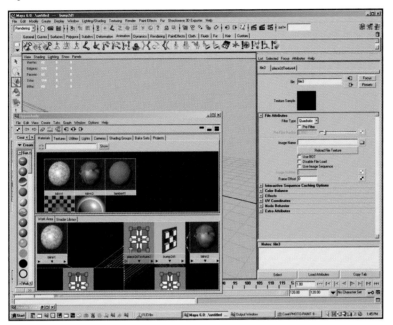

Figure 9.40 Click the file folder icon.

14. Texture maps for the Bump feature in Maya are called bump maps, and they are grayscale images. Maya interprets the light areas as protrusions and the dark areas as recesses. This gives the image the appearance of 3D even though it is only a flat plane as shown in Figure 9.41.

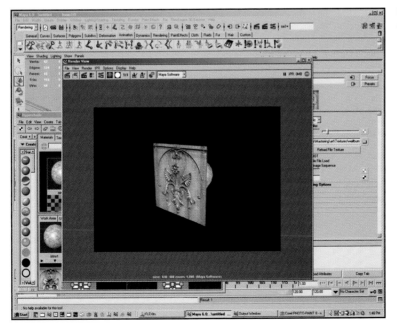

Figure 9.41 Bump maps give 2D images the appearance of 3D.

15. Now let's look at transparency. Bring up Hypershade and select the Blinn2 material to reset the Attribute Editor.

16. Move the slider next to Transparency as shown in Figure 9.42.

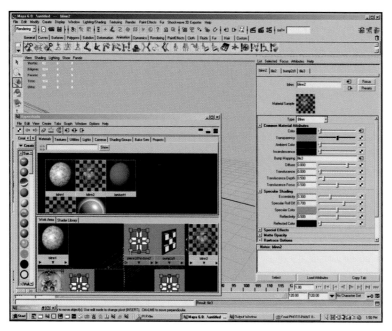

Figure 9.42 Move the Transparency slider to the right.

17. Now when the scene is rendered as shown in Figure 9.43, the wall polygon is transparent and the sphere can be seen through it.

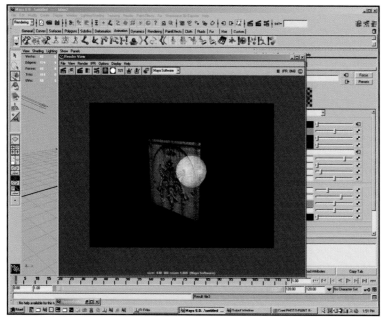

Figure 9.43 The wall is transparent.

18. Go back to Hypershade and this time select the material used on the sphere instead of the wall.

19. Move the slider next to Incandescence to the right, as shown in Figure 9.44. Incandescence is an attribute that gives a material a brightness quality similar to a light in real life.

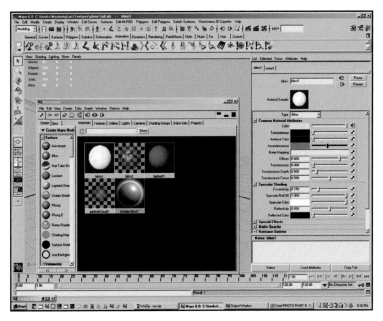

Figure 9.44 Move the Incandescence slider to the right.

20. Render the scene to see how it is changed. It should look similar to Figure 9.45.

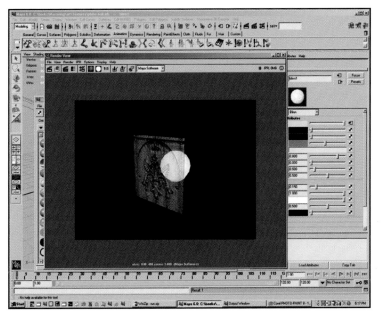

Figure 9.45 The sphere is now bright.

21. Go back to the Attribute Editor and scroll down to the Special Effects group. Click the arrow to open the group.

22. Move the slider next to Glow Intensity as shown in Figure 9.46. Click the check box next to Hide Source. Glow is an attribute that gives the material qualities similar to a light source. It causes the material to cast light on its surroundings.

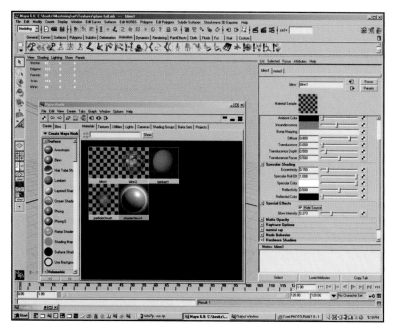

Figure 9.46 Move the slider next to Glow Intensity to the right.

23. Render the scene again to see the changes. Notice that the sphere is now gone and is replaced by a glowing light, as shown in Figure 9.47. The glowing light is not actually a light but acts similar to one. The sphere is not actually gone; it is just not rendered.

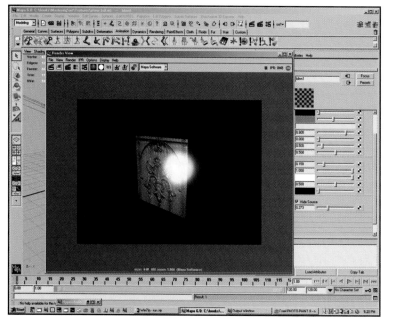

Figure 9.47 A glowing nimbus replaces the sphere.

These exercises have covered only a small portion of the many methods of creating and editing materials. The possibilities are almost endless. The exercises covered should give you a basic understanding of how to create and edit materials. With a little experimentation, you should be able to understand most of the features.

Mapping Complex Geometry

After creating the materials for a model, the next question becomes "How do I apply the material to the model?" Applying materials to a single polygon or a simple shape like a sphere is relatively easy, but it becomes infinitely more complex when the model is a complex model like the human head you created in Chapter 7. This section explains how the UV Editor is used to position textures correctly on an organic surface.

1. Start by loading the human head model you created in Chapter 7. It should look similar to Figure 9.48.

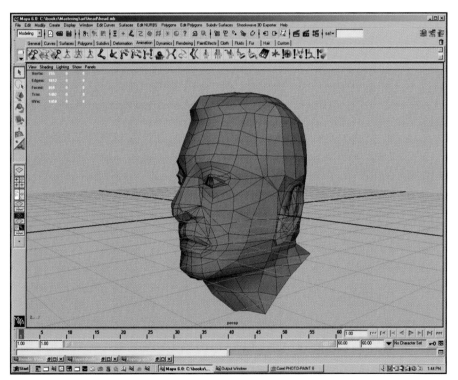

Figure 9.48 Load the head model.

2. Duplicate the model and move the duplicate forward as shown in Figure 9.49. The duplicate model will be textured first and then the UVs will be transferred to the original model. This is because the duplicate will be modified to make it easier to map.

3. Now the original model should be hidden so that it will be easier to work on the duplicate. Select the original model and then select Hide Selected, as shown in Figure 9.50.

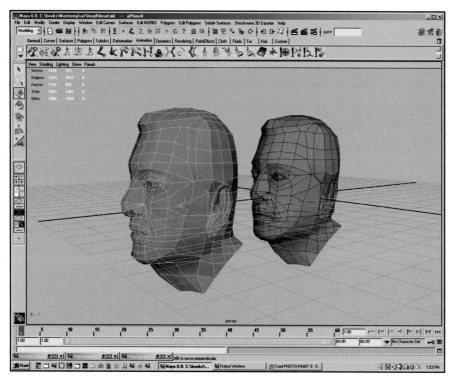

Figure 9.49 Duplicate the model.

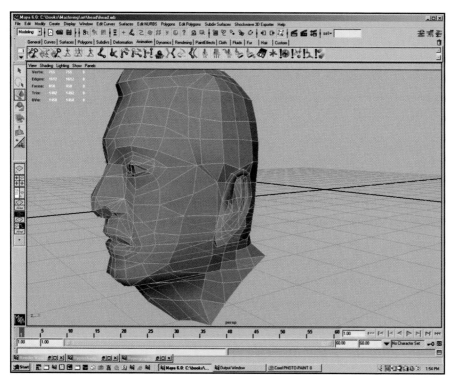

Figure 9.50 Hide the original model.

4. Overlapping UVs can be a real problem to untangle. To avoid the problem that can result in areas like ears, nose, and eyes, the model needs to be adjusted before mapping takes place. Start with the ears. From the side view, select the vertices around the ears as shown in Figure 9.51.

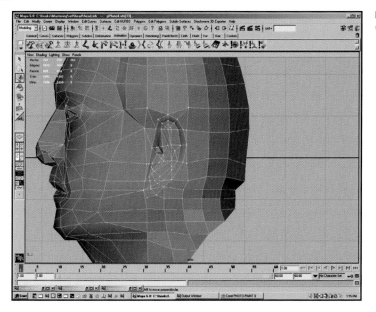

Figure 9.51 Select the vertices around the ears.

5. From the Polygon Menu bring up the Polygon Average Vertices Options box. Make sure you are in the Modeling Menu set.

6. Set the Iteration option to 10 and click Apply three or more times to eliminate overlapping geometry, as shown in Figure 9.52. The Polygon Average Vertices function averages the distance between selected vertices.

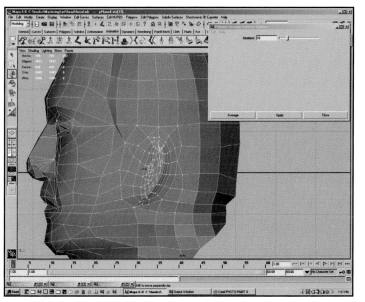

Figure 9.52 Remove overlapping geometry.

7. Select the vertices around the nose and remove the overlapping geometry as shown in Figure 9.53.

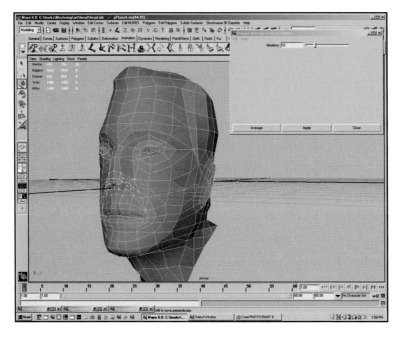

Figure 9.53 Remove the overlapping geometry around the nose.

8. Do the same process on the eyes. Now the model is ready for texturing.

9. Change the selection mode to Faces and select all of the faces on the model, as shown in Figure 9.54.

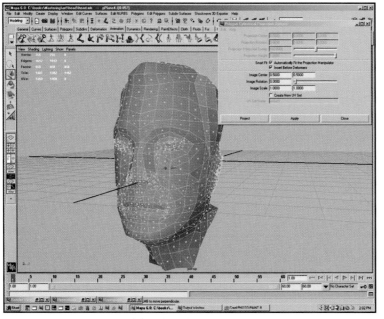

Figure 9.54 Select all the faces of the model.

10. In the Texture submenu under Edit Polygon are several mapping tools. Bring up the Polygon Cylindrical Projection Options box.

11. Apply cylindrical projection at the setting shown in Figure 9.55. Even though most people think of the head as a sphere, it is more like a cylinder with an enclosed rounded top.

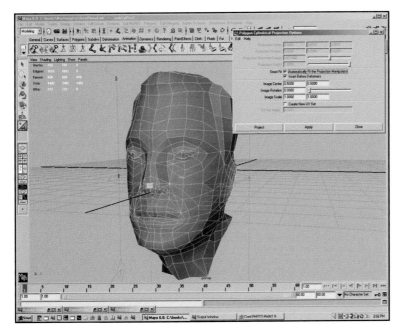

Figure 9.55 Apply cylindrical projection to the model.

12. Maya has a tool for editing UVs called the UV Texture Editor. You will use this tool to set up the UV map of the model. The tool is found in the Window Menu, as shown in Figure 9.56.

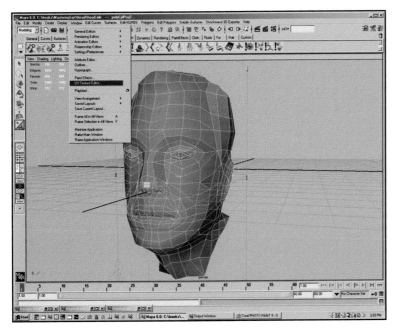

Figure 9.56 The UV Texture Editor is found in the Window Menu.

13. The UV Texture Editor shows the UVs of a model in a flat 2D view with the texture map that is attached to the UVs, as shown in Figure 9.57. Right-click on the editor window and change the selection mode to UVs in the Marking Menu.

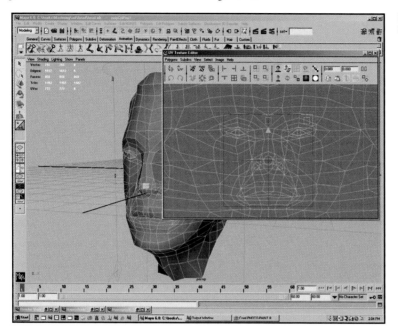

Figure 9.57 The UV Texture Editor is a 2D view of the UVs.

14. Hold down the Alt key and the left and middle mouse buttons to zoom in and out of the editor. Pull the view back until all of the UVs are shown.

15. Select all of the UVs as shown in Figure 9.58.

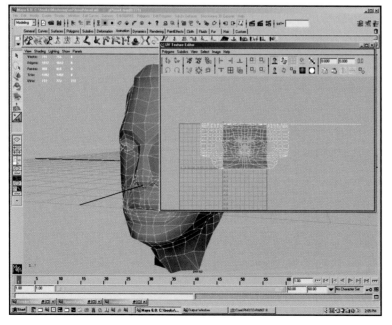

Figure 9.58 Select all of the UVs in the editor.

16. Use the Scale tool to scale the UV set until if fits in the gray box, as shown in Figure 9.59.

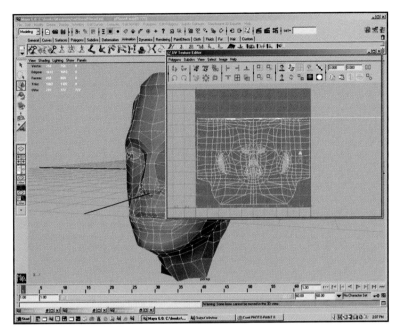

Figure 9.59 Scale the UVs to fit in the gray box in the Editor.

17. The Cylindrical Projection tool does not do a very good job of mapping UVs that are perpendicular to it. That is why some of the UVs are in a line off the gray square. Change the selection mode to Faces and select the faces on the top of the head in the Panel, as shown in Figure 9.60.

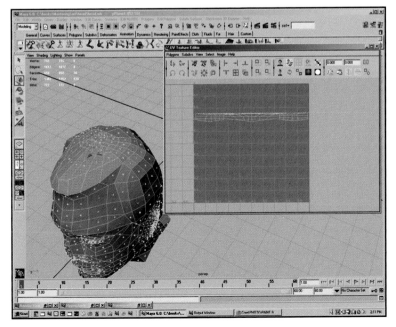

Figure 9.60 Select the faces at the top of the head.

18. Go back to the Edit Polygons > Texture Menu and bring up the Polygon Planar Projection Options box.

19. Set the projection tool to the setting shown in Figure 9.61 and apply the projection to the top of the model's head.

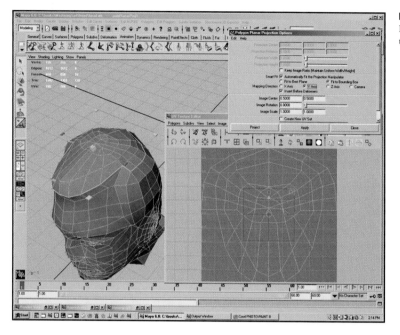

Figure 9.61 Use the Polygon Planar Projection tool to map the faces of the top of the head.

20. Change the selection mode in the editor to UV and scale the projected UV map as shown in Figure 9.62.

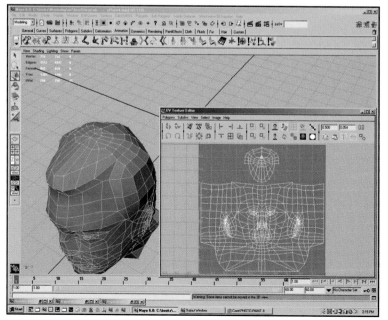

Figure 9.62 Scale the new UV set.

21. It is always a good idea to make as few separate UV sections as possible in the UV Editor to help reduce the potential for seams. The next few steps show how to join the two separate UV maps into one map. Scale the map of the top of the head sideways as shown in Figure 9.63.

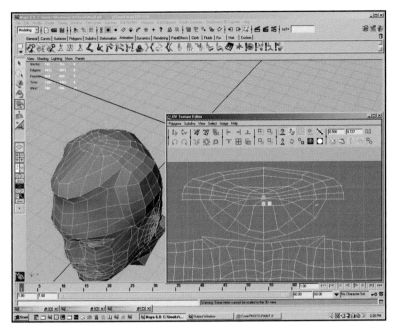

Figure 9.63 Scale the UV set sideways to fit better above the other UV set.

22. Now select matching UVs from both sets and use the Scale tool to align them closer with each other, as shown in Figure 9 64. A matching UV is a UV from one set that matches up with a UV from another set.

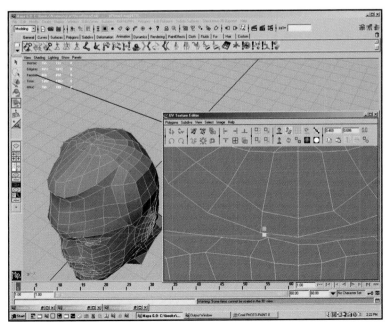

Figure 9.64 Align matching UVs.

23. Continue to scale matching UVs until your UV sets look similar to those in Figure 9.65.

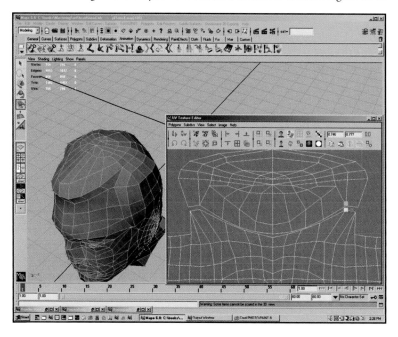

Figure 9.65 Scale the UVs from the front of the head.

24. On the top UV set, select the top four UVs running down the center line. Use the Cut UVs feature from the Polygons Menu in the editor as shown in Figure 9.66 to split the UVs into their individual polygons.

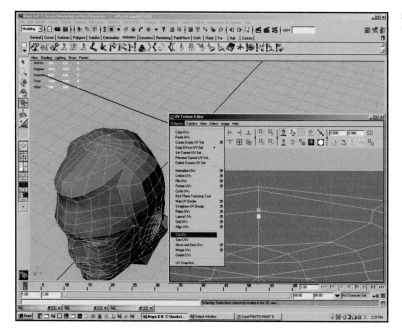

Figure 9.66 Use the Cut UVs feature to split the UVs.

25. Select individual UVs from the area just split and separate them as shown in Figure 9.67 so they can be moved to a better location.

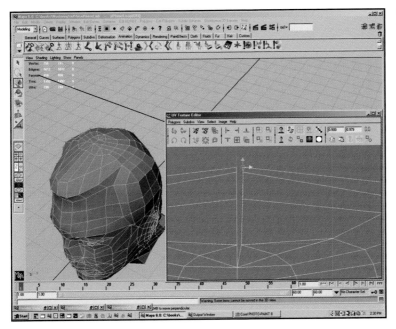

Figure 9.67 Separate the UVs along the back top of the head.

26. Scale the UVs along the top set to line up vertically with their matching UVs in the bottom set, as shown in Figure 9.68.

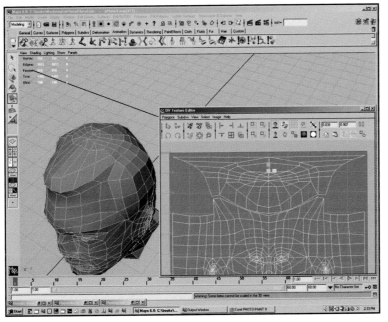

Figure 9.68 Line up matching vertices.

27. Scale all of the UVs in the upper set to be more evenly spaced, as shown in Figure 9.69. Also scale and move the split UVs along the top of the set as shown.

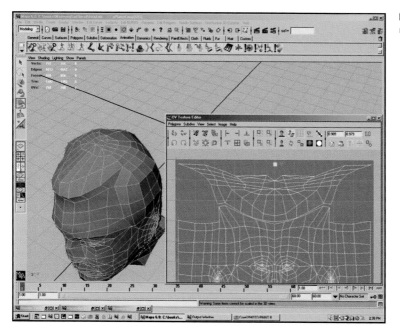

Figure 9.69 Move the UVs to be more evenly spaced.

28. Move the matching UVs from the top set down to match up with their corresponding UVs in the bottom set.

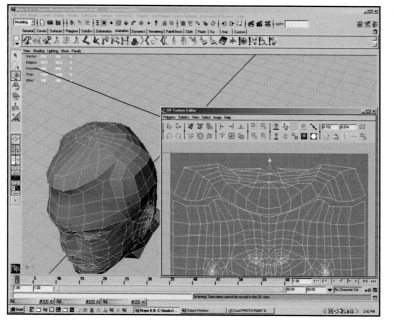

Figure 9.70 Move the UVs from the top set down to the bottom set.

29. Change the selection mode in the editor to Edges and select the edges along the border between the two sets. Notice that selecting an edge on one set automatically selects its matching edge in the other set. When all edges are selected, the result should look the same as Figure 9.71.

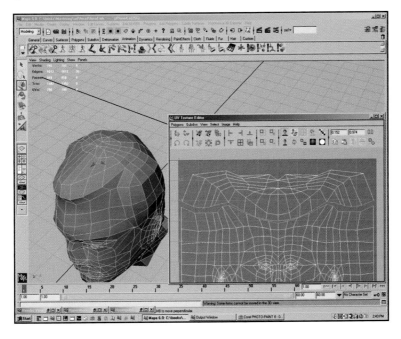

Figure 9.71 Select the edges along the border of the two sets.

30. Now go to the Polygon Menu in the editor and use the Move and Sew UVs feature as shown in Figure 9.72 to merge the selected edges.

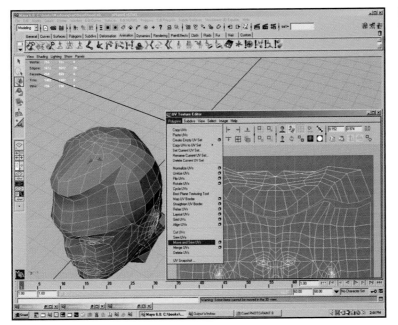

Figure 9.72 Use the Move and Sew UVs feature in the Polygon Menu.

31. In Polygon Menu in the editor there is a feature that will save the UV map out as a 2D image. It is the UV Snapshot feature. Selecting it brings up a dialog box to set the options for saving a 2D image as shown in Figure 9.73. Set the options as shown and click OK to save your image. The saved image will be useful in creating the texture map for the head.

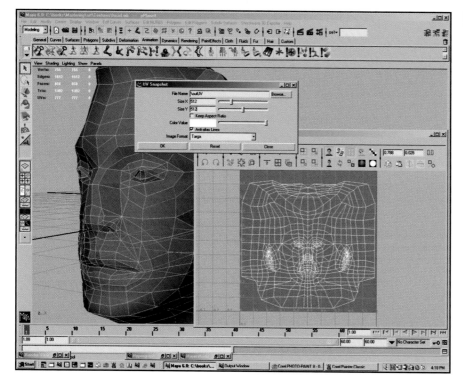

Figure 9.73 Save a snapshot of the UV map.

Creating the Texture Map

The model is ready now for you to apply a texture map to it. The next step is to create a texture map. Using the snapshot of the UV map as a guide is the best way to create an accurate texture map for the model. Figure 9.74 shows the snapshot of the UV map.

1. Use the snapshot as a guide to paint in the major features of the texture map in flat colors, as shown in Figure 9.75.

2. This is a model of an old man, so the skin texture needs to look weathered with age spots and wrinkles. Figure 9.76 shows the next step in creating the texture map with the addition of a mottled flesh tone and features. The hair is also detailed.

3. Next the facial wrinkles are added along with some other facial detail as shown in Figure 9.77. Use the techniques taught in the 2D section of the book to paint the texture map.

If the texture map was created correctly, it should match up with the UV map. Figure 9.78 shows the texture map with the UV map overlaid.

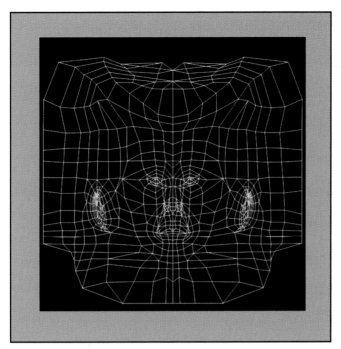

Figure 9.74 The UV snapshot shows the UV map in a 2D image.

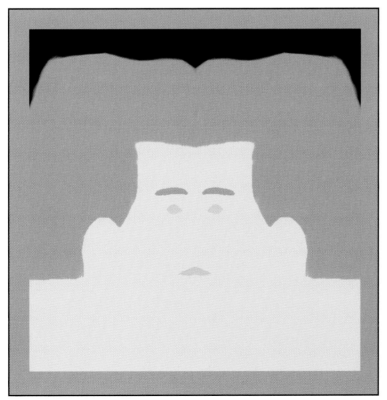

Figure 9.75 Use the snapshot as a guide to block in the base colors of the texture map.

Figure 9.76 Add flesh tones, features, and hair to the texture map.

Figure 9.77 Wrinkles and highlights are added to the texture map.

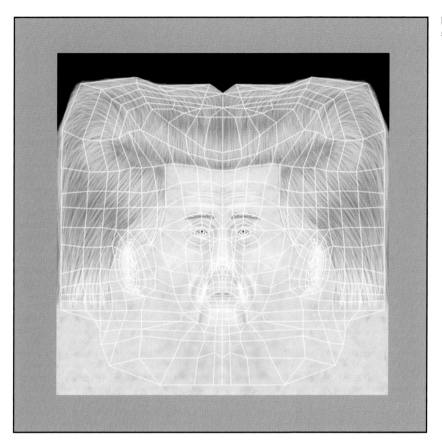

Figure 9.78 The UV snapshot is shown over the 2D image.

Finishing the Model

With the texture map ready, the model can now be textured. This section shows how a texture is applied and how the material can be adjusted to make the model look more realistic.

1. Create a Blinn material and load the texture map as shown in Figure 9.79.

2. Select the model and apply the material to the model.

3. Now bring back the original model by selecting Show Last Hidden from the Display Menu as shown in Figure 9.80.

4. Apply the material to the original model. The two models should look similar to Figure 9.81. Notice that the maps on the original model are incorrect. We will need to transfer the correct UV information to fix the problem.

5. Maya has a feature that allows for transferring elements from one object to another if the objects have exactly the same polygon set. That is why the model was duplicated earlier. As long as there are no changes in the duplicate mesh, the duplicate and original will have the same polygon set. Go to the Transfer dialog box in the Polygon Menu.

6. Make sure that only UV is selected, as shown in Figure 9.82. Now select the duplicate first and then the original and click Apply. The UVs from the duplicate should transfer to the original as shown in the figure.

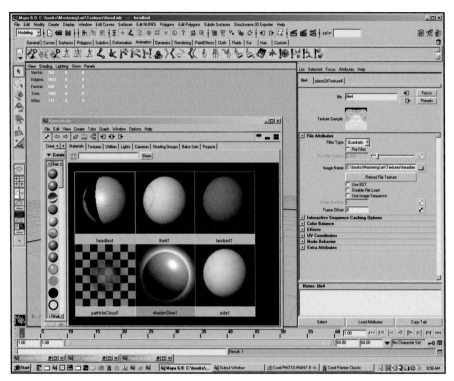

Figure 9.79 Load the texture map of the head into the Blinn material.

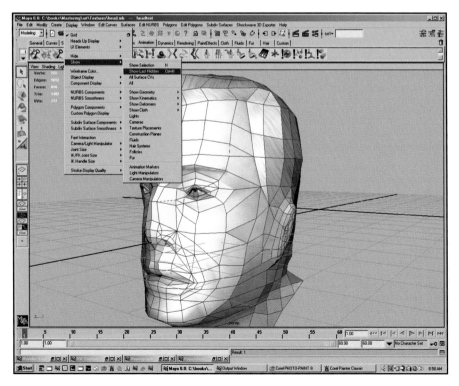

Figure 9.80 Use Show Last Hidden to bring the original model back.

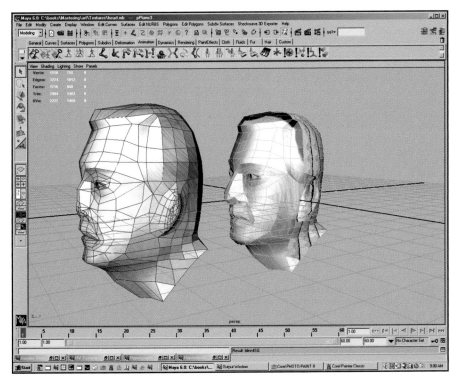

Figure 9.81 Apply the material to the original model.

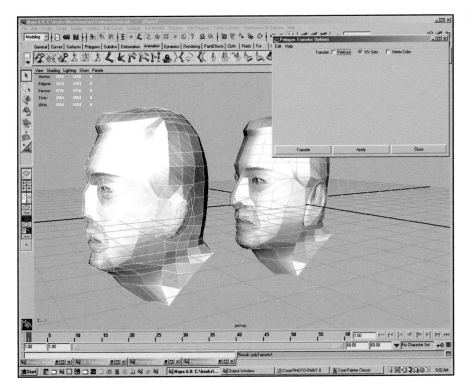

Figure 9.82 Transfer the UVs from the duplicate to the original model.

7. The Duplicate model can now be deleted. Currently the model has the Wireframe on Shaded option on. Turn this option off by selecting it from the Shading Menu in the Panel as shown in Figure 9.83.

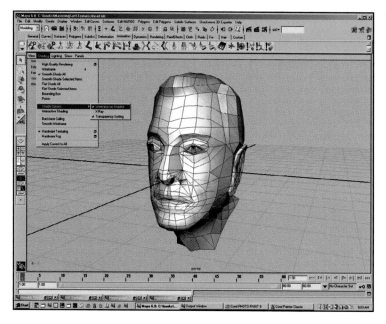

Figure 9.83 Turn off Wireframe on Shaded.

8. Notice that the model is highly faceted. This is the same problem that the ball had in the earlier exercise. Change the selection mode to Edges and select all the edges in the model.

9. Now bring up the Polygon Soften/Harden Edge Options box and set it at 90. Click Apply. The model should now look similar to Figure 9.84.

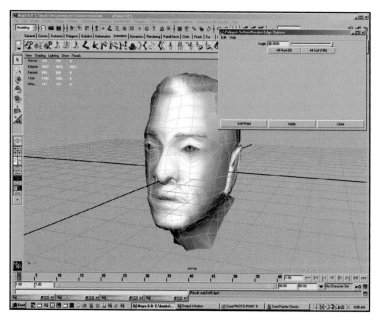

Figure 9.84 Soften the edges of the model.

10. Some of the UVs on the head need a little fine-tuning. Adjust them in the UV Editor as shown in Figure 9.85.

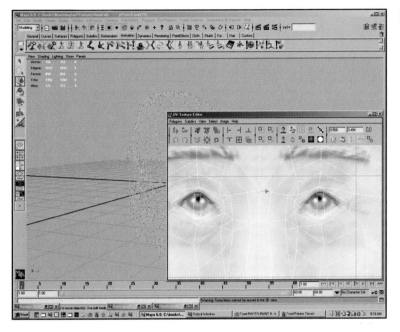

Figure 9.85 Adjust the UVs in the UV Editor.

11. A few edges need to have a hard edge, like in between the lips as shown in Figure 9.86. Select these edges and use the Soften/Harden command set to 0 to harden these edges.

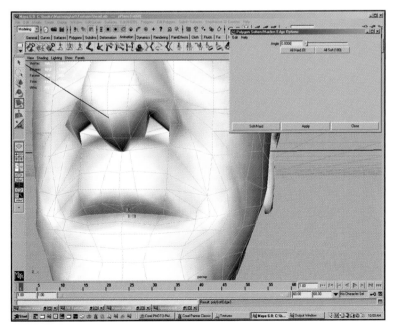

Figure 9.86 Some of the edges will need to be hardened.

12. Next add some lighting. First create a directional light as shown in Figure 9.87.

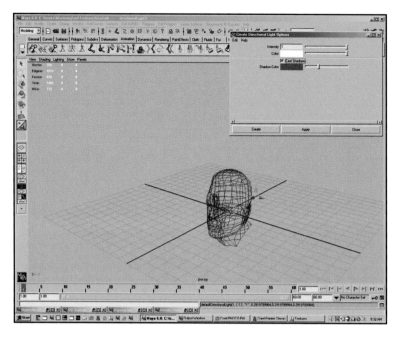

Figure 9.87 Create a directional light to light the head for rendering.

13. Position the light as shown in Figure 9.88.

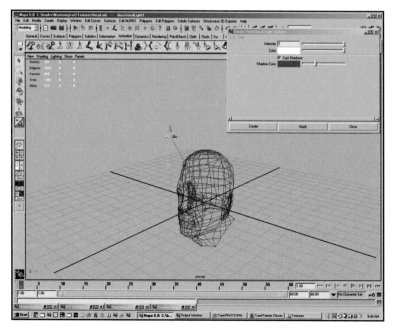

Figure 9.88 Position the directional light.

14. Now create a second directional light and position it as shown in Figure 9.89. Set the color and intensity as shown in the figure. The second light will illuminate the shadow areas of the first light.

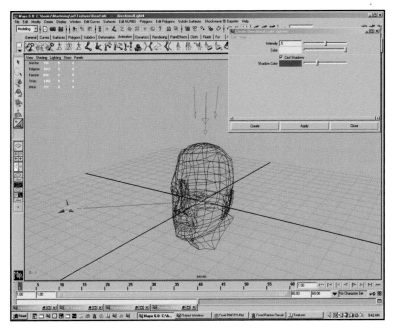

Figure 9.89 Create a second directional light.

15. Render the image. It should look similar to Figure 9.90. Notice that there are some weird lighting effects around the ears.

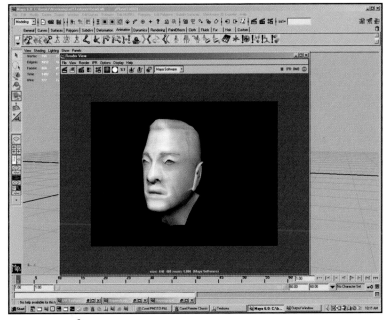

Figure 9.90 Render the head.

16. The problem with the ears is that there are multiple overlapping vertices. These vertices were never merged when the head was created in Chapter 7. That is why there is now a problem with the lighting on them. To fix the problem, select the vertices around the ears and merge them using the Merge Vertex feature in the Edit Polygon Menu, as shown in Figure 9.91.

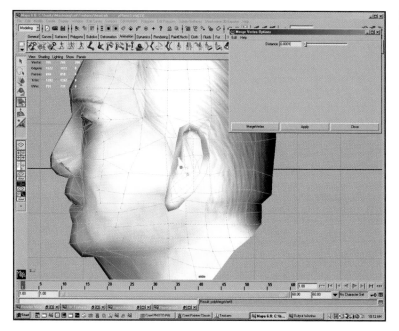

Figure 9.91 Merge the overlapping vertices of the ear.

17. Another problem with the head is that it looks too shiny, like it is made out of plastic. Adjust the Specular Rolloff, Reflectivity, and Eccentricity settings of the material as shown in Figure 9.92.

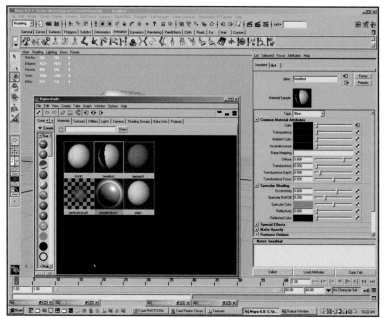

Figure 9.92 Adjust the specular settings of the material.

18. Render the scene again. The model should look better without the weird lighting around the ear and not as shiny. See Figure 9.93.

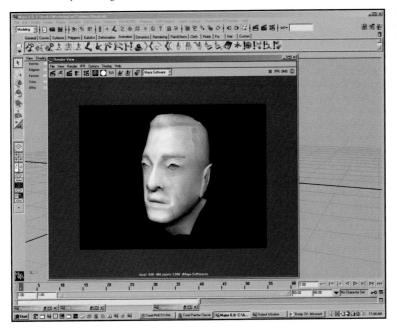

Figure 9.93 Render the scene again to see if the changes make the model look better.

19. The model looks too smooth. To look right it needs to have some crags and ridges in the skin. A simple way to achieve the desired look is to use a bump map. Figure 9.94 shows a bump map for the model. The bump map is a grayscale map showing highlights and dark areas. It was painted using the texture map as a base and decreasing the contrast dramatically. Bump maps use grayscale data to give the appearance of surface texture to models.

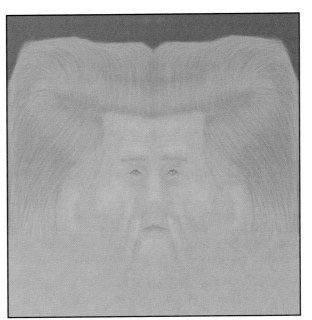

Figure 9.94 The bump map is a grayscale map showing highlights and dark areas.

20. Load the bump map into the material as shown in Figure 9.95.

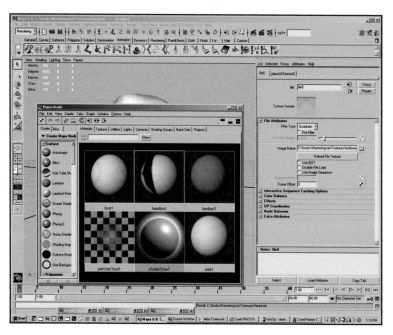

Figure 9.95 Load the bump map into the material.

21. Render the scene again. It now has a much more realistic appearance. See Figure 9.96.

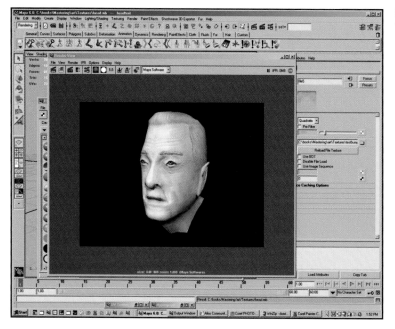

Figure 9.96 Render the scene with the bump map.

Experiment texture mapping a few more complex models. Try out a few of the different projection tools in Maya. In the preceding exercise the Cylindrical and Planar Projection tools were used. There is also a tool for Spherical projections that works well for ball-shaped objects. In addition there is a tool called Automatic Mapping, which automatically lays out the UVs in the UV Editor. I don't often use Automatic Projections because I like having more control over the UVs.

Summary

This chapter covered many concepts related to texturing models, including the following:

- Color
- Saturation
- Value
- Roughness
- Transparency
- Reflectivity
- Luminance

Through explanations and exercises, you learned how to create materials in Maya and apply them to a model. You saw how adjusting material attributes can change the way a material looks with examples of changing attributes like color, transparency, luminance, bump, and glow.

You learned how to texture complex models with an example of texturing the model of a human head created in Chapter 7. You also learned how to use the UV Editor. A snapshot of the UVs was used as a guide to paint a texture for the model and then the texture was applied to the model. Finally, a bump map was applied to the model to add realism.

This chapter covered many aspects of texture mapping 3D models, but it has not covered every aspect. Hopefully it has covered enough of the subject that you will be able to experiment with the many other features in Maya to learn how they work. Think of it as a starting off point of a great adventure.

10

Lighting and Rendering

The final step in creating 3D digital art before rendering is to light the scene. Like a dark room with the lights turned off, without lights there will be nothing to render. This chapter deals with lighting and rendering 3D digital art.

Lighting in 3D digital art is similar to lighting found in the real world. In real life there are many types of lights—large powerful lights like the sun, and smaller lights like a reading lamp. Lights can be directed like a spotlight or they can be colored like a neon sign.

Maya has to have a light in a scene to render the scene. Without a light, the scene would just be black. By default, Maya has a set of lights that will automatically light any object. These lights are okay to check your work, but they are not good enough for most finished projects. So just placing a light in a scene is not enough. The type of light, where that light is placed, and the number of lights in a scene make a big difference in how the scene is rendered.

Lighting 3D Digital Art

Lights in 3D programs are objects. They exist in 3D space like any other object. They also have attributes like other objects. These attributes can be adjusted to give a light different qualities depending on the light. For example, an area light might have a diffuse rate set to diminish the light as it goes away from a light source. The diffuse rate can be adjusted to extend or diminish the area affected by the light.

To really understand how lights work in Maya, you need to try lighting a scene. The following examples will help to explain how lights work and many of their attributes.

Building a Scene

Before you can light a scene you need to have a scene. Bring up Maya and go to the Modeling
Menu set.

1. Create a polygon plane using the options shown in Figure 10.1.

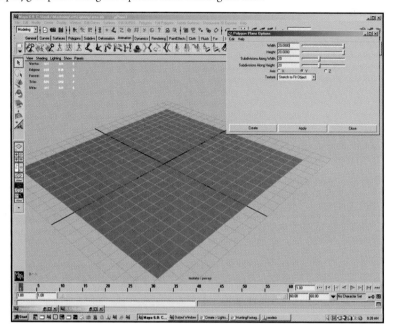

Figure 10.1 Create a polygon plane.

2. Create a polygon cube using the options shown in Figure 10.2. Move the cube so it sits
on top of the plane as shown in the figure.

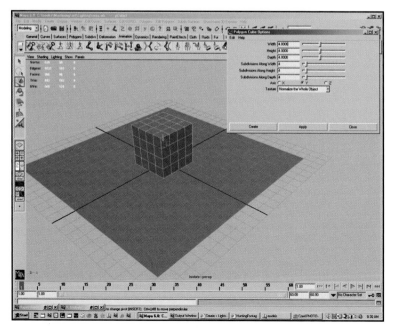

Figure 10.2 Create a polygon cube.

3. Create a polygon sphere using the options shown in Figure 10.3. Move the sphere so it sits on top of the cube as shown in the figure.

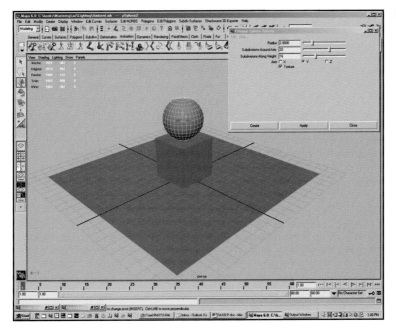

Figure 10.3 Create a polygon sphere.

4. Load the textures for this chapter, supplied online at www.courseptr.com/downloads, into Hypershade as Blinn materials. Rename them as brick, door, stones, and wall as shown in Figure 10.4.

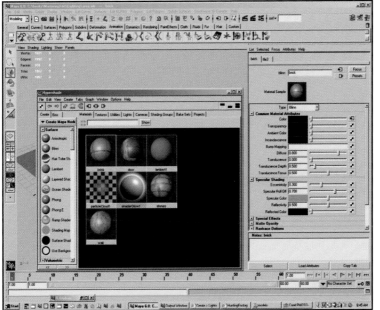

Figure 10.4 Load the supplied textures.

5. Apply the stones material to the plane using the Planar Projection tool at the settings shown in Figure 10.5. Chapter 9 has more detail on applying materials.

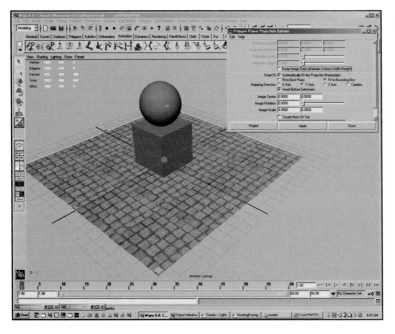

Figure 10.5 Apply the stones material to the plane.

6. Select the polygons on the cube with the exception of those on the top of the cube.

7. Apply the door material to the cube. The cube should look like Figure 10.6 without using any projection tools.

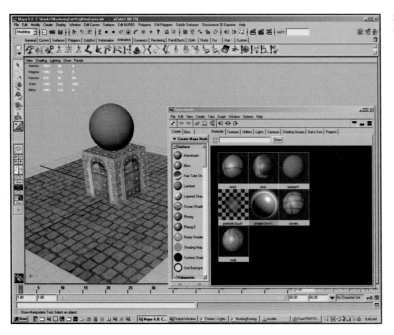

Figure 10.6 Apply the door material to the walls of the cube.

8. Now select the top faces of the cube and apply the wall material to them as shown in Figure 10.7.

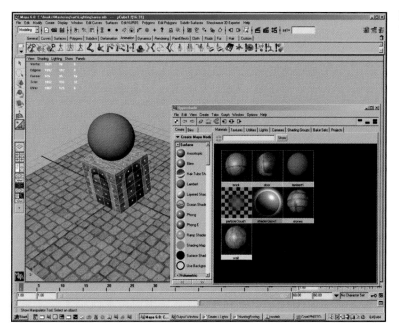

Figure 10.7 Apply the wall texture to the top of the cube.

9. Apply the brick material to the sphere using the Cylindrical Projection tool set to the options shown in Figure 10.8.

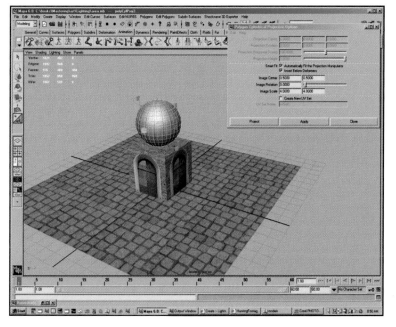

Figure 10.8 Apply the brick material to the sphere.

The scene is now finished and ready to light. Save the scene. It is always a good idea to save a scene before lighting so that if something doesn't work right the original scene can be reloaded.

Creating Lights

Lights are created like other objects in Maya. The exercises in the last chapter included the creation of very simple lighting. This section covers lighting in more detail.

Ambient Light

In nature, light is refracted in many directions. During the day the sun is the major light source. As light from the sun bounces off objects on the earth, it illuminates other objects from different angles. This is why we can turn off lights in buildings during the day even if the windows are not facing the sun and still see. It is also why we can see detail in the shadows cast from the sun. Maya has a light called Ambient Light, which simulates the general lighting found in nature.

Create an ambient light in the scene using the setting shown in Figure 10.9. Set the color as shown in the color picker. Move the ambient light up and to the right as shown in the figure so that it is above the plane object.

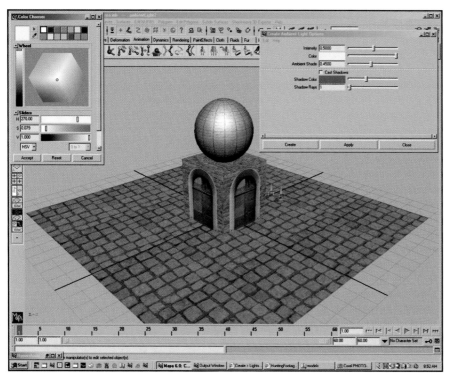

Figure 10.9 Create an ambient light for the scene.

To see how the ambient light affects the scene, go to the Rendering Menu set and render the scene. The results should look like Figure 10.10.

The ambient light casts a soft blue light across the objects. Notice that it is a little brighter around the light source and then evenly lit throughout the rest of the scene. The color of the light mixed with the color of the materials give the scene a bluish look.

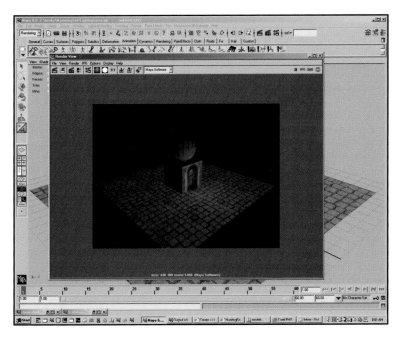

Figure 10.10 Render the scene to see the ambient light.

Now that the ambient light is set, we can move on to look at the other lights.

1. Create a directional light using the setting and color shown in Figure 10.11.

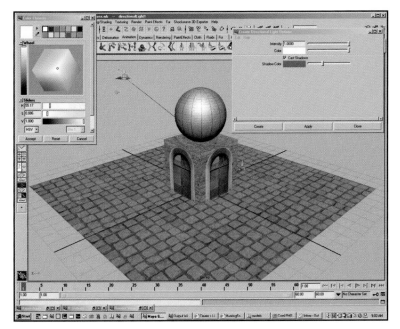

Figure 10.11 Create a directional light.

2. Now render the scene to see the results of adding the directional light. Directional lights have parallel light rays. This results in a flat, even lighting. Directional lights are good for outdoor scenes because they simulate the light of the sun. Figure 10.12 shows the scene rendered. Notice that the ambient light gives the scene lighting in the shadow areas.

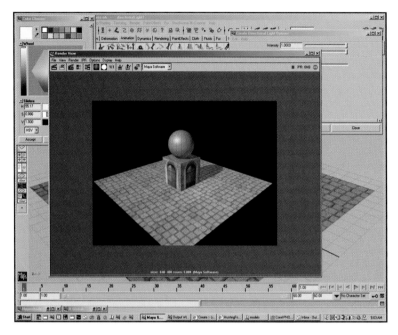

Figure 10.12 Render the scene with the directional light.

3. Hide the ambient light and render the scene as in Figure 10.13. Without the ambient light the shadows are almost completely black.

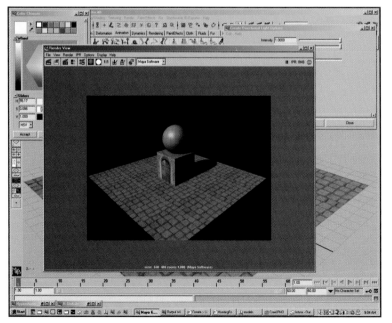

Figure 10.13 Without the ambient light the shadows are black.

4. Bring the ambient light back into the scene.

5. Select the directional light and bring up the Attribute Editor as shown in Figure 10.14.

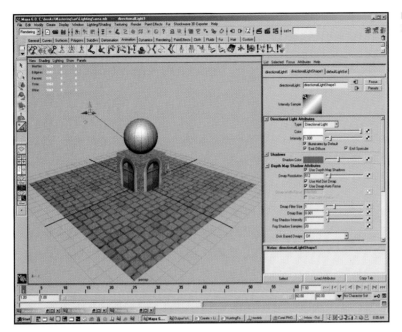

Figure 10.14 Bring up the Attribute Editor for the directional light.

6. Under Type choose Area Light as shown in Figure 10.15. An area light sends light out from a square light source. It is great for simulating the light from a window.

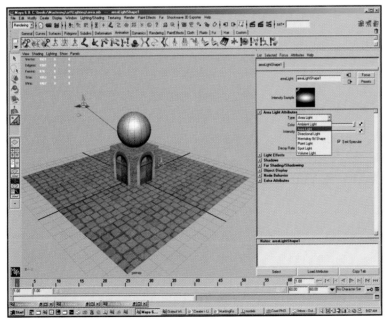

Figure 10.15 Area lights are great for simulating the light from a window.

7. Render the scene again to see how the area light is different from the directional light. Notice that the area light produces a strong highlight on the sphere. The light also diminishes with distance from the source. See Figure 10.16.

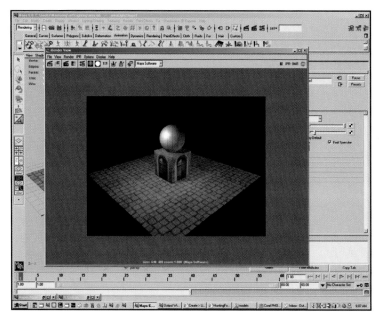

Figure 10.16 The area light produces a strong highlight in this scene.

8. Now change the light to a point light. Point lights shine evenly in all directions. They are great for simulating light from a lightbulb.

9. Render the scene with the point light. The highlight on the sphere is not as intense as it was with the area light. There is also a reflection of the light from the ground. See Figure 10.17.

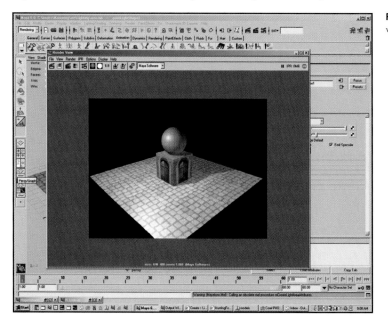

Figure 10.17 Render the scene with a point light.

10. Change the light to a spotlight. Spotlights are similar to directional lights except that they only shine in a defined circle of light. They are used often for flashlights or car headlights.

11. Render the scene with the spotlight. The spotlight sends a cone of light across the scene as shown in Figure 10.18. The edges of a spotlight can be adjusted so they are not so harsh as in this scene.

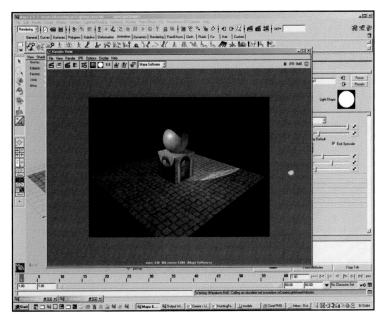

Figure 10.18 The spotlight shines light in a cone of light.

12. Now try a volume light. Notice that the volume light has a light envelope. This is the area in which the light will shine. Expand the light envelope to the size shown in Figure 10.19.

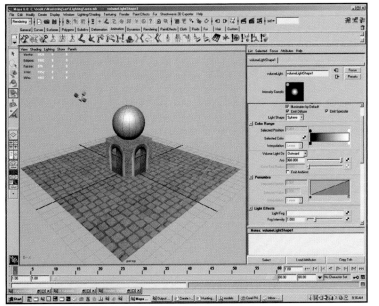

Figure 10.19 Expand the light envelope.

13. Volume lights are great for any lighting that needs to be in a defined area. Render the scene to see how the volume light affects the scene. It should look like Figure 10.20.

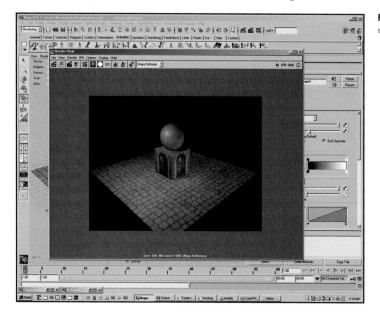

Figure 10.20 Render the scene with the volume light.

Each light has had a different effect on the scene. The type of light chosen for lighting a scene should be based on the type of light it is simulating.

Raytracing

Now for a little fun, scroll down on the Attribute Editor and check Use Ray Trace Shadows as shown in Figure 10.21.

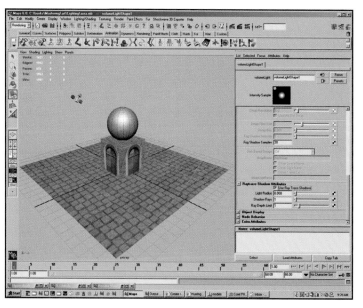

Figure 10.21 Use Ray Trace Shadows.

Raytracing is a high-end rendering technique for rendering reflections and shadows.

In the Render view select Render Globals from the Options Menu. An options window appears. Go to the second tab labeled Maya Software and check the Raytracing checkbox, as shown in Figure 10.22. Raytracing is a more precise method of simulating light than other methods. Because it is more precise, it takes much longer to render.

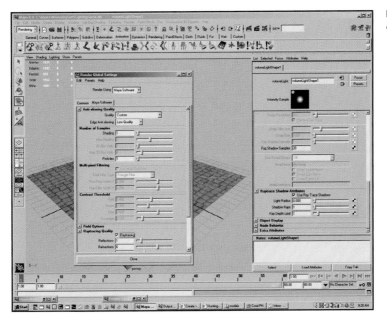

Figure 10.22 Check the Raytracing checkbox.

Render the scene with raytracing. Notice the reflections on the floor and on the sphere. See Figure 10.23.

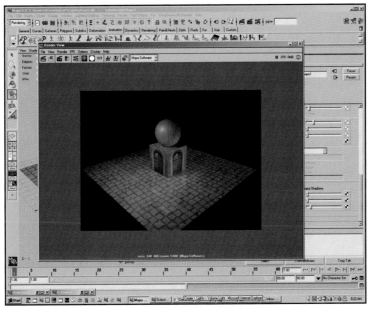

Figure 10.23 Raytracing enables reflections.

Raytracing is a very sophisticated method of rendering scenes. Because of the sophistication it will take much longer to render a scene with raytracing turned on than it will with it turned off. Even this simple scene took longer to render with it turned on. Raytracing can be used in most rendering situations, if rendering time is not an issue.

Diffusion

Diffusion or attenuation is the phenomenon in light where light rays become more scattered as they spread over space. This causes the light to diminish with distance from the light source. Diffusion is why streetlights light only a portion of the road. It is also why light is much stronger close to the light source. The amount of diffusion from a given light source depends on the scattering of the light rays. A laser, for example, does not have much diffusion because all the light rays are traveling in the same direction. A lightbulb, on the other hand, has a high rate of diffusion because the light rays spread out from it in all directions.

Some lights in Maya, such as point lights and area lights, have built-in diffusion, whereas others, such as directional lights, do not. Volume lights have an envelope that controls the diffusion of the light. Scaling the light itself controls area lights. Other lights such as spotlights and point lights use the Decay function found in the Attribute Editor.

1. Change the light source in the scene back to the point light as shown in Figure 10.24.

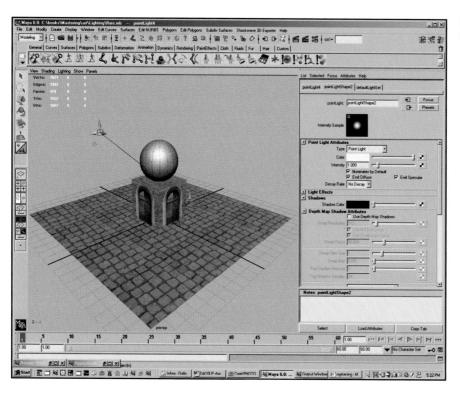

Figure 10.24 Change the light source to a point light.

2. Render the scene again to see what the default rate of decay for a point light looks like. Notice that the light is brighter near the middle of the ground and darker around the sides and back, as shown in Figure 10.25.

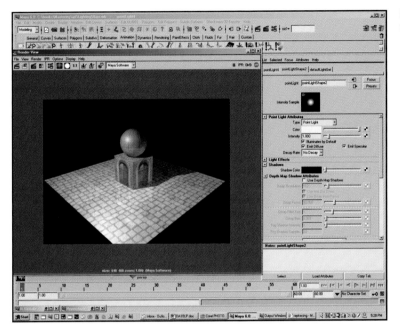

Figure 10.25 The light is brighter in the middle of the scene.

3. Find Decay Rate in the Attribute Editor and change the rate to Linear as shown in Figure 10.26. Maya has several preset decay rates as shown in the figure including Linear, Quadratic, and Cubic.

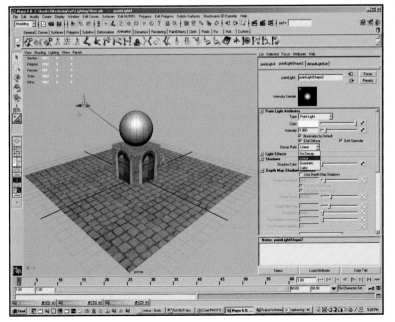

Figure 10.26 Change the decay rate to Linear.

4. Now change the scene a little to better show the decay rate in action. Duplicate the ground plane and using the Channel Box rotate and move it as shown in Figure 10.27. To better see the effects of the decay rate, hide the ambient light. Select the point light and in its Attribute Editor change the decay rate to Linear. Because the light will be decaying more rapidly, the intensity will need to be raised. Change the intensity to 6.

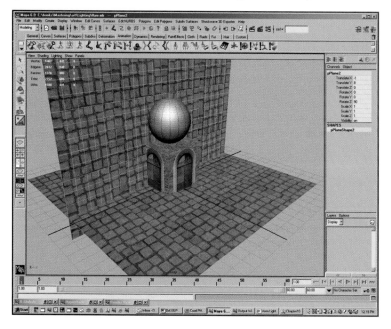

Figure 10.27 Change the scene to better show the decay rate of the light.

5. Render the scene as shown in Figure 10.28. Notice how the light diminishes as distance increases from the light source.

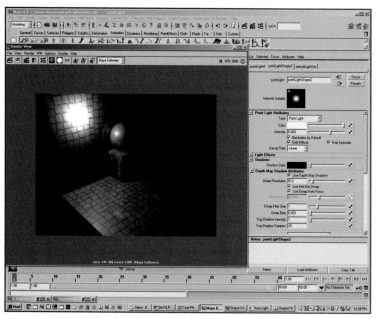

Figure 10.28 Render the scene with linear decay.

6. Change the decay rate to Quadratic and render the scene again. See Figure 10.29. Notice that the decay rate with Quadratic is much faster and therefore, the scene is much darker. In fact, the light doesn't even hit most of the scene at all.

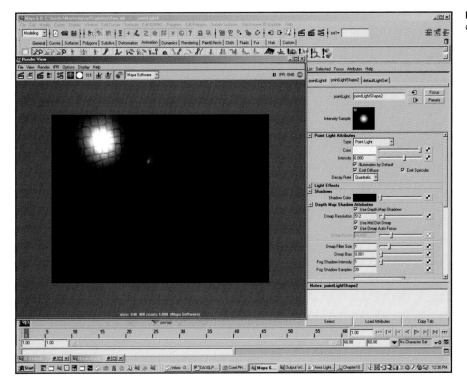

Figure 10.29 Render the scene with Quadratic decay.

Cubic decay is even more rapid than Quadratic. Use the decay rate to control point lights and spotlights in your scenes; they work great for when you need to have a limited area of light like in night scenes. Decay is very useful in creating night scenes where the area of the individual lights might need to be small compared to the rest of the scene.

Fog and Flares

Air is not always clear. Often air is filled with haze, smoke, fog, or dust. Maya has many features that help to simulate fine particles in the air. The following exercise shows how to add fog and light flares to your scenes. To prepare for the exercise, delete the vertical plane from the scene, bring the ambient light back, and change the decay rate to No Decay and the light intensity to 1.

1. Select the point light and bring up its Attribute Editor.

2. Open the Light Effects area in the Attribute Editor. Change the Fog Type to Linear and click the checkered icon next to Light Fog. This will apply a fog around the light source. A spherical envelope will represent it in the scene.

3. Change the envelope size, color, and density to those shown in Figure 10.30. Also check the checkbox next to Fast Drop Off.

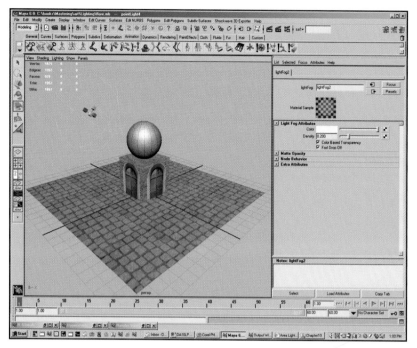

Figure 10.30 Change the setting and size of the fog envelope.

4. Render the scene. Notice the foggy glow around where the light is in the rendering. It is nice but out of place without a light source. See Figure 10.31.

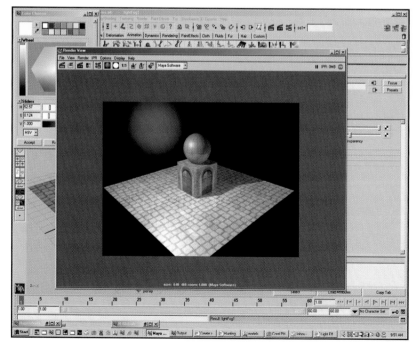

Figure 10.31 Render the light fog.

5. Select the light again and in the Attribute Editor click the checkered icon to the right of Light Glow. This will add another area envelope around the point light. The new envelope shows the extent of the glow.

6. Render the scene. The fog now looks better because there is a light source. See Figure 10.32.

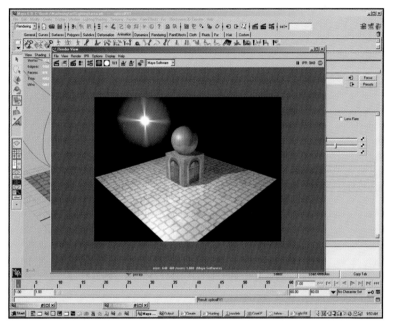

Figure 10.32 Add a glow around the light source.

7. Change the Glow Type to Lens Flare as shown in Figure 10.33 and render the scene again.

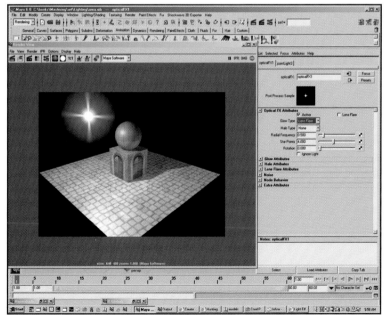

Figure 10.33 Change the glow to Lens Flare.

8. Now give the point light a halo. Change the Halo Type to Lens Flare and render the scene again as shown in Figure 10.34. The glow is now much too bright.

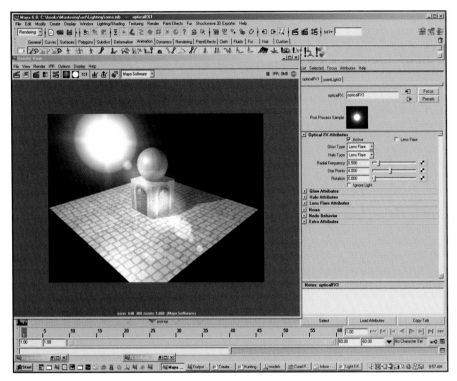

Figure 10.34 Add a halo effect to the scene.

9. Open the Glow Attributes and the Halo Attributes.

10. Change the Glow Intensity to .5.

11. Change the Halo Intensity to .4

12. Change the Halo Spread to .5

13. Render the scene with the new settings. The light looks much better. See Figure 10.35.

14. Now change the Star Point to 6.

15. Change the Rotation to 20.

16. Render the scene again to see the effect of the changes. See Figure 10.36.

Flares are a neat effect but they are not always appropriate for every scene. They don't work well for soft lights or when there are more dominant lights off the scene.

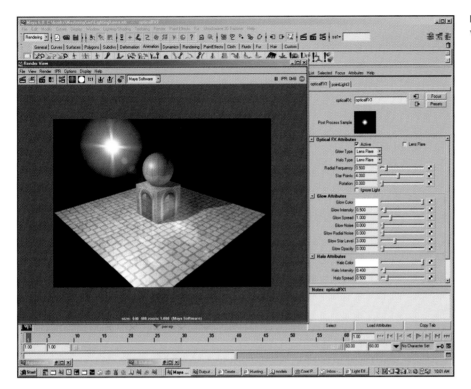

Figure 10.35 Render the scene with the new settings.

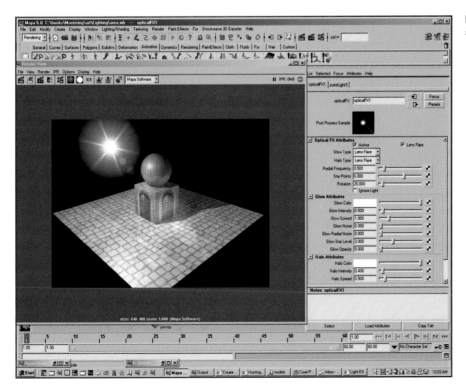

Figure 10.36 The flare now has six points.

Rendering Quality

Even a great picture may not look very good if the quality of the rendering is not good. You have already explored rendering quality a little with Raytracing. Another important issue surrounding rendering is anti-aliasing. Anti-aliasing is the process of smoothing the edges of a digital rendering. Because a digital picture is made up of square pixels, the edges for diagonal and rounded lines can often become jagged. Maya uses blending programs to smooth out the jaggedness caused by pixels. Because these blending programs can take a long time to render, they are turned off by default in Maya.

To change the quality of the anti-aliasing in a picture, go to the Render Globals Settings box found in the Options Menu in the Render view. On the second tab labeled Maya Software the first option settings are for anti-aliasing. Change the quality to Production Quality as shown in Figure 10.37.

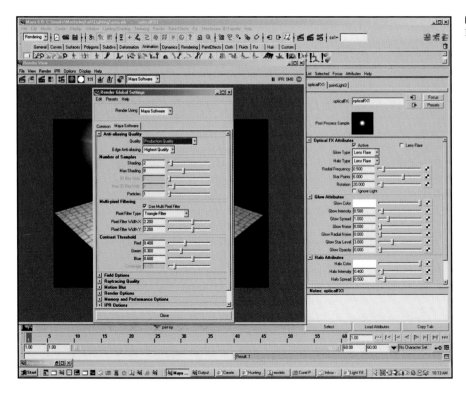

Figure 10.37 Change the quality to Production Quality.

Figure 10.38 shows the scene rendered at production quality. All of the edges are smooth and clean.

It may be a little difficult to see the difference between the scenes rendered at production quality versus it rendered before. Figure 10.39 shows a close-up of an earlier render and the one done at production quality. The difference in the close-up is obvious.

Production Quality takes a long time to render, particularly for complex scenes. For most quick renders, I tend to use Low Quality to see the progress of a scene until I am ready for the final rendering, at which time I change to Production Quality.

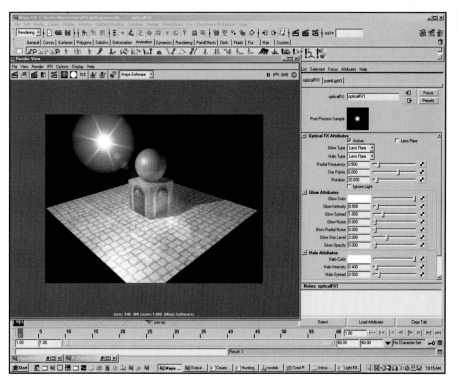

Figure 10.38 The rendering of the scene is cleaner.

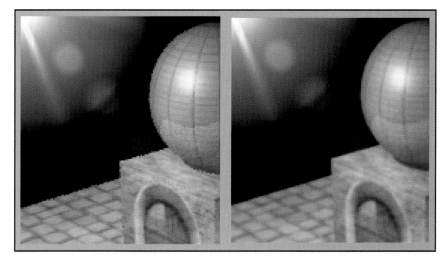

Figure 10.39 The Production Quality rendering is much cleaner than the earlier render.

Environment Fog

Environment Fog is a simulation of fog. It gives the 3D space a fogging effect as objects recede from the camera. Go back to the Render Globals Settings box and scroll down to the Render options group. Open the group and click the checkered icon to the right of Environment Fog. Keep the Attribute Editor open so the fog can be adjusted. See Figure 10.40.

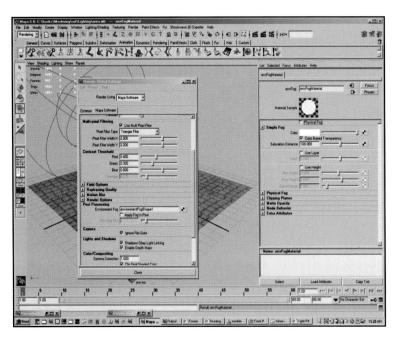

Figure 10.40 Click the checkered icon to the right of Environment Fog.

Figure 10.41 shows the scene rendered with Environment Fog. The fog is definitely there but it is way too harsh. It needs to be adjusted.

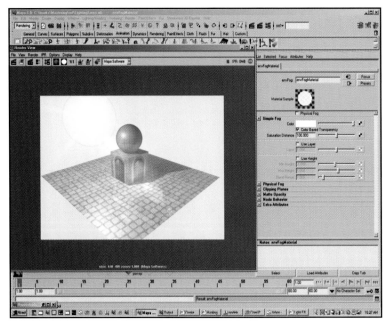

Figure 10.41 The fog is too harsh.

In the Attribute Editor, close Simple Fog and open Physical Fog. Physical Fog has several types of fog that can be used in a picture. It is worth experimenting with each type. For this exercise use Uniform Fog. Set the Fog Density to .5 and the Fog Light Scatter to .35. Try rendering with the new settings. See Figure 10.42.

Figure 10.42 Now the fog looks better.

The fog looks much better now. It lends a nice soft feel to the scene as if there is some mist in the air but not as heavy as the earlier render. This is a good technique to use in any scene where the feeling of atmosphere or fine particles in the air is important.

Summary

This chapter covered a lot of ground. Compare Figure 10.43 with Figure 10.44. Figure 10.43 is one of the first renderings made at the beginning of the chapter and Figure 10.44 is the last rendering. Although Figure 10.43 looks nice, Figure 10.44 is a lot nicer. The geometry didn't change; the only difference was the lighting and the rendering techniques.

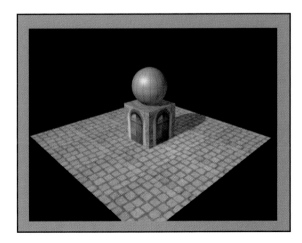

Figure 10.43 The early rendering looks nice.

Figure 10.44 The last rending looks much nicer.

This chapter covered many important aspects of lighting and rendering a scene. The topics explored included:

- Developing a simple scene from basic primitive shapes
- Adding textures
- Using a variety of lights and some purposes for each light type
- Changing light attributes
- Raytracing
- Rendering quality
- Adding fog and flares

The chapter was only able to cover a small amount of the total options available in Maya for creating 3D digital art. Maya is a very powerful and flexible software program. Most artists don't even come close to using everything in the program. Hopefully this chapter was able to give you enough information to feel comfortable using Maya. Experimenting and learning the program features is key to unlocking the full potential of the program.

Book Summary

Mastering digital art is a huge subject, especially when both 2D and 3D digital art are considered. Hopefully you have enjoyed reading this book and it has helped you on your way to becoming a better artist.

There is a bright future for digital art. More and more applications for digital art are created every day. Many pictures that once were created using traditional methods are now created on the computer. We hope that this book has helped to make your future bright as well. Good luck in your art.

Index